BE YOUR OWN LAWYER

BOOK FOR LAYMAN

BE YOUR OWN LAWYER

BOOK FOR LAYMAN

BY

KUSH KALRA

LUV KALRA

Foreword by

Dr. Adish C Aggarwala
Chairman All India Bar Association

Vij Books India Pvt Ltd
New Delhi (India)

Published by

Vij Books India Pvt Ltd
2/19, Ansari Road, Darya Ganj
New Delhi - 110002
Phones: 91-11- 43596460, 47340674
Fax: 91-11-47340674
e-mail : vijbooks@rediffmail.com
web : www.vijbooks.com

First Published   : 2013

ISBN   : 978-93-82652-10-6 (Paperback)

Acknowledgements

My special thanks to Chhaya Kirti (Student of Law, CNLU) for helping me in research work and making me realize the importance of being Positive.

Contents

Foreword

In a day and age when the laws of this country are becoming increasingly more complex, one wonders about the strict applicability of the old maxim "Ignorantia juris non excusat" (ignorance of law is no excuse). Even the seasoned lawyer has to sometimes struggle in interpreting the serpentine alleys and by-alleys of a piece of ill-considered and confusing legislation. The need, therefore, arises for a simple exposition of at least the more vital provisions of law. The author of this book Mr. Kush Kalra, has tried to fulfill this need.

It is essential for the layman to have at least a broad prospective of the provisions of law which come into play in our daily lives and work. The lay reader will surely find this book very useful as most interesting judgments of courts are laid out in this book in a very simple and effective manner. One can profitably read through this book and also dip into its pages when confronted with a legal problem. This book will also benefit young students of law, as well as junior legal practitioners who need to brush up on what may have been missed in the classroom or in the course of preparing for a law exam as the book deals with judgments of various courts in a very simple and effective manner.

"Be Your Own Lawyer" is an attempt to provide a forum for discussion and debate on all kinds of legal and social issues that confront us today. In the first issue of the book varied subjects like criminal law, the constitution, right to information, family law, medical negligence, justification of various theories of punishment and powers of the Police to arrest and detain have been covered. This book shall help the common man in his day to day life.

I wish the book the wide circulation which it deserves.

(Dr. Adish C Aggarwala)
Chairman All India Bar Association

10 Feb 2013

Preface to the First Edition

It is important that citizens must obey the law. It is even more important that citizens must obey the high standards of decency which are not enforced by the law but are the hallmark of a truly civilized and mature democracy. Maintenance of standards of decency dictated by a high moral sense is impossible unless the people have a sense of discipline and knowledge of law. A democracy without discipline is a democracy without a future. We must remember that democracy, with freedom of opinion and opposition, is not the normal way of organizing society, but it is a rare achievement. It involves the co-operation of large number of citizens in the active work of the government. The State has a claim on our energy, time and thought. The law moves on a different plane. It is a great anthropological document. It reflects man's sense of order and justice; embodies rules and traditions which hold society together; and supplies the enduring element, the dimension of performance, in history. There can be no government without order; there can be no order without law; and there can be no administration of law without lawyers. For almost 3,000 years, the law has stood sentinel over the progress of man.

The law cannot but throb with human interest, for its sole concern is men and women and their affairs. It touches life at countless points. Justice Holmes expressed his conviction that "a man may live greatly in the law as well as elsewhere". The legal profession at the highest level develops absorptive and analytic capacities of the human mind and offers great intellectual stimulus. It is no small service to be called upon to defend life, liberty and the other fundamental rights. The administration of justice has become so obsolescent that most people regard the law as an enemy rather than as a friend. The law may not be an ass but it is certainly a snail: the operation of our legal system is not merely slow but is susceptible to the most shameless delaying tactics, and resort to the courts has become a costly lottery which takes years in the drawing. As on December 12, 2012 there were no fewer than 43 lakhs[1] cases pending in the different High Courts of India, not to speak of the far greater number of cases pending in the subordinate courts.

Education has been called the technique of transmitting civilization. In order that it may transmit civilization, it has to perform two major functions: it must enlighten the understanding, and it must enrich the character. The two marks of a truly educated man, whose understanding has been enlightened, are the capacity to think clearly and intellectual curiosity. Growth of knowledge is a continuous and endless process. We have made great strides in acquiring knowledge, especially in the fields of science and technology, broadening the vistas of our information and understanding. Many mysteries of the nature stand unraveled but many remain in veil. Yet another aspect of knowledge is that its perfection has always been allusive to humans-the reason that our knowledge of things, facts and phenomena has remained imperfect and everchanging. Our efforts towards world peace and order, social welfare, and satisfaction of human needs and desires have never been fully successful. The United Nations Organizations (UNO) and its supplementary institutions, founded on the UN Charter, were set up with the aim of obtaining a world order based on peaceful co-existence of nations-where sovereignty of nations would be settled peacefully, natural resources would not be evolved for administration of justice, human wants and desires would not be abused and efforts would be made to eradicate poverty. Circumstances were sought to be created for all to engage themselves in pursuit of their interest, actualize their potentials and realize their aspirations of material and spiritual development. It is with this aim that conventions treaties and agreements, both at the regional and international level, were made between countries. This civilized society set the Millennium Development Goals (MDGs) for the whole of the world community to achieve within a target time, for standard education, health care, good governance, openness and accountability.

An evaluation of these goals and objectives reflects an utter failure. Despite setting up of basic institutions of democracy, Secularism and rule of

---

[1] http://articles.timesofindia.indiatimes.com/2012-10-05/india/34278926_1_high-courts-crore-cases-supreme-court, accessed on 14/1/2013

law, we are still faced with poverty, malnutirition, discrimination, criminalization, corruption, judicial delays, over exploitation of natural resources, mismanagement of environment, nexus between politics and crime, abuse of power, non-protection of minorities and a biased world order. Nevertheless the failure of the efforts thus far should not discourage us, the efforts have to be persistent. Ours is a country with a penchant for drafting and changing laws. Too frequently, there is a torrent of legislation, accompanied by a barrage of rules and regulations. In the present exciting times, when liberalization and globalization are counted as the great powerhouses of change, we are saddled with the problems of understanding the legal position regarding a number of minor subjects with which we come in regular contact—Negligence of Doctors, RTI, Harrasment of Women, Arrest and Detention by Police among others. Even the seasoned lawyer has sometimes to struggle in interpreting the serpentine alleys and by-alleys of a piece of ill-considered and confusing legislation. The need therefore exists for a simple exposition of atleast the more vital provisions of law, in a manner that he runs may read. It is essential for the layman to have atleast a broad prospective of the provisions of law which come into play in our daily lives and work.

" Be Your Own Lawyer" book is an attempt to provide a forum for discussion and debate on all kinds of legal and social issues that confront us today. In the first issue of the book varied subjects like criminal, constitution, Right to Information, Family Law, Medical Negligence, Justification of various theories of Punishment and Power of Police to Arrest and Detention have been covered. Various Judgments of Courts are presented in this book which will help common man in their day to day life.

When we live in a democracy, we live in hazard. There is no amenable god in it, no particular concern or particular mercy. Democracy involves the cooperation of all perceptive citizens in the active work of running the country. It means the payment to the state, not only in taxes but in time and in thought. In Daniel Webster's memorable words in the U.S. Senate in March 1834, "Nothing will ruin the country if the people themselves will undertake its safety; and nothing can save it if they leave that safety in any hands but their own". When new dangerous tremors are working their way through the subsoil of our national life, it is only the knowledge and character that can ensure the survival of the freedom. Always keep before your mind's eye Buddha's last words to his disciples: "Look at for refuge to anyone besides yourselves". These words contain a world of timeless wisdom.

In the end we would welcome suggestions from our esteemed readers for further improvement of the book.

Kush Kalra
Law Graduate
Pursuing LL.M
India
Email: krrish.kush@gmail.com

List of Abbreviations

AIR	-	All India Reporter
Bom	-	Bombay
D.B.	-	Division Bench
Govt.	-	Government
ILR	-	Indian Law Reporter
IPC	-	Indian Penal Code
Lah	-	Lahore
LJ	-	Law Journal
LR	-	Law Reporter
Mah	-	Maharashtra
M.P.	-	Madhya Pradesh
P&H	-	Punjab and Haryana
Sec	-	Section
SC	-	Supreme Court
SCC	-	Supreme Court Cases
SCR	-	Supreme Court Reporter

Family Law

Indian family law is complex, with each religion adhering to its own specific laws. In most states, registering of marriages and divorces is not compulsory. Separate laws govern Hindus, Muslims, Christians, Sikhs, and followers of other religions. The exception to this rule is in the state of Goa, where a uniform civil code is in place, in which all religions have a common law regarding marriages, divorces, and adoption.

Family laws in India are different when Warren Hastings in 1772 created provisions prescribing Hindu law for Hindus and Islamic law for Muslims, for litigation relating to personal matters. However, after independence, efforts have been made to modernise various aspects of personal law and bring about uniformity among various religions. Recent reform has affected custody and guardianship laws, adoption laws, succession law, and laws concerning domestic violence and child marriage.

Hindu Law

As far as Hindus are concerned Hindu Law is a specific branch of law. Though the attempt made by the first parliament after independence did not succeed in bringing forth a Hindu Code comprising the entire field of Hindu family law, laws could be enacted touching upon all major areas that affect family life among Hindus in India. Jains, Sikhs and Buddhists are also covered by Hindu law.

Muslim law

Indian Muslims' personal laws are based on the Sharia, which is partially applied in India. The portion of the fiqh applicable to Indian Muslims as personal law is termed Mohammedan law. Despite being largely uncodified, Mohammedan law has the same legal status as other codified statutes. The development of the law is largely on the basis of judicial precedent, which in recent times has been subject to review by the courts. The contribution of Justice V.R. Krishna Iyer in the matter of interpretation of the statutory as well as personal law is significant. The very Source of the Muslim law are divided into two categories : (1) Primary Source (2) Secondary Source

1. "Primary Source" As per Sunni Law:

- Quran
- Sunna or Ahdis (Tradition of the Prophet)
- Ijma (Unanimous Decision of the Jurists)
- Qiyas (Analogical deduction)

As per Shia Law:

- Quran
- Tradition (only those that have come from the family of the Prophet)
- Ijma (only those confirmed by Imams)
- Reasons

2. "Secondary Source"

- Custom
- Judicial Decisions
- Legislation

Salient Feature of Quran:

- Divine Origin
- First Source
- Structure
- Mixture of Religion, Law and Morality
- Different Forms of Legal Rules
- Unchangeable

Christian Law

For Christians, a distinct branch of law known as Christian Law, mostly based on specific statutes, applies. Christian law of Succession and Divorce in India have undergone changes in recent years. The Indian Divorce (Amendment) Act of 2001 has brought in considerable changes in the grounds available for divorce. By now Christian law in India has emerged as a separate branch of law. It covers the entire spectrum of family law so far as it concerns Christians in India. Christian law, to a great extent is based on English law but there are laws that originated on the strength of customary practices and precedents. Christian family law has now distinct sub branches like laws on marriage, divorce, restitution, judicial separation, succession, adoption, guardianship, maintenance, custody of minor children and relevance of canon law and all that regulates familial relationship.

The Problem in Brief

Many a man and woman of this land with different personal laws have migrated and are migrating to different countries either to make their permanent abode there or for temporary residence. Likewise there is also immigration of the nationals of other countries. The advancement in communication and transportation has also made it easier for individuals to hop from one country to another. It is also not unusual to come across cases where citizens of this country have been contracting marriages either in this country or abroad with nationals of the other countries or among themselves, or having married here, either both or one of them migrate to other countries. There are also cases where parties having married here have been either domiciled or residing separately in different foreign countries. This migration, temporary or permanent, has also been giving rise to various kinds of matrimonial disputes destroying in its turn the family and its peace.[1]

Abandoned bride in distress due to runaway foreign country resident Indian spouse, stressed non-resident Asian parent frantically searching spouse in India who has removed their child from a foreign jurisdiction in violation of a foreign court order, desperate parent seeking child support

---

[1] *Y. Narasimha Rao* vs. *Y. Venkata Lakshmi*, JT 1991 (3) SC 33

and maintenance, non-resident spouse seeking enforcement of foreign divorce decree in India, agitated children of deceased non-resident Indian turning turtle in trying to seek transfer of property in India and its repatriation to foreign shores, anxious and excited foreign adoptive parents desperately trying to resolve Indian legal formalities for adopting a child in India, bewildered officials of a foreign High Commission trying to understand the customary practices of marriage and divorce exclusively saved by Indian legislation, foreign police officials trying to understand intricacies of Indian law in apprehending offenders of law on foreign soil: these are some instances of problems arising every day from cross-border migration.

There are a large number of legal issues that concern a sizeable section of the Global Indian Community residing abroad. Though the non-resident Indians have increased multifold in foreign jurisdictions, family law disputes and situations are handicapped for want of proper professional information and advice on Indian laws. The lure for settling in foreign jurisdictions attracts a sizeable Indian population but the problems created by such migration largely remain unresolved.

The Search for Solution in Law

Solicitors and litigants overseas worldwide frantically look for professional opinions and advice when the problems come to the Indian resident abroad. Instances of conditions of validity of marriages solemnized in India, modes and means of divorce under Indian law, legal formalities to be complied with for adopting children from India, remedies available in Indian law for enforcing parental rights in child abduction and other family law issues relating to non-resident Indians abound. Likewise, there are a plethora of problems in matters concerning succession and transfer of property, banking affairs, taxation issues, execution and implementation of wills and other commercial propositions for non-resident Indians. However, application of multiple laws, their judicial interpretation & other legalities often leave the problems unresolved even though remedies partially exist in Indian law and partly need new urgent legislation.

The number of non-resident Indians (NRI) has multiplied in every jurisdiction abroad. However, family, property, kith and kin or the love for the motherland keeps bringing the NRI back on Indian soil in body or in soul. With this return the NRI seeks a remedy for his legal problem connected with his temporary or permanent return to India. This invariably makes the NRI import the foreign law of the overseas jurisdiction from where he has migrated. Such a situation is created because either Indian law provides him no remedy or because he finds it easier and quicker to import a foreign court judgment to India on the basis of alien law which has no parallel in the Indian jurisdiction. This clash of jurisdictional law is commonly called Conflict of Laws in the realm of Private International Law which is not yet a developed jurisprudence in the Indian territory.

Difficulties Faced under Indian Law

Areas of family law in which the problems of jurisdiction are seen occurring very frequently relate to dissolution of marriage, inter-parental child abduction, inter country child adoption and succession of property of non-resident Indians. In matters of divorce, since irretrievable breakdown of marriage is not a ground for dissolving the marriage under Indian law, Indian Courts in principle do not recognise foreign matrimonial judgments dissolving marriage by such breakdown. Surprisingly, even very little help is available in areas of matrimonial offences and problems arising out of child abduction. Leaving a helpless deserted Indian spouse on Indian shores confronted with a matrimonial litigation of a foreign court which he or she neither has the means or ability to invoke often results in despair, frustration and disgust. Likewise, enforcement of a foreign court order in whose violation a child of the family has been removed and brought to Indian soil brings a parent to India desperately seeking a legal remedy. The list of problems is myriad but the solutions are few or non-existent.

Unfortunately, no special Indian legislation exists to combat such remedies. The numbers of Indians on foreign shores have increased multifold but the multiple problems which bring them back to India are still left to be resolved by the conventional Indian legislation. Times have changed but laws have not. However, the dynamic, progressive and open minded judicial system in the Indian Jurisprudence often comes to the rescue of such problems by interpreting the existing laws with a practical application to the new generation problems of immigrant Indians. Fortunately, judicial legislation is the only crutch available.

1

Abortion Without Consent is A Ground For Divorce[1]

Facts in Nutshell: The matrimonial alliance was entered into between Suman Kapur and Sudhir Kapur the parties as per Hindu rites and rituals in Delhi on March 04, 1984. The marriage was inter-caste marriage. Though initially parents of both the parties were opposed to the marriage, subsequently, they consented. The parties have no issue from the said wedlock. Ms Suman Kapur conceived for the first time in 1984, within a period of about one month of the marriage, but on account of being exposed to harmful radiations as a part of lab work of her Ph.D. thesis, she decided to terminate the pregnancy. It was also mentioned by her that termination of pregnancy was done with the knowledge and consent of the husband.

Again, in 1985, she conceived. But even that pregnancy was required to be terminated on the ground of an acute kidney infection for which she had to undergo an IVP, which entailed six abdominal X-rays and radiometric urinary reflect test with radioactive drinking dye. She claimed that even the second pregnancy was terminated with the **knowledge** and **consent** of husband. Third time she became pregnant in 1989, but she suffered natural abortion on account of having a congenitally small uterus and thus prone to recurrent miscarriages.

The husband submission before the court, on the other hand was that since solemnization of marriage between the parties, the attitude, conduct and behaviour of the wife towards him and as well as his family members was indignant and rude. He also alleged that first pregnancy was terminated

---

[1] Appellants: **Suman Kapur Vs.** Respondent: **Sudhir Kapur** AIR2009SC589, 2009(1) ALD33(SC) **Hon'ble Judges:** C. K. Thakker and D. K. Jain, JJ.

in 1984 by his wife **without consent** and even **without knowledge** of him. Same thing was repeated at the time of termination of second pregnancy in 1985. He was kept in complete dark about the so-called miscarriage by the wife in 1989. The husband was thus very much aggrieved since he was denied the joy of feeling of fatherhood and his parents were also deprived of grand-parenthood of a new arrival.

Action by Respondent (Husband): The respondent-husband, herefore, filed HMA No. 322/2001/96 in the Court of Additional District Judge, Delhi under Section 13(1)(ia) and (ib)[2] of the Hindu Marriage Act, 1955 (hereinafter referred to as 'the Act') for getting divorce from the appellant-wife. Two grounds were taken by the respondent-husband in the said petition, i.e. (i) **cruelty and (ii) desertion.**

---

[2] **Section13 of Hindu Marriage Act, 1955 Divorce.-**

(1) Any marriage solemnized, whether before or after the commencement of this Act, may, on a petition presented by either the husband or the wife, be dissolved by a decree of divorce on the ground that the other party-

(i) is living in adultery; or

(ii) has ceased to be a Hindu by conversion to another religion; or

(iii) has been incurably of unsound mind for a continuous period of not less than three years immediately preceding the presentation of the petition; or

(iv) has, for a period of not less than three years immediately preceding the presentation of the petition, been suffering from a virulent and incurable form of leprosy; or

(v) had, for a period of not less than three years immediately preceding the presentation of the petition, been suffering from venereal disease in a communicable form; or

(vi) has renounced the world by entering any religious order; or

(vii) has not been heard of as being alive for a period of seven years or more by those persons who would naturally have heard of it, had that party been alive; or

(viii) has not resumed cohabitation for a space of two years or upwards after the passing of a decree for judicial separation against that party; or

(ix) has failed to comply with a decree for restitution of conjugal rights for a period of two years or upwards after the passing of the decree.

(2) A wife may also present a petition for the dissolution of her marriage by a decree of divorce on the ground,-

(i) in the case of any marriage solemnized before the commencement of this Act, that the husband had married again before such commencement or that any other wife of the husband married before such commencement was alive at the time of the solemnization of the marriage of the petitioner:

Provided that in either case the other wife is alive at the time of the presentation of the petition; or

(ii) that the husband has, since the solemnization of the marriage, been guilty of rape, sodomy or bestiality.

Decision by Trail Court: The trial Court after hearing the parties held that the husband was not entitled to a decree of divorce on the ground that the wife had deserted the husband for a continuous period of not less than two years immediately preceding the presentation of the petition. The Court, however, held that it was fully established by the husband that there was cruelty on the part of the wife. The wife without the knowledge and consent of the husband got her pregnancy terminated twice - firstly in 1984 and secondly in 1985. The husband was also not informed about natural miscarriage in 1989.

Decision by High Court: The wife preferred an appeal in the High Court of Delhi. The High Court again appreciated the evidence on record and confirmed the decree of divorce passed by the trial Court. The High Court, however, held that it was not necessary for the Court to consider mental cruelty so far as termination of pregnancy was concerned, since in the opinion of the High Court, even otherwise from the letters and entries in diary, it was proved that there was mental cruelty on the part of the wife. Accordingly, the decree of divorce passed by the trial Court was confirmed by the High Court.

Decision by Supreme Court: Confirming the decree of divorce on the ground of **mental cruelty**[3] as held by both the courts, i.e. the trial Court as well as by the High Court, no relief can be granted so far as the reversal of decree of the courts below is concerned. At the same time, however, in Supreme Court Judges opinion, the respondent-husband should not have re-married before the expiry of period stipulated for filling Special Leave to Appeal in this Court by the wife. Therefore to meet the ends of justice the respondent –husband to pay an amount of Rs Five lakhs to the appellant wife.

---

[3] In *V. Bhagat v. MANU/SC/0155/1994 : D. Bhagat (Mrs.)* AIR1994SC710, the Court observed;

Mental Cruelty in Section 13(1)(ia) can broadly be defined as that conduct which inflicts upon the other party such mental pain and suffering as would make it not possible for that party to live with the other. In other words, mental cruelty must be of such a nature that the parties cannot reasonably be expected to live together. The situation must be such that the wronged party cannot reasonably be asked to put up with such unintentional. If it is physical, it is a question of fact and degree. If it is mental, the enquiry must begin as to the nature of the cruel treatment and then as to the impact of such treatment on the mind of the spouse.

2

Benefit of Maintenance Cannot be Denied to Minor [1]

Facts in Nutshell: This case was an appeal by petitioner against order dated 2nd March, 2009 passed by the Learned Metropolitan Magistrate granting of Rs. 2000 per month for the minor daughter of the petitioner who is living separate from petitioner with the mother. The sole Contention raised by the petitioner before High Court is that in view of Section 3(1)(b) of Muslim Women (Protection of Rights on Divorce) Act, 1986[2] the right of the child to claim maintenance from father after two years of divorce of the mother does not survive.

Decision by High Court: The court held that Even a wife who has been divorced under Muslim Law is entitled to claim maintenance under Section 125 Cr.P.C.[3] after Iddat period. The court makes it crystal clear that even a

---

[1] Appellants: **Gulam Rashid Ali** Vs. Respondent: **Kaushar Parveen and Anr.** 171(2010)DLT340 **Hon'ble Judges:** Shiv Narayan Dhingra, J.

[2] **Section 3. Mahr or other properties of Muslim woman to be given to her at the time of divorce.** - (1) Notwithstanding anything contained in any other law for the time being in force, a divorced woman shall be entitled to-

(b) where she herself maintains the children born to before or after the divorce, a reasonable and fair provision and maintenance to be made and paid by her former husband for a period of two years from the respective date of birth of such children;

[3] **Section 125 Cr.P.C., 1973**: Order for Maintenance of wives, children and parents

(1) If any person leaving sufficient means neglects or refuses to maintain-

(a) his wife, unable to maintain herself, or

(b) his legitimate or illegitimate minor child, whether married or not, unable to maintain itself, or

(c) his legitimate or illegitimate child (not being a married daughter) who has attained majority, where such child is, by reason of any physical or mental abnormality or injury unable to maintain itself, or

(d) his father or mother, unable to maintain himself or herself,

Muslim divorced woman would be entitled to claim maintenance from a Muslim husband till she has not married.

The court also held that benefit under Section 125 Cr.P.C. cannot be denied to a **minor daughter**. The petition was dismissed by court.

Reference by High Court to Supreme Court Judgment: Supreme Court in *Shabana Bano v Imran Khan*[4] had observed that petition under Section 125 Cr.P.C would be maintainable (for the wife) before Family Courts so long as she does not remarry and the amount of maintenance to be awarded under Section 125 Cr.P.C. cannot be restricted for Iddat period only.

---

note 3 contd/-

A Magistrate of' the first class may, upon proof of such neglect or refusal, order such person to make a monthly allowance for the maintenance of his wife or such child, father or mother, at such monthly rate[***] as such magistrate thinks fit, and to pay the same to such person as the Magistrate may from time to time direct

Provided that the Magistrate may order the father of a minor female child referred to in clause (b) to make such allowance, until she attains her majority, if the Magistrate is satisfied that the husband of such minor female child, if married, is not possessed of' sufficient means.

[4] Crl. Appeal No. 2309/2009 decided on 4th December, 2009

3

Infertility is Not a Ground for Divorce[1]

Facts in Nutshell: In this matter wife filed an appeal challenging the judgment and decree passed by the Family Court, Pune. Wife challenged: the judgment and decree of nullity under Section 12[2] of the Hindu Marriage Act on the ground of impotency under Section 12(1)(a), and also the judgment

---

[1] Appellants: **Sou. Pramila Shankar Ghante**, Age : 45 years, Occ. Service, R. No. 2, Behind Laxmi Departmental Stores, Alandi Road, Kalaz, Pune 15 Vs. Respondent: **Shri Shankar Vishwanath Ghante**, Age : 42 years, Occ. Service, R/o Plot No. 191, Phulewadi, The House of Shri Desai, Kolhapur 416 410 MANU/MH/1090/2012

Hon'ble Judges: A.M. Khanwilkar and A.R. Joshi, JJ.

[2] **Section 12 of Hindu Marriage Act, 1955: Voidable Marriages**

(1) Any marriage solemnized, whether before or after the commencement of this Act, shall be voidable and may be annulled by a decree of nullity on any of the following grounds, namely:-

(a) that the respondent was impotent at the time of the marriage and continued to be so until the institution of the proceedings; or

(b) that the marriage is in contravention of the condition specified in clause (ii) of section 5; or

(c) that the consent of the petitioner, or where the consent of the guardian in marriage of the petitioner is required under section 5, the consent of such guardian was obtained by force or fraud; or

(d) that the respondent was at the time of the marriage pregnant by some person other than the petitioner. 0

(2) Notwithstanding anything contained in sub-section (1), no petition for annulling a marriage-
(a) on the ground specified in clause (c) of sub-section (1) shall be entertained if-

(i) the petition is presented more than one year after for force had ceased to operate or, as the case may be, the fraud had been discovered; or

(ii) the petitioner has, with his or her full consent, lived with the other party to the marriage as husband or wife after the force had ceased to operate or, as the case may be, the fraud had been discovered;

(b) on the ground specified in clause (d) of sub-section (1) shall be entertained unless the court is satisfied-

(i) that the petitioner was at the time of the marriage ignorant of the facts alleged;

(ii) that proceedings have been instituted in the case of a marriage solemnized before the commencement of this Act within one year of such commencement and in the case of marriages solemnized after such commencement within one year from the date of the marriage; and

(iii) that marital intercourse with the consent of the petitioner has not taken place since the discovery by the petitioner of the existence of the grounds for a decree.

and decree of divorce on the ground of cruelty and desertion under Section 13(1)(ia)(ib)[3] of the Hindu Marriage Act, 1955.

One petition was filed by husband for nullity and alternatively for divorce. One petition was filed by wife for restitution of conjugal rights. Both petitions were jointly heard and by the common judgment the marriage between the parties was annulled and also divorce was granted. Petition for restitution of conjugal rights was dismissed.

Court Observation on laws delays (Paragraph 3): It is rather a disturbing state of affair that there is laws delay. This Family Court Appeal has reached final hearing after about 18 years of the dissolution of marriage. The spouses then in the year 1992 were 42 years (husband) and 45 years (wife), when the petitions were filed. However, presently both the parties have become or about to become senior citizens.

Decision by Family Court: Family court held that inability to give birth to a child presupposes that the woman is **impotent** and as such a valid ground as contemplated by Section 12 of the Hindu Marriage Act, 1955 for divorce.

Case cited by Learned Advocate: V. (Wife) vs. S. (Husband)[4] in which Impotence is defined as physical incapacity of accomplishing the sexual act, while sterility means inability for procreation of children. Impotence in males is the persistent inability to develop or maintain a penile creation sufficient to conclude coitus to orgasm and ejaculation.

Impotence has been described in Halsbury's Laws of England to be such a state of mental or physical condition which makes consummation of the marriage a practical impossibility.

---

[3] **Section 13 Hindu Marriage Act, 1955**: Divorce

(1) Any marriage solemnized, whether before or after the commencement of this Act, may, on a petition presented by either the husband or the wife, be dissolved by a decree of divorce on the ground that the other party-

(i) 1[has, after the solemnization of the marriage, had voluntary, sexual intercourse with any person other than his or her spouse; or

(ia) has, after the solemnization of the marriage, treated the petitioner with cruelty; or

(ib) has deserted the petitioner for a continuous period of not less than two years immediately preceding the presentation of the petition; or]

(ii) has ceased to be a Hindu by conversion to another religion;

[4] 1994 MLJ 1513

Decision by High Court: Court held that Family court committed an error by treating **impotency** and **infertility** at par. Family Court committed an error by giving divorce on ground of impotency. High Court also set aside the judgment of family court where family court granted divorce and annulled the marriage between husband and wife on grounds of impotency . Petition by husband was dismissed with costs quantified at Rs 10,000 to be paid to the wife.

4

Muslim Girl Can Marry At the Age of 15 without the Parental Consent[1]

Facts in Nutshell: The petitioner seeks a writ of habeas corpus[2] for the production of her daughter (Shumaila). It was alleged that Shumaila was a minor (aged 15) when she was kidnapped by Mehtab on 12.04.2011 along with Rs. 1,50,000. The petitioner's husband reported the kidnapping to the Gokalpuri police and on 14.04.2011 got FIR registered. It was alleged that after the abduction of Shumaila, the petitioner received telephonic threats from Mehtab stating that if the petitioner took any legal action against him, he would kidnap her other daughter. The police did not take any action and hence the petitioner approached Court through writ petition. Petitioner relies on the birth certificate on record of Shumaila issued by the Delhi Government which shows that her date of birth was 10.06.1996. It was submitted by the petitioner that the age of her daughter at the time of kidnapping was 15 years.

Shumaila statement in Court: Shumaila told the Court on 18th April, 2012 that she did not wish to go back to her parents and that she wanted to continue to stay with her husband. According to available records, Shumaila's

---

[1] Appellants: **Mrs. Tahra Begum Vs.** Respondent: **State of Delhi & Ors.** MANU/DE/2154/2012

Hon'ble Judges: Mr. Justice S. Ravindra Bhat and Mr. Justice S.P. Garg

[2] **Habeas Corpus** is a Latin term which literally means "you should have the body".In India the power to issue a writ of Habeas Corpus is vested only in the Supreme Court and the High Court. The writ is a direction of the Court to a person who is detaining another, commanding him to bring the body of the person in his custody a specified time to a specified place for a specified purpose.The writ has only one purpose: to set at liberty a person who is confined without legal justification; to secure release from confinement of a person unlawful detained. The writ is issued not only against the State and its authorities but also to private individuals or organization, if necessary.

age was 15 years, 10 months and 23 days.

Issue to be decided by the Court: Issue to be decided by this Court, in view of these developments is, whether Shumaila should be directed to return to her parental home. Court notes that according to Mohammedan Law a girl can marry without the consent of her parents once she attains the age of puberty and she has the right to reside with her husband even if she is below the age of 18.[3]

Case Refereed: In *Vivek Kumar @ Sanju and Anjali @ Afsana vs. The State and another*[4] observed that: There is no law which prohibits a girl under 18 years from falling in love with someone else. Neither falling in love with somebody is an offence under IPC or any other penal law. Desiring to marry her love is also not an offence. A young girl, who is in love has two courses available to her one is that she should marry with the consent of her parents after obtaining the consent of her parents. If her parents do not agree to persuade them or to wait for attaining the age of majority and then exercise her right as a major to marry the person of her own choice.

If a girl around 17 years of age runs away from her parents house to save herself from the onslaught of her father or relatives and joins her lover or runs away with him, it is no offence either on the part of girl or on the part of boy with whom she ran away and married.

Decision by Court: It is clear that a Muslim girl who has attained puberty i.e. 15 years can marry and such a marriage would not be a void marriage[5].

---

3   In this connection reference can be made to Artcle 251 of Mulla's Principles of Mahomedan Law which says that every Mahomedan of sound mind, who has attained puberty, may enter into a contract of **marriage**. The explanation to the said Article says that puberty is presumed, In absence of evidence, on completion of the age of 15 years. Even in Tyabji's Muslim Law under Artcle 27 is mentioned that a girl reaching the age of puberty can marry without the consent of her guardian. Artcle 268 of Mulla's Principles of Mahomedan Law says that the marriage will be presumed, in the absence of direct proof, by mere fact of acknowledgment by the man of the woman as his wife. Article 90 of Tyabji's Muslim Law also says that a marriage Is to be presumed on the acknowledgment of either party to the marriage. As such, it has to be held that under Mahomedan Law a girl, who has reached the age of puberty, i.e., in normal course at the age of 15 years, can marry without the consent of her guardian.

4   Crl. M.C. No. 3073-74 of 2006, decided on 23.02.2007

5   In law, void means of no legal effect. An action, document or transaction which is void is of no legal effect whatsoever: an absolute nullity - the law treats it as if it had never existed or happened.

However, she has the option of treating the marriage as voidable[6], at the time of her attaining the age of majority, i.e 18 years. Direction was give to Mehtab, Shumaila and either of her in-laws to be present once in six months, in order to ascertain Shumaila well being till she attains the age of majority before the Child Welfare Committee. Shumaila was allowed to live with Mehtab, in the matrimonial home. The writ petition was disposed.

---

[6]   Black's Law Dictionary defines voidable as follows:

Voidable. That which may be avoided, or declared void; not absolutely void, or void in itself. It imports a valid act which may be avoided rather than an invalid act which may be ratified. Simply it means (Voidable) In law, a transaction or action which is **voidable** is valid, but may be annulled by one of the parties to the transaction.

5

Marriage with Minor under Hindu Law[1]

Facts in Nutshell:

A letter was addressed by Smt. Lajja Devi to the Hon'ble the Chief Justice of Delhi High Court. In the letter, it was alleged by Smt. Lajja Devi that her daughter named Ms.Meera, who was around 14 years of age (date of birth being 6.7.1995) was kidnapped by Promod, Vinod, Satish, Manoj S/o Shri Raj Mal. On the basis of the information, an FIR bearing No. 113/2008 under Section 363 IPC[2] had been registered. The letter was treated as a Writ Petition.

Statement of Girl (Meera who was Minor[3]):

The girl made a statement under Section 164 of Cr.P.C., 1973[4] before the learned Metropolitan Magistrate, Rohini Courts Delhi that she had gone along with the accused Charan Singh of her own free will as her Uncle and Aunt were marrying her against her wishes.

---

[1] Appellants: **Court on its Own Motion (Lajja Devi) Vs.** Respondent: **State AND** Appellants: **Smt. Laxmi Devi and Another Vs.** Respondent: **State (GNCT of Delhi) & Ors.** MANU/DE/3556/2012

Hon'ble Judges: Hon'ble A.K. Sikri, Acting Chief Justice, Hon'ble Mr. Justice Sanjiv Khanna and Hon'ble Mr. Justice V.K. Shali

[2] **Section 363, IPC, 1860**

Whoever kidnaps any person from [India] or from lawful guardianship, shall be punished with imprisonment of either description for a term which may extend to seven years, and shall also be liable to fine.

[3] According to Section 3 of The Majority Act, 1875 every person domiciled in India shall attain the age of majority on his completing the age of eighteen years and not before.

[4] **Section 164 of Cr.P.C, 1973**: Recording of Confessions and Statements

Any Metropolitan Magistrate or Judicial Magistrate may, whether or not he has jurisdiction in the case, record any confession or statement made to him in the course of an investigation under this Chapter or under any other law for the time being in force, or at any time afterwards before the commencement of the inquiry or trial:

Provided that no confession shall be recorded by a police officer on whom any power of a Magistrate has been conferred under any law for the time being in force.

Question of Law:

1) Whether a marriage contracted by a boy with a female of less than 18 years and a male of less than 21 year could be said to be valid marriage and the custody of the said girl be given to the husband (if he is not in custody)?

2) Whether a minor can be said to have reached the age of discretion and thereby walk away from the lawful guardianship of her parents and refuse to go in their custody?

Definition of Child under Prohibition of Child Marriage Act, 2006

According to Section 2 (a) of the Prohibition of Child Marriage Act, 2006, a "child" means a person who, if a male, has not completed twenty-one years of age, and if female, has not completed eighteen years of age.

Marriage with a minor child would not be valid but voidable and would become valid if within two years from the date of attaining 18 years in the case of female and 21 years in the case of male if she or he elects to accept the marriage, the marriage shall become a full-fledged valid marriage. Until such an event of acceptance of the marriage or lapse of limitation period, the marriage shall continue to remain as a voidable marriage.[5]

Case Referred: In *Amnider Kaur and Anr. v. State of Punjab and Ors.*,[6] decided by Punjab and Haryana High Court, the Single Judge of the said Court has taken a view that having regard to the provisions of Section 12 of the PCM Act, 2006[7] marriage with a minor girl would be void.

Ill-effects of child marriage can be summarized as under (Para 41 of the Judgment)[8] :

    (i)   Girls who get married at an early age are often more susceptible to

---

[5]   Section 3, The Prohibition Of Child Marriage Act, 2006

[6]   2010 Crl.L.J. 1154

[7]   **Section 12, The Prohibition Of Child Marriage Act, 2006**

    Marriage of a minor child to be void in certain circumstances.- Where a child, being a minor-

    (a) is taken or enticed out of the keeping of the lawful guardian; or

    (b) by force compelled, or by any deceitful means induced to go from any place; or

    (c) is sold for the purpose of marriage; and made to go through a form of marriage or if the minor is married after which the minor is sold or trafficked or used for immoral purposes, such marriage shall be null and void.

[8]   Ill effects of the child marriage were taken note of in the case of Association for Social Justice & Research v.Union of India & others, [W.P. (Crl.) No. 535/2010]

the health risks associated with early sexual initiation and childbearing, including HIV and obstetric fistula.

(ii) Young girls who lack status, power and maturity are often subjected to domestic violence, sexual abuse and social isolation.

(iii) Early marriage almost always deprives girls of their education or meaningful work, which contributes to persistent poverty.

(iv) Child Marriage perpetuates an unrelenting cycle of gender inequality, sickness and poverty.

(v) Getting the girls married at an early age when they are not physically mature, leads to highest rates of maternal and child mortality.

Decision by High Court:

Marriage which has been solemnised by petitioner No. 2 with petitioner No. l, who is child and a minor, is unsustainable in the eyes of law and is thus, declared as void. Court also held where the allegation against the husband is of enticing away minor girl from the lawful keeping of guardian/ parents and a case has been registered under Sections 363[9] / 366-A IPC[10], no protection under Section 482 Cr.P.C., 1973[11] can be granted by Court because in that eventuality police protection has to be granted to a fugitive of law.

Since girl has not attained majority and is residing with her parents, arrangement would continue. When girl becomes major it would be for her to exercise her right under the PCM, Act 2006 (Section 3) if she so desires and future course of action would depend threon. Petition was disposed of.

6

DNA Test and Powers of the Court[1]

Facts in Nutshell:

The case relates to refusal by a party to the litigation to comply with the court direction made in accordance with law to furnish a blood sample for DNA testing which would enable authoritative adjudication on the real issue in the matter. The Plaintiff has filed the suit seeking declaration that the Plaintiff is the naturally born son of the Defendants and that the Defendant No. 1 is the father of the Plaintiff. It is asserted that, though he was born to Smt. Ujjwala Sharma, Defendant No. 1 whilst her marriage to Sh. B.P. Sharma subsisted, the Plaintiff was not born from their wedlock. Reliance in this behalf has been placed on the report of blood samples drawn from Shri B.P. Sharma and DNA profiling which have been compared with the DNA profiling of the Plaintiff's blood sample which report reflects that Sh. B.P. Sharma cannot be his (the Plaintiff's) biological father. The Plaintiff has categorically asserted that he was born from an extramarital relationship between the Defendants. In this regard, he places reliance on the proximity between the parties in the plaint and relies on photographs which according to the Plaintiff manifest that the Defendants as well as the Plaintiff shared an intimate relationship.

The Defendant No. 1 does not dispute that the Plaintiff is the biological son of the Defendant No. 2, but denies relationship or intimacy with her as well as the Plaintiff. During the pendency of the suit, the Plaintiff filed IA No. 4720/2008 on 11th April, 2008 seeking a direction to the Defendant No. 1 to submit to DNA testing.

---

[1] Appellants: **Rohit Shekhar Vs.** Respondent: **Shri Narayan Dutt Tiwari and Anr.** 2011(4)RCR(Civil)459

Hon'ble Judges: Gita Mittal, J.

Short Summary of Case:

It is the case of the Plaintiff and Defendant No. 2 that the Plaintiff was born outside of marriage. He was born from a relationship between the Defendant Nos. 1 and 2. The Defendant No. 2 has stated that though she was married to Sh. B.P. Sharma from which marriage they were blessed with one son Siddharth on 30th October, 1968; that the Defendant No. 2 and her ex-husband did not have marital relationship or co-habitation since 1970; that the Defendant No. 1 became close to the Defendant No. 2 from 1968 and they entered into an intimate relationship in 1977 which resulted in the birth of Rohit Shekhar, the present Plaintiff on 15th February, 1979.

Decision by High Court:

The parties or their counsel are directed to appear before the Joint Registrar on 8th February, 2011. The Joint Registrar shalll obtain particulars and details to facilitate the DNA testing of the first Defendant; the said Defendant is directed to furnish such sample on a date and time to be designated by the Joint Registrar, by taking or drawing appropriate samples after ascertaining the details from the concerned accredited agency i.e. Centre for Cellular & Molecular Biology (Constituent Laboratory of the Council of Scientific Industrial Research, Government of India, Habsiguda Uppal Road, Hyderabad -500 007, Andhra Pradesh, India. The said institution shall furnish the report to this Court within six weeks of receiving the samples.

Defendant challenged the order of the court by way of special leave petition[2] in Supreme Court of India.

The Defendant No. 1 put forth the following reasons for the application:

(i) no useful purpose would be served to subject Defendant No. 1 to the test

---

2 **Article 136 in The Constitution Of India**

136. Special leave to appeal by the Supreme Court(1) Notwithstanding anything in this Chapter, the Supreme Court may, in its discretion, grant special leave to appeal from any judgment, decree, determination, sentence or order in any cause or matter passed or made by any court or tribunal in the territory of India

(2) Nothing in clause (1) shall apply to any judgment, determination, sentence or order passed or made by any court or tribunal constituted by or under any law relating to the Armed Forces

(ii) final relief cannot be granted to the Plaintiff because of Section 112of the Evidence Act[3]

(iii) no sample can be obtained from the Defendant No. 1 per force without his express consent or else it would violate fundamental rights of the Defendant No. 1 protected under Article 21 of the Constitution[4].

(iv) for the above reasons, not to pressurise, coerce or force the Defendant No. 1 to provide blood and/or tissue sample for DNA testing

Question before the Court:

The application therefore raises the question as to whether a person can be physically compelled to give a blood sample for DNA profiling in compliance with a civil court order in a paternity action? If it were held that the same was permissible, how is the court to mould its order and what would be the modalities for drawing the involuntary sample?

Submission by Plaintiff Counsel:

The Plaintiff submits that the Court has power under Section 75(e)[5] of the Code of Civil Procedure (CPC) read with Order-XXVI, Rule-10 (A) to issue a direction for holding a scientific technical or expert investigation.

Another question before the court was if a third party (to a marriage, like the first Defendant here) may be compelled to undergo scientific tests of the nature of giving blood samples for the purpose of DNA testing. In the case of *Goutam Kundu v. State of West Bengal and Anr.*[6] court held that

---

[3] **Birth during marriage, conclusive proof of legitimacy**

The fact that any person was born during the continuance of a valid marriage between his mother and any man, or within two hundred and eighty days after its dissolution, the mother remaining unmarried, shall be conclusive proof that he is the legitimate son of that man, unless it can be shown that the parties to the marriage had no access to each other at any time when he could have been begotten.

[4] **Article 21 in The Constitution Of India**

Protection of life and personal liberty No person shall be deprived of his life or personal liberty except according to procedure established by law

[5] **Section 75(e) of CPC: Power of the Court to issue Commissions**

(e) to hold a scientific, technical, or expert investigation;

[6] MANU/SC/0345/1993 : (1993) 3 SCC 418

1. A matrimonial court has the power to order a person to undergo medical test.

2. Passing of such an order by the court would not be in violation of the right to personal liberty under Article 21 of the Indian Constitution.

3. However, the Court should exercise such a power if the applicant has a strong prima facie case and there is sufficient material before the Court. If despite the order of the court, the Respondent refuses to submit himself to medical examination, the court will be entitled to draw an adverse inference against him.

In *Goutam Kundu v. State of West Bengal and Anr.*[7], it has been laid down that courts in India cannot order blood test as a matter of course and such prayers cannot be granted to have roving inquiry; there must be strong prima facie case and court must carefully examine as to what would be the consequence of ordering the blood test.

Submissions by Defendant No.1 Counsel:

Learned Counsel cited *Selvi v. State of Karnataka*[8] and placed observations of the Supreme Court in para 264 of the judgment:

264. In light of these conclusions, we hold that no individual should be forcibly subjected to any of the techniques in question, whether in the context of investigation in criminal cases or otherwise. Doing so would amount to an unwarranted intrusion into personal liberty. However, we do leave room for the voluntary administration of the impugned techniques in the context of criminal justice provided that certain safeguards are in place. Even when the subject has given consent to undergo any of these tests, the test results by themselves cannot be admitted as evidence because the subject does not exercise conscious control over the responses during the administration of

---

[7] MANU/SC/0345/1993 : (1993) 3 SCC 418

[8] MANU/SC/0325/2010 : (2010) 7 SCC 263

[9] **Section 27 of the Evidence Act**: How much of information received from accused may be proved.- Provided that, when any fact is deposed to as discovered in consequence of information received from a person accused of any offence, in the custody of a police- officer, so much of such information, whether it amounts to a confession or not, as relates distinctly to the fact thereby discovered, may be proved.

the test. However, any information or material that is subsequently discovered with the help of voluntary administered test results can be admitted in accordance with Section 27[9] of the Evidence Act, 1872.

Miss. Swati Lodha v. State of Rajasthan and Anr.[10] In this case the court was concerned with the refusal to submit to a blood test by a person accused of the offence of rape in which a child had been born to the victim. In para 16 of the pronouncement, the court considered the value to be attached to the test also and held as follows:

16. A review of the above law, would go to show the following propositions are well-settled:

(1) Report of a blood-test is capable of amounting to corroboration of the statement of the complainant. It amounts to corroboration even under the common law. The nature of the corroboration would necessarily vary according to the particular circumstances of the offence charged. The test applicable to determine the nature and extent of the corroboration is the same whether the case falls within the rule of common law or within that class of offences for which corroboration is required by statute. A Criminal Court can make a direction for a blood-test to be taken by taking blood-sample of the complainant, accused and of the child. In certain cases, where it is contrary to the interest of a minor, the Court may not make a blood-test direction.

(2) The Court cannot order an adult to submit to blood test. A blood-test which involves insertion of a needle in the veins of a person, is an assault, unless consented to. It would need express statutory authority to require an adult to submit to it. This is based on the fundamental that human body is inviolable and no one can prick it.

(3) Where a Court makes a direction for a blood-test, and the accused fails or refuses to comply with the blood-test direction, the Court can in the circumstances of the case, use the refusal

---

[10] MANU/RH/0088/1990 : 1991 Cri.L.J. 939

or failure of the accused to submit to blood test as a corroborative evidence against him. If a party refuses to submit to blood-test, the Court may infer that some impediment existed which pointed out towards the implication of the accused.

Decision by Court:

Court held that refusal by the Defendant No. 1 to submit the blood sample is wilful, malafide, unreasonable and unjustified. It held that ordering a test upon a person to determine biological relationships between him and the Plaintiff would not attract the sanction of Article 21 of the Constitution of India. Hence the prayer of Defendant No.1 for not doing DNA testing was rejected by court.

7

Women can get Divorce if Husband Aboard[1]

Question before the Court:

The legality of a matrimonial proceeding initiated by the Wife before a family court in India invoking the provisions of the Hindu Marriage Act against her Hindu husband having his domicile in New Jersey in the United States of America is the substantial issue raised in the writ appeal.

Facts in Nutshell:

The appellant was an Indian Citizen and on his migration to the United States of America, he was granted US Citizenship. The second respondent was residing adjacent to the residence of the appellant at Madras. Their marriage was solemnized on 17 April, 2002. The marriage was conducted in accordance with the Hindu Rites and custom in the Balaji Temple at New Jersey. The parties were living happily as husband and wife. Subsequently, during the second week of January, 2003 the second respondent came to India for a short visit promising to return after completing her dance program. However all of a sudden, she changed her mind and contrary to the promise made, began to act in films with no idea of returning to States. She also filed divorce petition in before the Principal Family Court, Chennai on the ground of cruelty. Since the petitioner was residing in United States, he was not aware of the proceedings initiated by the second respondent. Summons was not served on him. However, an ex parte order[2] of divorce was granted on 19 July, 2004. When the appellant came to know the said

---

[1] Appellants: **R. Sridharan** Vs. Respondent: **The Presiding Officer, Principal Family Court and R. Sukanya** MANU/TN/0976/2010

Hon'ble Judges: Elipe Dharma Rao and K.K. Sasidharan, JJ.

[2] **Exparte Order**: Refers to situations in which only one party (and not the adversary) appears before a judge.

order, he took necessary steps for setting aside the ex parte order. The learned Family Court Judge was pleased to set aside the ex parte order of divorce. The appellant filed writ petition for issuance of a writ of prohibition[3]. According to the appellant, the Family Court at Chennai has no jurisdiction to entertain the divorce proceedings, as he is a citizen of United States of America and a permanent resident in the said Country. The Court in India had no jurisdiction to take up the matter involving American citizens, having his domicile in United States of America. Therefore, the Family Court proceedings at Chennai was one without jurisdiction and as such, he prayed for a writ to direct the first respondent to abstain from taking up the matrimonial proceedings.

Counter Statement by Second Respondent:

The second respondent filed a counter opposing the plea made by the appellant. According to the second respondent, the marriage was solemnized in Balaji Temple at Bridge Water, New Jersey in United States of America as per the Hindu Rites and Customs. Therefore the rights and obligations of the parties runs from the provisions of the Hindu Marriage Act. As per Section 19(iii-a) of the Hindu Marriage Act, 1955[4], she was competent to institute proceedings for dissolution of marriage at the place where she is residing on the date of presentation of the divorce proceedings. It was her further contention that it was not open to the appellant to raise the question of jurisdiction after submitting to the jurisdiction of the Family Court by filing counter. Accordingly, she prayed for dismissal of the writ petition.

---

[3] **Writ of Prohibition**: A writ of prohibition is a writ directing a subordinate to stop doing something the law prohibits.

[4] Court to which petition shall be presented: Every petition under this Act shall be presented to the District Court within the local limits of whose ordinary original civil jurisdiction-

(i) the marriage was solemnized, or

(ii) the respondent, at the time of presentation of the petition, resides, or

(iii) the parties to the marriage last resided together, or

[(iii-a) in case the wife is the petitioner, where she is residing on the date of presentation of the petition, or]

(iv) the petitioner is residing at the time of the presentation of the petition, in a case where the respondent is, at that time, residing outside the territories to which this Act extends, or has not been heard of as being alive for a period of seven years or more by those persons who would naturally have heard of him if he were alive.

Decision by Court in writ:

The learned Single Judge opined that the appellant had his domicile of India by origin and the marriage was solemnised as per Hindu vedic rights and customs and as such the parties are governed by their personal law. Therefore the Court in India exercising jurisdiction under Hindu Marriage Act had jurisdiction to entertain the divorce petition irrespective of the present residence of the opposite party. Accordingly, the writ petition was dismissed.

Decision by High Court in writ appeal:

The question raised by the appellant before the writ court was as to whether the Family Court in India has got jurisdiction to try the matter involving a foreign citizen whose domicile is outside the territory to which the Hindu Marriage Act extends. There is no dispute that the appellant and the second respondent are governed by the provisions of the Hindu Marriage Act. The appellant was originally an Indian citizen and on his migration to United States of America, he acquired citizenship in the said country. When the marriage was solemnized under the Hindu law, the proceedings for divorce has also to be made under the Hindu Marriage Act. The appellant cannot take any exception to the proceedings in India under the provisions of the Hindu Marriage Act, merely on account of his US citizenship or domicile.

The Hindu Marriage Act applies to all Hindus domiciled in the territory to which the act extends. Section 19 gives a right to the wife to present the petition to the District Court within whose jurisdiction she is residing. When the wife was given the right to initiate the proceedings before the local District Court where she is actually residing, such a provision cannot be defeated by taking a technical plea that no such proceeding would lie on account of Foreign Citizenship of the husband or his domicile in another country.

Court also took strong note of the *Y. Narasimharao v. Y. Venkatalakshmi*[5] case where the issue before the Supreme Court was regarding recognition of foreign judgment on matrimonial disputes granted by a Foreign Court. In the said case, the marriage was as per the

---

[5] 1991(3) S.C.C. 451

provisions of the Hindu Marriage Act. However the decree of divorce was granted by the Court at Missouri. The Supreme Court held that the Court at Missouri has no jurisdiction to entertain a petition under the Hindu Marriage Act. . In Narasimha Rao's case the Supreme Court categorically stated that marriages performed under the Hindu Marriage Act can be dissolved only under the said Act.

Therefore on a true construction of Section 19 read with Sections 1 and 2 of the Hindu Marriage Act, court was of the view that the Family court at Chennai has got jurisdiction to try the matrimonial litigation initiated by the second respondent not withstanding the fact that the appellant is a citizen of United States of America and not an ordinary resident of India. Writ appeal was dismissed by court.

8

Cruelty by Wife[1]

Ratio Decidendi[2]:

"If from the conduct of the spouse, an inference can be legitimately drawn that the treatment of the spouse is such that it causes an apprehension in the mind of the other spouse, about his or her mental welfare, then this conduct amounts to cruelty."

Facts in Nutshell:

Husband (Respondent[3]) filed an application for divorce on the ground of cruelty alleging that because of the acts of cruelty on several occasions perpetuated by the wife (appellant[4]), the husband (respondent) was under apprehension that it would not be desirable and safe to stay with the wife (appellant) and to continue their marital relationships. Husband also alleged that the wife (appellant) used to keep the children tied by ropes and she attempted to throw them down from the rooftop and used to physically torture them. She was temperamentally very cruel and used to behave cruelly with the children also. She always used to threaten that she will destroy the whole family of the respondent and that there would be no successor left in the family.

---

[1] Appellants: **Smt. Mayadevi** Vs. **Respondent: Jagdish Prasad** AIR2007SC1426
  Hon'ble Judges: Dr. Arijit Pasayat and Dalveer Bhandari , JJ.

[2] **Meaning of Ratio Decidendi**
  Ratio decidendi is a Latin phrase meaning "the reason" or "the rationale for the decision." The ratio decidendi is "[t]he point in a case which determines the judgment" or "the principle which the case establishes."

[3] A person against whom a petition or complaint is filed in a court.

[4] One who appeals, or asks for a rehearing or review of a cause by a higher tribunal.

On 5.4.2002 she left her parental home along with three children. Since she did not return the husband (respondent), started searching for her. Police was informed and on search dead bodies of the three children were recovered from the well and appellant(wife) was also taken out of the well. A criminal case was instituted and she was convicted for an offence under Section 302 of the Indian Penal Code, 1860[5] (in short the 'IPC'). Meanwhile, she filed a false case alleging dowry demand[6] against the respondent (husband) and his family members.

Decision by Trail Court and High Court:

The trial Court and High Court clearly made out a case for dowry.

Meaning of Cruelty:

The expression "cruelty" has not been defined in the Hindu Marriage Act, 1955. Cruelty can be physical or mental. Cruelty which is a ground for dissolution of marriage may be defined as wilful and unjustifiable conduct of such character as to cause danger to life, limb or health, bodily or mental, or as to give rise to a reasonable apprehension of such a danger. The question of mental cruelty has to be considered in the light of the norms of marital ties of the particular society to which the parties belong, their social values, status, environment in which they live. Cruelty, as noted above, includes mental cruelty, which falls within the purview of a matrimonial wrong. Cruelty need not be physical. If from the conduct of his spouse same is established and/or an inference can be legitimately drawn that the treatment of the spouse is such that it causes an apprehension in the mind of the other spouse, about his or her mental welfare then this conduct amounts to cruelty. Cruelty may be physical or corporeal or may be mental. In physical cruelty, there can be tangible and direct evidence, but in the case of mental cruelty there may not at the same time be direct evidence. Physical violence is not absolutely essential to constitute cruelty and a consistent course of conduct inflicting immeasurable mental agony and torture may well constitute cruelty

---

[5] **Section 302 I.P.C 1860**

Punishment for murder: Whoever commits murder shall be punished with death, or [imprisonment for life] and shall also be liable to fine.

[6] Material assets such as money or property that is provided by a bride to her husband at the time of their marriage.

within the meaning of Section 10 of the Hindu Marriage Act, 1955[7]. Mental cruelty may consist of verbal abuses and insults by using filthy and abusive language leading to constant disturbance of mental peace of the other party.

Every matrimonial conduct, which may cause annoyance to the other, may not amount to cruelty. Mere trivial irritations, quarrels between spouses, which happen in day-to-day married life, may also not amount to cruelty.

Decision of the Court:

Court rejected the appeal[8] of wife and held that the foundation of a sound marriage is tolerance, adjustment and respecting one another. Court also held that husband (respondant) was subjected to cruelty by wife.

---

[7] **Section 10 in The Hindu Marriage Act, 1955**
Judicial separation.

(1) Either patty to a marriage, whether solemnized before or after the commencement of this Act, may present a petition praying for a decree for judicial separation on any of the grounds specified in sub- section (1) of section 13, and in the case of a wife also on any of the grounds specified in sub- section (2) thereof, as grounds on which a petition for divorce might have been presented.]

(2) Where a decree for judicial separation has been passed, it shall no longer be obligatory for the petitioner to cohabit with the respondent, but the court may, on the application by petition of either party and on being satisfied of the truth of the statements made in such petition, rescind the decree if it considers it just and reasonable to do so. NULLITY OF MARRIAGE AND DIVORCE

[8] **Meaning of Appeal**
To make application for the removal of (a cause) from an inferior to a superior judge or court for a rehearing or review on acco unt of alleged injustice or illegality in the trial below.

CRIMINAL LAW

Criminal Law

The Indian Penal Code formulated by the British during the British Raj in 1860, forms the backbone of criminal law in India. It has since been amended several times and is now supplemented by other criminal provisions. In the state of Jammu and Kashmir, the IPC is known as Ranbir Penal Code (RPC). The Code of Criminal Procedure, 1973 governs the procedural aspects of the criminal law. The criminal justice system descends from the British model. The judiciary and the bar are independent although efforts have been made by some politicians to undermine the autonomy of the judiciary. Under the constitution, criminal jurisdiction belongs concurrently to the central government and the states. The prevailing law on crime prevention and punishment is embodied in two principal statutes: the Indian Penal Code and the Code of Criminal Procedure of 1973. These laws take precedence over any state legislation, and the states cannot alter or amend them. Separate legislation enacted by both the states and the central government also has established criminal liability for acts such as smuggling, illegal use of arms and ammunition, and corruption. All legislation, however, remains subordinate to the constitution.

The Indian Penal Code came into force in 1862; as amended, it continued in force in 1993. Based on British criminal law, the code defines basic crimes and punishments, applies to resident foreigners and citizens alike, and recognizes offenses committed abroad by Indian nationals.

The penal code classifies crimes under various categories: crimes against the state, the armed forces, public order, the human body, and property; and crimes relating to elections, religion, marriage, and health, safety, decency, and morals. Crimes are cognizable or noncognizable, comparable to the distinction between felonies and misdemeanors in legal use in the United States. Six categories of punishment include fines, forfeiture of property, simple imprisonment, rigorous imprisonment with hard labor, life imprisonment, and death. An individual can be imprisoned for failure to pay fines, and up to three months' solitary confinement can occur during rare rigorous imprisonment sentences. Commutation is possible for death and life sentences. Executions are by hanging and are rare—there were only three in 1993 and two in 1994—and are usually reserved for crimes such as political assassination and multiple murders.

Courts of law try cases under procedures that resemble the Anglo-American pattern. The machinery for prevention and punishment through the criminal court system rests on the Code of Criminal Procedure of 1973, which came into force on April 1, 1974, replacing a code dating from 1898. The code includes provisions to expedite the judicial process, increase efficiency, prevent abuses, and provide legal relief to the poor. The basic framework of the criminal justice system, however, was left unchanged.

Constitutional guarantees protect the accused, as do various provisions embodied in the 1973 code. Treatment of those arrested under special security legislation can depart from these norms, however. In addition, for all practical purposes, the implementation of these norms varies widely based on the class and social background of the accused. In most cases, police officers have to secure a warrant from a magistrate before instituting searches and seizing evidence. Individuals taken into custody have to be advised of the charges brought against them, have the right to seek counsel, and have to appear before a magistrate within twenty-four hours of arrest. The magistrate has the option to release the accused on bail. During trial a defendant is protected against self-incrimination, and only confessions given before a magistrate are legally valid. Criminal cases usually take place in open trial, although in limited circumstances closed trials occur. Procedures exist for appeal to higher courts.

India has an integrated and relatively independent court system. At the apex is the Supreme Court, which has original, appellate, and advisory jurisdiction. Below it are eighteen high courts that preside over the states and union territories. The high courts have supervisory authority over all subordinate courts within their jurisdictions. In general, these include several district courts headed by district magistrates, who in turn have several subordinate magistrates under their supervision. The Code of Criminal Procedure established three sets of magistrates for the subordinate criminal courts. The first consists of executive magistrates, whose duties include issuing warrants, advising the police, and determining proper procedures to deal with public violence. The second consists of judicial magistrates, who are essentially trial judges. Petty criminal cases are sometimes settled in panchayat courts.

Hierarchy of Courts in India

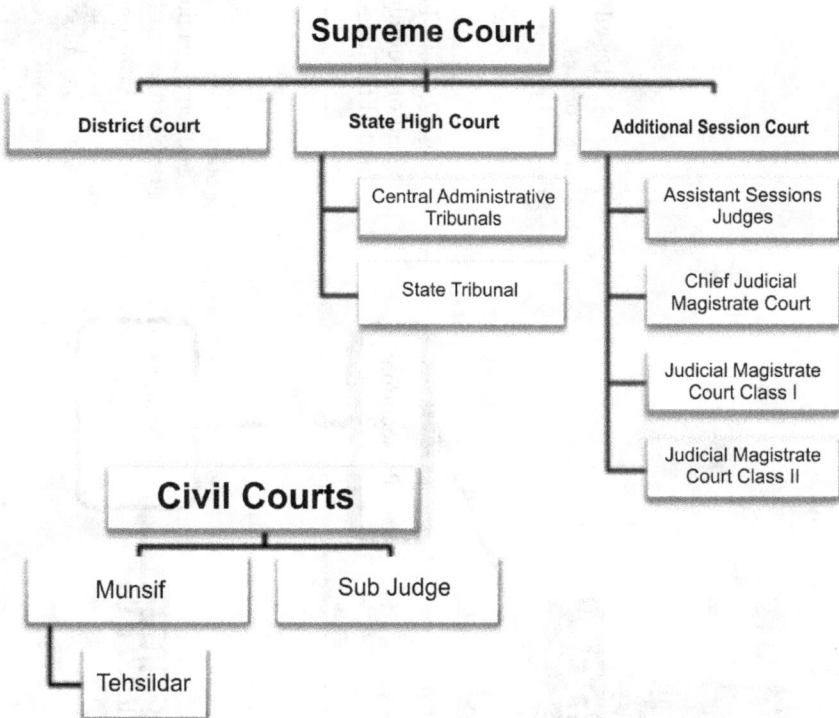

```
                        ┌──────────────────────┐
                        │    Supreme Court     │
                        └──────────────────────┘
        ┌───────────────────────┼────────────────────────┐
┌───────────────┐      ┌──────────────────┐      ┌────────────────────────┐
│ District Court │     │ State High Court │      │ Additional Session Court │
└───────────────┘      └──────────────────┘      └────────────────────────┘
```

District Court	State High Court	Additional Session Court
	Central Administrative Tribunals	Assistant Sessions Judges
	State Tribunal	Chief Judicial Magistrate Court
		Judicial Magistrate Court Class I
		Judicial Magistrate Court Class II

Civil Courts

Munsif	Sub Judge
Tehsildar	

Legal Procedure

Stage 3: Based on the Evidence the judge passes the judgments bases on the legal provision pertaining that conflict.

Stage 2: Both Legal Representations on behalf of their clients present their case in front of the judge.

Stage 1: In case of a dispute where the conflicting parties seek a Legal Solution Both parties constitutionally have a right to choose their own legal representative, if either one is unable to find representation, the judiciary allocates a Legal representative on his behalf

JUDGE

Prosecution

Defense

Disputing Party 2

Disputing Party 1

DISPUTE

Criminal law, one of two broad categories of law, deals with acts of intentional harm to individuals but which, in a larger sense, are offences against us all. It is a crime to break into a home because the act not only violates the privacy and safety of the home's occupants - it shatters the collective sense that we are secure in our own homes. A crime is a deliberate or reckless act that causes harm to another person or another person's property, and it is also a crime to neglect a duty to protect others from harm. Canada's Criminal Code, created in 1892, lists hundreds of criminal offences - from vandalism to murder - and stipulates the range of punishment that can be imposed. Since crimes are an offence against society, normally the state or Crown investigates and prosecutes criminal allegations on the victim's behalf. The police gather evidence and, in court, public prosecutors present the case against the person accused of the crime. For someone to be convicted of a crime, it must be proven that a crime was committed and, for most offences, that the person meant to commit the crime. For instance, striking another person is the crime of assault but it is only a crime if the blow was intentional.

Criminal law is that part of the law which characterizes certain kinds of wrongdoings as offences the state, not necessarily violating any private right, and punishable by the state. Crime is "an unlawful act or default which is an offence against the public and renders the person guilty of the act liable to legal punishment "Criminal law is a part of public law, as the society or 'the people, are directly involved. Their interests are represented by some governmental agency, officers or official whose obligation is to see that justice is accomplished and the ends of the society fulfilled.

Thus, crimes are thought of as wrongs not only against the injured parties but also against the society. Generally, it is the police, as public servants, whose duty is the (i) prevention and detection of crime and (ii) Prosecution of offences before the court of law.

As the maintenance of law and order in a society is the primary function of the state it is inevitable that prosecution is the exclusive right of the state. However, the injure individual may legally enforce the criminal law by beginning proceedings himself under section 200 of the Criminal procedure code but rarely do so in practice. In a criminal case, a prosecutor representing the state brings suit against the defendant for an alleged violation of the criminal law. The prosecutor, in effect, represents the public at large. The law penalizes a violation of the criminal law with a fine or imprisonment. The victim is not, as a general rule, compensated for the injury suffered by him.

9

Acid Throwers May Get Life Sentence[1]

Ratio Decidendi: "Prosecution shall proved guilt of Accused beyond reasonable doubt."

Facts in Nutshell: Mr Om Prakash (accused), was charged for having murdered his wife Kaushalya and 2 minor children; Vikram and Vickey and for having caused simple hurt to 2 women; Usha and Asha. The motive attributed for the crime pertaining to the murder of Kaushalya was that Om Prakash suspected Kaushalya of having illicit relation with a neighbour named Jogi.

When Kaushalya was sitting on a dari (mattress) on the ground floor i.e. the residence of Usha and Asha and when Vikram and Vickey, aged 3 years and 11/2 years respectively, sons of Usha were sleeping on either side of Kaushalya, having an intention to kill Kaushalya Om Prakash came down from the top floor with a jug full of acid and threw the same on Kaushalya; needless to state the acid caused corrosive burn injuries to the 2 infant boys. Usha and Asha also received acid burn injuries on their person when they intervened to save the infant boys and Kaushalya. After committing the dastardly act Om Prakash fled from the place.

Decision by Trail Court: The learned Court of Sessions has convicted the Appellant for the offence of having murdered Kaushalya, Vikram and Vicky and for having caused simple hurt to Usha and Asha. For the offence

---

[1] Appellants: **Om Prakash Vs.** Respondent: **State** MANU/DE/3248/2011
Hon'ble Judges: Pradeep Nandrajog and Sunil Gaur, JJ.

of murder[2] the Appellant has been sentenced to undergo imprisonment for life and for the offence of causing simple hurt to Usha and Asha has been sentenced to undergo rigorous imprisonment for 1 Year.

Decision by Delhi High Court: The quantity of **acid** thrown is so huge, a fact which can be gleaned from the extensive burn injuries suffered by Kaushalya, Vikram and Vickey, that it must be inferred that the Appellant desired to kill his wife. *In any case, a person who throws a jug full of acid on a person has to be saddled with the knowledge that he is doing an imminently dangerous act which would in all probability cause the death of the person on whom acid is thrown.* The Hon'ble Judges of Delhi High Court concur with the reasoning of the learned Trial Judge that qua Kaushalya, the act of the Appellant constitutes an offence of murder.

If a man, having intention to kill his wife, **throws** a jug full of **acid** on his wife on seeing her sitting in the middle of 2 infants, it certainly would be said that the act is so imminently dangerous even as regards the children that the man ought to know that in all probability even the 2 infants would be the victims of the imminently dangerous act. Thus, Section 300 of I.P.C[3] fourthly stands attracted.

---

[2] **Section 302 of I.P.C, 1860**: Punishment for Murder

Whoever commits murder shall be punished with death, or [imprisonment for life] and shall also be liable to fine.

[3] **Section 300 I.P.C, 1860** : Murder

Except in the cases hereinafter excepted, culpable homicide is murder, if the act by which the death is caused is done with the intention of causing death, or—

Secondly.—If it is done with the intention of causing such bodily injury as the offender knows to be likely to cause the death of the person to whom the harm is caused, or—

Thirdly.—If it is done with the intention of causing bodily injury to any person and the bodily injury intended to be in-flicted is sufficient in the ordinary course of nature to cause death, or—

Fourthly.—If the person committing the act knows that it is so imminently dangerous that it must, in all probability, cause death or such bodily injury as is likely to cause death, and commits such act without any excuse for incurring the risk of causing death or such injury as aforesaid.

10

Live-in Relationships among adults fine[1]

Facts in Nutshell: A well known actress (S. Khushboo) approached Hon'ble Supreme Court to seek quashing of criminal proceedings pending against her. As many as 23 Criminal Complaints were filed against her, mostly in the State of Tamil Nadu, for the offences contemplated under Sections 499[2], 500[3] and 505[4] of the Indian Penal Code, 1860 [hereinafter 'IPC'] and

---

[1] Appellants: **S. Khushboo** Vs. Respondent: **Kanniammal and Anr**. 2010(2)ACR2082(SC), AIR2010SC3196

   Hon'ble Judges: K. G. Balakrishnan, C.J., Deepak Verma and B. S. Chauhan, JJ.

[2] **Section 499 of I.P.C, 1860**, Defamation: Whoever, by words either spoken or intended to be read, or by signs or by visible representations, makes or publishes any imputation concerning any person intending to harm, or knowing or having reason to believe that such imputation will harm, the reputation of such person, is said, except in the cases hereinafter expected, to defame that person.

[3] **Section 500 of I.P.C, 1860** Punishment for defamation: Whoever defames another shall be punished with simple imprisonment for a term which may extend to two years, or with fine, or with both.

[4] **Section 505 of I.P.C, 1860** : Statements conducting to public mischief: [(1) Whoever makes, publishes or circulates any statement, rumor or report,-

   (a) with intent to cause, or which is likely to cause, any officer, soldier, [sailor or airman] in the Army, [Navy or Air Force] [of India] to mutiny or otherwise disregard or fail in his duty as such; or

   (b) with intent to cause, or which is likely to cause, fear or alarm to the public, or to any section of the public whereby any person may be induced to commit an offence against the State or against the public tranquility; or

   (c) with intent to incite, or which is likely to incite, any class or community of persons to commit any offence against any other class or community;

   shall be punished with imprisonment which may extend to [three years], or with fine, or with both.

   [(2) Statements creating or promoting enmity, hatred or ill-will between classes Whoever makes, publishes or circulates any statement or report containing rumor or alarming news with intent to create or promote, or which is likely to create or promote, on grounds of religion, race, place of birth, residence, language, caste or community or any other ground whatsoever, feelings of enmity, hatred or ill-will between different religious, racial, language or regional groups or castes or communities, shall be punished with imprisonment which may extend to three years, or with fine, or with both.

   (1) Offence under sub-section (2) committed in place of worship, etc- Whoever commits an offence specified in sub-section (2) in any place of worship or in an assembly engaged in the performance of religious worship or religious ceremonies, shall be punished with imprisonment which may extend to five years and shall also be liable to fine.]

Sections 4[5] and 6[6] of the Indecent Representation of Women (Prohibition) Act, 1986[hereinafter 'Act 1986']. The trigger for the same were some remarks made by her in an interview to a leading news magazine and later on the same issue was reported in a distorted manner in another periodical.

Decision of High Court: Faced with the predicament of contesting the criminal proceedings instituted against her in several locations, the appellant(S. khushboo) had approached the High Court of Madras, praying for the quashing of proceedings through the exercise of its inherent power under Section 482 of the Code of Criminal Procedure, 1973[7]. The High Court rejected her plea vide impugned judgment and order dated 30.4.2008.

Submission by Counsel appearing for the Appellant: It was stated that the appellant had made a fair and reasonable comment as a prudent person, and therefore, the opinion expressed by the appellant is fully protected under Article 19(1)(a) of the Constitution of India which guarantees freedom of speech and expression to all citizens.

Submission by Counsel appearing for the Respondents:

Since the High Court has refused to quash the complaints, the Court should not interfere either since the complaints require determination of factual controversies that are best left to be decided by a court of first instance. It was contended that the constitutional protection for speech and expression is not absolute and that it is subject to reasonable restrictions based on considerations of 'public order', 'defamation', 'decency and morality' among other grounds.

---

[5] **Section 4 of the Indecent Representation of Women Act, 1986**: Prohibition of publication or sending by post of books, pamphlets, etc. containing indecent representation of women- No person shall produce or cause to be produced, sell, let to hire, distribute, circulate or send by post any book, pamphlet, paper, slide, film, writing, drawing, painting, photograph, representation or figure which contains indecent representation of women in any;

[6] **Section 6 of the Indecent Representation of Women Act, 1986:** Any person who contravenes the provisions of section 3 or section 4 shall be punishable on first conviction with imprisonment of either description for a term which may extend to two years, and with fine which may extend to two thousand rupees, and in the event of a second or subsequent conviction with imprisonment for terms of not less than six months but which may extend to five years and also with a fine not less than ten thousand rupees but which may extend to one lakh rupees.

[7] **Section 482 of Cr.PC, 1973:** Saving of inherent powers of High Court. Nothing in this Code shall be deemed to limit or affect the inherent powers of the High Court to make such orders as may be necessary to give effect to any order under this Code, or to prevent abuse of the process of any Court or otherwise to secure the ends of justice.

Observation by Hon'ble Supreme Court: At the outset, the court is of the view that there is absolutely no basis for proceeding against the appellant in respect of some of the alleged offences. For example, the Act, 1986 was enacted to punish publishers and advertisers who knowingly disseminate materials that portray women in an indecent manner. However this statute cannot be used in the present case where the appellant has merely referred to the incidence of pre-marital sex in her statement which was published by a news magazine and subsequently reported in another periodical. It would defy logic to invoke the offences mentioned in this statute to proceed against the appellant, who cannot be described as an 'advertiser' or 'publisher' by any means. Similarly, Section 509 IPC criminalises a 'word' gesture or act intended to insult the modesty of a woman' and in order to establish this offence it is necessary to show that the modesty of a particular woman or a readily identifiable group of women has been insulted by a spoken word, gesture or physical act. Clearly this offence cannot be made out when the complainants' grievance is with the publication of what the appellant had stated in a written form. Likewise, some of the complaints have mentioned offences such as those contemplated by Section 153A IPC ('Promoting enmity between different groups etc.,') which have no application to the present case since the appellant was not speaking on behalf of one group and the content of her statement was not directed against any particular group either.

Coming to the substance of the complaints, we fail to see how the appellant's remarks amount to 'obscenity' in the context of Section 292 IPC. Clause (1) to Section 292 states that the publication of a book, pamphlet, paper, writing, drawing, painting, representation, figure, etc., will be deemed obscene, if -

- It is lascivious (i.e. expressing or causing sexual desire) or

- Appeals to the prurient interest (i.e. excessive interest in sexual matters), or

- If its effect, or the effect of any one of the items, tends to deprave and corrupt persons, who are likely to read, see, or hear the matter contained in such materials.

In the present case, the appellant takes full responsibility for her statement which was published in 'India Today', a leading news magazine.

It would be apt to refer back to the decision of this Court in *Samaresh Bose v. Amal Mitra*[8] where the Court held that in judging the question of obscenity, the judge in the first place should try to place himself in the position of the author and from the viewpoint of the author, the judge should try to understand what is it that the author seeks to convey and whether what the author conveys has any literary and artistic value. Judge should thereafter place himself in the position of a reader of every age group in whose hands the book is likely to fall and should try to appreciate what kind of possible influence the book is likely to have on the minds of the reader.

In the present case, the appellant has merely referred to the increasing incidence of pre-marital sex and called for its societal acceptance. At no point of time appellant described the sexual act or said anything that could arouse sexual desires in the mind of a reasonable and prudent reader. It is difficult to appreciate the claim that the statements published as part of the survey were in the nature of obscene communications.

Paragraph 29 of the Judgment : While there can be no doubt that in India, marriage is an important social institution, we must also keep our minds open to the fact that there are certain individuals or groups who do not hold the same view. To be sure, there are some indigenous groups within our country wherein sexual relations outside the marital setting are accepted as a normal occurrence. Even in the societal mainstream, there are a significant number of people who see nothing wrong in engaging in premarital sex.

Decision by Supreme Court: Various complaints filed against the appellant do not support o even draw a prima facie case for any of the statutory offences as alleged. Therefore, the appeals are allowed and the impugned judgment and order of the High Court dated 30.4.2008 is set aside. The impugned criminal proceedings were quashed.

---

[8] MANU/SC/0102/1985 : AIR 1986 SC 967

11

Duty of the Husband to Protect his Wife when Harrased by In-Laws[1]

Ratio Decidendi[2] : "Benefit of doubt shall always be given to accused."

Facts in Nutshell: This case was an appeal against the judgment and orders of learned Additional Sessions Judge where judge convicted all the accused under Section 235(2) of the Code of Criminal Procedure[3], for the offence punishable under Section 498(a)[4] read with Section 34[5] of Indian Penal Code and sentenced them to suffer rigorous imprisonment for three years and a fine of Rs. 1,000/- was imposed on each of the accused and in default to suffer rigorous imprisonment for three months. Similarly, the

---

[1] Appellants: **Anantrao Gyanaba Pawar, Sou. Savitribai Anantrao Pawar, Mrityanjay @ Sambhaji Anant Pawar and Sau. Vijaya Vishwasrao Salunkhe** Vs. Respondent: **The State of Maharashtra** AND

Appellants: The State of Maharashtra Vs. Respondent: Anantrao Gyanaba Pawar, Sou. Savitribai Anantrao Pawar, Mrityanjay @ Sambhaji Anant Pawar and Sau. Vijaya Vishwasrao Salunkhe II(2011)DMC277

Hon'ble Judges: P.B. Majmudar and Anoop V. Mohta, JJ.

[2] **Meaning of Ratio Decidendi**

Ratio decidendi is a Latin phrase meaning "the reason" or "the rationale for the decision." The ratio decidendi is "[t]he point in a case which determines the judgment" or "the principle which the case establishes."

[3] **Section 235 Cr.P.C , 1973** : Judgment of acquittal or conviction (2) If the accused is convicted, the Judge shall, unless he proceeds in accordance with the provisions of section 360 hear the accused on the question of sentence, and then pass sentence on him according to law.

[4] **Section 498 (A) of the IPC 1860**: Husband or relative of husband of a woman subjecting her to cruelty. Whoever, being the husband or the relative of the husband of a woman, subjects such woman to cruelty shall be pun-ished with imprisonment for a term which may extend to three years and shall also be liable to fine.

[5] **Section 34 of I.P.C , 1860**: Acts done by several persons in furtherance of common intention

When a criminal act is done by several persons in furtherance of the common intention of all, each of such persons is liable for that act in the same manner as if it were done by him alone.

accused have also been convicted under Section 306[6] read with Section 34 of Indian Penal Code, for which also same sentence is awarded. Being aggrieved by the order appeal is filed.

During the pendency of appeal, the original accused No. 2 Savitribai Anantrao Pawar has died. Therefore the appeal is required to be considered in connection with appellant/accused Nos. 1, 3 'and 4 only. The appellant/ accused No. 1 is the father of appellant/accused Nos. 3 and 4. Appellant/ accused No. 2 i.e. mother-in-law of the deceased, has already died during the pendency of the appeal.

Case of Prosecution: The marriage of Sushma (deceased) with accused No. 3 was solemnized in the year 1987. The complainant Vithoba Gangadhar Surve, father of the deceased, had given various household items to her daughter at the time of marriage, including the gold ornaments. Initially, for some time, the deceased was treated with love and affection after the marriage. Thereafter, accused started illtreating the victim by demanding certain items, which ultimately were given by the brother of the deceased. On 14-06-1989 at about 8.30 a.m., the deceased committed suicide by pouring kerosene on her body and set herself ablaze on fire and died in hospital.

Case cited by Additional Public Prosecutor: *Pawan Kumar and Ors. v. State of Haryana*[7] wherein it was held that cruelty or harassment need not be physical. Mental torture would be sufficient.

Decision by High Court: The court held that there was ground for presuming that the appellant had instigated the deceased i.e. wife (demand from the husband's side from the girl and her parents for the various articles as aforesaid and on failure, the girl was tortured, harassed by words and deeds amounting to cruelty.) to commit suicide and therefore the appellant has committed the offence under Section 306 read with Section 34 IPC. Appeallant No.1 and 4 were acquitted by court on the reason of benefit of doubt. Appellant No. 3 was put in jail .

---

[6] **Section 306 of I.P.C , 1860**: Abetment of Suicide

If any person commits suicide, whoever abets the commission of such suicide, shall be punished with imprisonment of either description for a term which may extend to ten years, and shall also be liable to fine.

[7] AIR 1998 SC 958

Court Observed (Para 50 of the Judgment): The husband should always be at the side of the wife and even if there is any harassment or ill treatment on the part of the other family members, it is the duty of the husband to protect his wife.

12

Indian Committing Crime abroad can be tried in India[1]

Facts in Nutshell: The Petitioner, Thota Venkateswarlu, was married to the Respondent No. 2, ParvathareddySuneetha, on 27th November, 2005, as per Hindu traditions and customs in Andhra Pradesh. At the time of marriage 12 lakhs in cash, 45 sovereigns of gold and 50,000/- as Adapaduchu Katnam is alleged to have been given to the Accused Nos. 1 to 4, who are the husband, the mother-in-law and other relatives of the husband. According to the Respondent No. 2, the Petitioner left India for Botswana in January 2006 without taking her along with him. However, in February,2006, he Respondent No. 2 went to Botswana to join the Petitioner. While in Botswana, the Respondent No. 2 is alleged to have been severely ill-treated by the Petitioner and apart from the above, various demands were also made including a demand for additional dowry of 5 lakhs. On account of such physical and mental torture not only by the Petitioner/husband, but also by his immediate relatives, who continued to demand additional dowry by way of phone calls from India, the Respondent No. 2 addressed a complaint to the Superintendent of Police, Ongole, Prakasam District, Andhra Pradesh, from Botswana and the same was registered as Case(Crl.) No. 25 of 2007 under Sections 498A[2] and 506[3] Indian Penal Code ('I.P.C.' for short) together with Sections 3[4] and 4[5] of the Dowry Prohibition Act, 1986, by the Station

---

[1] Appellants: **ThotaVenkateswarlu** Vs. Respondent: **State of A.P. tr. Princl Sec. and Anr.** AIR2011SC2900

Hon'bleJudges: Altamas Kabir, Cyriac Joseph and Surinder Singh Nijjar, JJ.

[2] **Section 498A of the IPC**: Husband or Relative of the Husband of a woman subjecting her to cruelty

Husband or relative of husband of a woman subjecting her to cruelty.—Whoever, being the husband or the relative of the husband of a woman, subjects such woman to cruelty shall be punished with imprisonment for a term which may extend to three years and shall also be liable to fine.

House Officer, Medarametla Police Station, on the instructions of the Superintendent of Police. Father, mother and sister, were named as Accused Nos. 2, 3 and 4. The Additional Munsif Magistrate, ordered issuance of summons against the accused.

Decision by High court

The High Court by its order allowed Criminal Petition filed by the Accused Nos. 2 to 4 and quashed the proceedings against them. Criminal Petition filed by Petitioner was dismissed. Petitioner field the special leave petition[6] against the order of the High Court rejecting the Petitioner's petition under Section 482[7] Code of Criminal Procedure.

Explanation

For the purpose of this section, "cruelty" means—

(a) any wilful conduct which is of such a nature as is likely to drive the woman to commit suicide or to cause grave injury or danger to life, limb or health (whether mental or physical) of the woman; or

(b) harassment of the woman where such harassment is with a view to coercing her or any person related to her to meet any unlawful demand for any property or valuable security or is on account of failure by her or any person related to her to meet such demand

[3] **Section 506 of the IPC**: Criminal Intimidation

Whoever commits, the offence of criminal intimidation shall be punished with imprison-ment of either description for a **term which may extend to two years, or with fine, or with both;**

[4] **Section 3 Dowry Prohibition Act**: Penalty for giving or taking dowry

Penalty for giving or taking dowry. If any person, after the commencement of this Act, gives or takes or abets the giving or taking of dowry, he shall be punishable with imprisonment which may extend to six months, or with fine which may extend to five thousand rupees, or with both.

[5] **Section 4 Dowry Prohibition Act**: Penalty for demanding dowry.

Penalty for demanding dowry. If any person, after the commencement of this Act, demands, directly or indirectly, FROM the parents or guardian of a bride or bridegroom, as the case may be, any dowry, he shall be punishable with imprisonment which may extend to six months, or with fine which may extend to five thousand rupees, or with both:

Provided that no court shall take cognizance of any offence under this section except with the previous sanction of the State Government or of such officer as the State Government may, by general or special order, specify in this behalf.

[6] **Article 136 of the Constitution**

Under Article 136 of the Constitution of India any person aggrieved by any judgment, decree, determination or order in any cause or matter passed or made by any Court or Tribunal in the territory of India may appeal to the Supreme Court of India. Accordingly a person aggrieved by any order or judgment of High Court or of Tribunal may appeal to the Supreme Court by filing Special Leave Petition.

[7] **Section 482 of the Criminal Procedure Code**: Saving of Inherent power of High Court

Nothing in this Code shall be deemed to limit or affect the inherent powers of the High Court to make such orders as may be necessary to give effect to any order this Code, or to prevent abuse of the process of any court or otherwise to secure the ends of justice.

Submissions by Petitioner Counsel

Learned Counsel urged that Section 188 Code of Criminal Procedure[8] recognizes that when an offence is committed outside India by a citizen of India, he would have to be dealt with as if such offence had been committed in any place within India at which he maybe found. Learned Counsel, however, laid stress on the proviso which indicates that no such offence could be inquired into or tried in India except with the previous sanction of the Central Government.

Question raised before Supreme Court

Whether in respect of a series of offences arising out of the same transaction, some of which were committed within India and some outside India, such offences could be tried together, without the previous sanction of the Central Government as envisaged in the proviso to Section 188 Code of Criminal Procedure.

Decision by Supreme Court

Court held that it may be said that the alleged offences under Sections 3 and 4 of the Dowry Prohibition Act occurred within the territorial jurisdiction of the Criminal Courts in India and could, therefore, be tried by the Courts in India without having to obtain the previous sanction of the Central Government. Cases relating to alleged offences under Section 498A and 506 I.P.C. had been committed outside India in Botswana. Therefore, the learned Magistrate shall not proceed with the trail where previous sanction of the Central government is required in cases related to offences committed outside India under Section 498A and 506 I.P.C. The Magistrate is, therefore, free to proceed against the accused in respect of offences having been committed in India. i.e. Offences relating to Sections 3 and 4 of the Dowry Prohibition Act.

The Special Leave Petition was disposed off.

---

[8] **Section 188 of the Criminal Procedure Code:** Offences Committed Outside India
When an offence is committed outside India-

(a) By a citizen of India, whether on the high seas or elsewhere; or

(b) By a person, not being such citizen, on any ship or aircraft registered in India.

He may be dealt with in respect of such offence as if it had been committed at any place within India at which he may be found:

Provided that, notwithstanding anything in any of the preceding sections of this Chapter, no such offence shall be inquired into or tried in India except with the previous sanction of the Central Government.

13

Bail is the Rule Jail is an Exception[1]

Ratio Decidendi [2]:

"Right to Bail is not to be denied merely because of the sentiments of the community against the accused. The primary purposes of bail in a criminal case are to relieve the accused of imprisonment, to relieve the State of the burden of keeping him, pending the trial, and at the same time, to keep the accused constructively in the custody of the Court, whether before or after conviction, to assure that he will submit to the jurisdiction of the Court and be in attendance thereon whenever his presence isrequired."

Facts in Nutshell:

1. The allegations against accused[3] Sanjay Chandra are that he entered into criminal conspiracy with accused A. Raja, R.K. Chandolia and other accused persons during September 2009 to get UAS licence for providing telecom services to otherwise an ineligible company to get UAS licence. The Unitech companies got benefit of spectrum in as many as 10 circles over the other eligible applicants.

2. The allegations against accused Vinod Goenka are that he carried forward the fraudulent applications of STPL (Swan Telecom (P)

---

[1] Appellants: **Sanjay Chandra** Vs. Respondent: **CBI**
AIR2012SC830

Hon'ble Judges: H.L. Dattu and G.S. Singhvi, JJ.

[2] **Meaning of Ratio Decidendi**

Ratio decidendi is a Latin phrase meaning "the reason" or "the rationale for the decision." The *ratio decidendi* is "[t]he point in a case which determines the judgment" or "the principle which the case establishes."

[3] A person charged with a crime.

Limited) submitted by previous management despite knowing the fact that STPL was ineligible company to get UAS licences by virtue of clause 8 of UASL(United Access Service License) guidelines 2005. Accused/applicant in conspiracy with accused Shahid Usman Balwa concealed or furnished false information to DoT regarding shareholding pattern of STPL as on the date of application thereby making STPL an eligible company to get licence on the date of application, that is, 02.03.2007. Accused/applicant was an overall beneficiary with accused Shahid Usman Balwa for getting licence and spectrum in 13 telecom circles.

3. Accused Gautam Doshi, Surendra Pipara and Hari Nath in furtherance of their common intention to cheat the Department of Telecommunications, structured/created net worth of M/s Swan Telecom Pvt. Ltd., out of funds arranged from M/s Reliance Telecom Ltd. or its associates, for applying to DoT for UAS Licences in 13 circles, where M/s Reliance Telecom Ltd. had no GSM spectrum, in a manner that its associations with M/s Reliance Telecom Ltd. may not be detected, so that DOT could not reject its application on the basis of Clause 8 of the UASL Guidelines dated 14.12.2005.

Decision by Special Judge & High Court:

The Special Judge, CBI, New Delhi, rejected **Bail** Applications filed by the Appellants[4]. The Appellants moved the High Court by filing applications under Section 439 of the Code of Criminal Procedure.[5]

---

[4] The party who appeals to a higher court from the decision of a lower tribunal

[5] **Section 439 of CrPC:** Special Powers of High Courts or Courts of Session regarding Bail

(1) A High Court or Court of Session may direct.

(a) That any person accused of an offence and in custody be released on bail, and if the offence is of the nature specified in sub-section (3) of section 437, may impose any condition, which it considers necessary for the purposes mentioned in that sub-section;

(b) That any condition imposed by a Magistrate when releasing any person on bail be set aside or modified:

Provided that the High Court or the Court of Session shall, before granting bail to a person who is accused of an offence which is triable exclusively by the Court of Session or which, though not so triable is punishable with imprisonment for life, give notice of the application for bail to the Public Prosecutor unless it is, for reasons to he recorded in writing, of opinion that it is not practicable to give such notice.

(2) A High Court or Court of Session may direct that any person who has been released on bail under this Chapter be arrested and commit him to custody.

Submission by Appellants Counsel:

1. Shri. Ram Jethmalani, learned senior counsel appearing for the Appellant Sanjay Chandra, urged that the impugned judgment(both by CBI Judge and High Court) has not appreciated the basic rule laid down by this Court (Hon'ble Supreme Court) that *grant of bail is the rule and its denial is the exception.*

2. Shri. Jethmalani submitted that if there is any apprehension of the accused of absconding from trial or tampering with the witnesses, then it is justified for the Court to deny **bail**.

3. The learned senior counsel stated that the trial Judge does not have the power to send a person, who he has summoned in pursuance of Section 87 Code of Criminal Procedure.[6]

4. The only power that the trial Judge had, he would contend, was to ask for a bond as provided for in Section 88 Code of Criminal Procedure[7] to ensure his appearance.

Learned Counsel Mukul Rohatgi stated that the only bar for bail pending trial in Section 437 CrPC[8] is for those persons who are charged with offences punishable with life or death, and there is no such bar for those persons who were charged with offences with maximum punishment of seven years.

---

[6] **Section 87 Cr.PC**: Issue of Warrant in lieu of, or in addition to, summons

A court may, in any case in which it is empowered by this Code to issue a summons for the appearance of any person, issue, after recording its reasons in writing, a warrant for his arrest-

(a) if either before the issue of summons, or after the issue of the same but before time fixed for his appearance, the court sees reason to believe that he has absconded or will not obey the summons; or

(b) if, at such time he fails to appear and the summons is proved to have been duly served in time to admit of his appearing in accordance therewith and no reasonable excuse is offered for such failure.

[7] **Section 88 CrPC**: Power to take bond for appearance

When any person for whose appearance or arrest the officer presiding in any court is empowered to issue a summons or warrant, is present in such court, such officer may require such person to execute a bond, with or without sureties, for his appearance in such court, or any other court to which the case may be transferred for trial.

[8] **Section 437 CrPC:** When Bail may be taken in case of Non Bailable offence

(1) When any person accused of, or suspected of, the commission of any non-bailable offence is arrested or detained without warrant by an officer in charge of a police station or appears or is brought before a court other than the High Court or Court of Session, he may be released on bail, but-

Judgments cited:

1. Judgment of the Delhi High Court in the *'Court on its own motion v. CBI*', by which the High Court gave directions to Criminal Courts to call upon the accused who is summoned to appear to apply for bail, and then decide on the merits of the bail application.

2. The concept and philosophy of **bail** was discussed by Court in *Vaman Narain Ghiya v. State of Rajasthan*[10], thus:

> *"**Bail**" remains **an** undefined term in Code of Criminal Procedure. Nowhere else has the term been statutorily defined. Conceptually, it continues to be understood as a right for assertion of freedom against the State imposing restraints. Since the UN Declaration of Human Rights of 1948, to which India **is** a signatory, the concept of **bail** has found a place within the scope of human rights. The dictionary meaning of the expression "**bail**" denotes a security for appearance of a prisoner for his release. Etymologically, the word **is** derived from **an** old French verb "bailer" which means to "give" or "to deliver", although another view **is** that its derivation **is** from the Latin term "baiulare", meaning "to bear a burden".*

> ***Bail** may thus be regarded as a mechanism whereby the State devolutes upon the community the function of securing the presence of the prisoners, and at the same time involves participation of the community in administration of justice.*

(i) Such person shall not be so released if there appear reasonable grounds for believing that he has been guilty of an offence punishable with death or imprisonment for life;

(ii) Such person shall not be so released if such offence is a cognizable offence and he had been previously convicted of an offence punishable with death, imprisonment for life or imprisonment for seven years or more, or he had been previously convicted on two or more occasions of [2][a cognizable offence punishable with imprisonment for three years or more but not less than seven years]:

Provided that the court may direct that a person referred to in clause (i) or clause (ii) be released on bail if such person is under the age of sixteen years or is a woman or is sick or infirm:

Provided further that the court may also direct that a person referred to in clause (ii) be released on bail if it is satisfied that it is just and proper so to do for any other special reason:

Provided also that the mere fact that an accused person may be required for being identified by witnesses during investigation shall not be sufficient ground for refusing to grant bail if he is otherwise entitled to be released on bail and gives an undertaking that the shall comply with such directions as may be given by the court.

[9] 2004 (I) JCC 308

[10] MANU/SC/8394/2008 : (2009) 2 SCC 281

The principles, which the Court must consider while granting or declining **bail**, have been culled out by this Court in the case of *Prahlad Singh Bhati* v. *NCT, Delhi*[11], thus:

The jurisdiction to grant bail has to be exercised on the basis of well-settled principles having regard to the circumstances of each case and not in an arbitrary manner. While granting the bail, the court has to keep in mind the nature of accusations, the nature of the evidence in support thereof, the severity of the punishment which conviction will entail, the character, behaviour, means and standing of the accused, circumstances which are peculiar to the accused, reasonable possibility of securing the presence of the accused at the trial, reasonable apprehension of the witnesses being tampered with, the larger interests of the public or State and similar other considerations. It has also to be kept in mind that for the purposes of granting the bail the legislature has used the words "reasonable grounds for believing" instead of "the evidence" which means the court dealing with the grant of bail can only satisfy it (sic itself) as to whether there is a genuine case against the accused and that the prosecution will be able to produce prima facie evidence in support of the charge. It is not expected, at this stage, to have the evidence establishing the guilt of the accused beyond reasonable doubt.

Decision by Supreme Court:

Court held that the accused are charged with economic offences of huge magnitude. Court were also conscious of the fact that the offences alleged, if proved, may jeopardize the economy of the country. At the same time, courts cannot lose sight of the fact that the investigating agency has already completed investigation and the charge sheet is already filed before the Special Judge, CBI, New Delhi. Therefore, their presence in the custody may not be necessary for further investigation. Appellants were released on **bail** on their executing a bond with two solvent sureties, each in a sum of ₹5 lakhs to the satisfaction of the Special Judge, CBI, New Delhi with some conditions.

---

[11] MANU/SC/0193/2001 : (2001) 4 SCC 280

14

Citizens need not be Coward[1]

Ratio Decidendi[2]: "Right to private defence could even extend to causing death if there is real apprehension that aggressor might cause death or grievous hurt."

Facts in Nutshell:

The dispute is between very close and intimate family members. Deceased Gurcharan Singh was the brother of Bakhtawar Singh and uncle of Darshan Singh. He was the father of Gurdish Singh, PW7, the informant. The agriculture fields of both brothers, Gurcharan Singh and Bakhtawar Singh were situated adjoining to each other. According to the prosecution, on 15.7.1991 at about 8 a.m. Gurdish Singh, PW7 and his father, Gurcharan Singh were irrigating their aforesaid fields and were also mending its ridges and at that time Gurdev Singh, PW8 and Ajit Singh were also present there. In the meantime, Darshan Singh and Bakhtawar Singh came there from the side of their fields raising lalkaras and abused the complainant party. Darshan Singh, accused was armed with D.B.B.L. gun and his father Bakhtawar Singh was carrying a Gandasa and they were saying that they would teach a lesson to the complainant party for cutting the ridges.

According to the further story of the prosecution, Bakhtawar Singh gave a Gandasa blow causing injuries on the chest of Gurcharan Singh. Gurcharan

---

[1] Appellants: **Darshan Singh** Vs. Respondent: **State of Punjab and Anr.**
AIR2010SC1212

Hon'bleJudges: Dalveer Bhandari and Asok Kumar Ganguly, JJ.

[2] **Meaning of Ratio Decidendi**

Ratio decidendi is a Latin phrase meaning "the reason" or "the rationale for the decision." The *ratio decidendi* is "[t]he point in a case which determines the judgment" or "the principle which the case establishes."

Singh was also having a Gandasa with him and in order to save himself he also caused injury on the head of Bakhtawar Singh. Thereafter, Darshan Singh fired two shots from his licensed gun which hit Gurcharan Singh in the chest and some of the pellets hit Gurdish Singh PW7 on his left upper arm and Gurdev Singh, PW8 on his left thigh. Gurcharan Singh fell down and died at the spot. Gurdish Singh and others retraced their steps in order to save themselves. Both the accused in order to save themselves ran towards their respective houses. Gurdish Singh, PW7 left the dead body of Gurcharan Singh and proceeded to the police station to lodge a report.

According to the prosecution, the motive of the crime was dispute regarding partition of land between both brothers Bakhtawar Singh and Gurcharan Singh. One year prior to the present incident, the village Panchayat had got the dispute compromised by a written agreement. There was a common well situated in the adjoining land. As a result of the compromise, the well along with a small piece of land attached to it was given to Gurcharan Singh and the land of common pathway leading to the well was given to the accused party. The compromise was not accepted by the accused party and they wanted repartition of the land attached to the well. This grievance led to this unfortunate incident.

Both Darshan Singh and Bakhtawar Singh were acquitted by the Sessions Court, Ludhiana but convicted by Punjab and Harayan High Court.

Decision by Trial Court

The trial court held that "if the accused were already cultivating the land as per compromise, then it does not appeal to reason as to why they would feel aggrieved. On the other hand there was strong motive for Gurcharan Singh to assault the accused person as he has resiled from the compromise."

The trial court came to the definite conclusion that Darshan Singh fired a shot in his right of private defence. Trial court orders for acquittal. The High Court in the impugned judgment reversed the trial court's judgment of acquittal and convicted the accused.

Provisions relating to Right to Private Defense under IPC

Relevant provisions dealing with the right of private defence are Sections

96[3] and 97[4] of the Indian Penal Code. Section 100 of IPC[5] talks about when the right of private defence of the body extends to causing death. Section 100 of the Indian Penal Code justifies the killing of an assailant when apprehension of atrocious crime enumerated in several clauses of the section is shown to exist.

Scope and Foundation of the Right to Private Defense[6]

...a man is justified in resisting by force anyone who manifestly intends and endeavours by violence or surprise to commit a known felony against either his person, habitation or property.

In these cases he is not obliged to retreat, and may not merely resist the attack where he stands but may indeed pursue his adversary until the danger is ended, and if in a conflict between them he happens to kill his attacker, such killing is justifiable.

The law does not require a law-abiding citizen to behave like a coward when confronted with an imminent unlawful aggression. There is nothing more degrading to the human spirit than to run away in face of danger. The

---

[3] **Things done in private defence.** - Nothing is an offence which is done in the exercise of the right of private defence.

[4] **Right of private defence of the body and of property.** - Every person has a right subject to the restrictions contained in Section 99, to defend—

First.- His own body, and the body of any other person, against any offence affecting the human body;

Secondly.- The property, whether moveable or immovable, of himself or of any other person, against any act which is an offence falling under the definition of theft, robbery, mischief or criminal trespass, or which is an attempt to commit theft, robbery, mischief or criminal trespass.

[5] The right of private defence of the body extends, under the restrictions mentioned in the last preceding section, to the voluntary causing of death or of any other harm to the assailant, if the offence which occasions the exercise of the right be of any of the descriptions hereinafter enumerated, namely:

First. — Such an assault as may reasonably cause the apprehension that death will otherwise be the onsequence of such assault;

Secondly. — Such an assault as may reasonably cause the apprehension that grievous hurt will otherwise be the consequence of such assault;

Thirdly. — An assault with the intention of committing rape;

Fourthly. — An assault with the intention of gratifying unnatural lust;

Fifthly. — An assault with the intention of kidnapping or abducting;

Sixthly. — An assault with the intention of wrongfully confining a person, under circumstances which may reasonably cause him to apprehend that he will be unable to have recourse to the public authorities for his release.

[6] Russel on Crime (11th Edn., Vol.1, p.491)

right of private defence is thus designed to serve a social purpose and deserves to be fostered within the prescribed limits.

Judgments Cited:

In *Laxman Sahu v. State of Orissa*[7] Court observed that it is needless to point out in this connection that the right of private defence is available only to one who is suddenly confronted with immediate necessity of averting an impending danger not of his creation.

In *Puran Singh and Ors. v. The State of Punjab*[8] this Court observed that in the following circumstances right of private defence can beexercised:

i. There is no sufficient time for recourse to the public authorities

ii. There must be a reasonable apprehension of death or grievous hurt to the person or danger to the property concerned.

iii. More harm than necessary should not have been caused.

Decision by Supreme Court:

Court framed some principles

(i) Self-preservation is the basic human instinct and is duly recognized by the criminal jurisprudence of all civilized countries. All free, democratic and civilized countries recognize the right of private defence within certain reasonable limits.

(ii) The right of private defence is available only to one who is suddenly confronted with the

necessity of averting an impending danger and not of self-creation.

(iii) A mere reasonable apprehension is enough to put the right of self defence into operation.

In other words, it is not necessary that there should be an actual commission of the offence in order to give rise to the right of private defence. It is enough if the accused apprehended that such an offence

---

[7] MANU/SC/0183/1986 : 1986 (1) Supp SCC 555

[8] MANU/SC/0184/1975 : (1975) 4 SCC 518

is contemplated and it is likely to be committed if the right of private defence is not exercised.

(iv) The right of private defence commences as soon as a reasonable apprehension arises and it is co- terminus with the duration of such apprehension.

(v) It is unrealistic to expect a person under assault to modulate his defence step by step with any arithmetical exactitude.

(vi) In private defence the force used by the accused ought not to be wholly disproportionate or much greater than necessary for protection of the person or property.

(vii) It is well settled that even if the accused does not plead self-defence, it is open to consider such a plea if the same arises from the material on record.

(viii) The accused need not prove the existence of the right of private defence beyond reasonable doubt.

(ix) The Indian Penal Code confers the right of private defence only when that unlawful or wrongful act is an offence.

(x) A person who is in imminent and reasonable danger of losing his life or limb may in exercise of self defence inflict any harm even extending to death on his assailant either when the assault is attempted or directly threatened.

Court held that Appellate Court or the High Court would not be justified in reversing the judgment of acquittal unless it comes to a clear conclusion that the judgment of the trial court is utterly perverse and, on the basis of the evidence on record, no other view is plausible or possible than the one taken by the Appellate Court or the High Court. Court allowed the appeal and the judgment of the High Court is set aside and the judgment of acquittal of the trial court is restored. Appellant was acquitted and released on bail.

15

Right to Life includes Right to live with Human Dignity[1]

Facts in Nutshell:

The petition under Article 32 of the Constitution[2] raised a question in regard of the right of a detenu under the Conservation of Foreign Exchange & Prevention of Smuggling Activities Act (hereinafter referred to as COFEPOSA Act) to have interview with a lawyer and the members of his family. The petitioner, who was a British national, was arrested and detained in the Central Jail, Tihar under an Order dated 23rd November 1979 issued under Section 3 of the COFEPOSA Act[3]. She preferred a petition in Court

---

[1] Appellants: **Francis Coralie Mullin Vs.** Respondent: **Administrator, Union Territory of Delhi and Ors.** AIR1981SC746a

Hon'ble Judges: P. N. Bhagwati and S. Murtaza Fazal Ali, JJ.

[2] **Article 32. Remedies for enforcement of rights conferred by this Part**

(1) The right to move the Supreme Court by appropriate proceedings for the enforcement of the rights conferred by this Part is guaranteed

(2) The Supreme Court shall have power to issue directions or orders or writs, including writs in the nature of habeas corpus, mandamus, prohibition, quo warranto and certiorari, whichever may be appropriate, for the enforcement of any of the rights conferred by this Part

(3) Without prejudice to the powers conferred on the Supreme Court by clause (1) and (2), Parliament may by law empower any other court to exercise within the local limits of its jurisdiction all or any of the powers exercisable by the Supreme Court under clause (2)

(4) The right guaranteed by this article shall not be suspended except as otherwise provided for by this Constitution

[3] **Section 3. Power to make orders detaining certain persons.**

(1) The Central Government or the State Government or any officer of the Central Government, not below the rank of a Joint Secretary to that Government, specially empowered for the purposes of this section by that Government, or any officer of a State Government, not below the rank of a Secretary to that Government, specially empowered for the purposes of this section by that Government, may, if satisfied, with respect to any person (including a foreigner), that, with a view to preventing him from acting in any manner prejudicial to the conservation or augmentation of foreign exchange or with a viewto preventing him from—

(i) smuggling goods, or

for a writ of habeas corpus[4] challenging her detention, but by a judgment delivered by Court on 27th February 1980, her petition was rejected with the result that she continued to remain under detention in the Tihar Central Jail. Whilst under detention, the petitioner experienced considerable difficulty in having interview with her lawyer and the members of her family. Some criminal proceeding was pending against the petitioner for attempting to smuggle hashish out of the country.

The petitioner was denied the facility of interview with her lawyer and even her young daughter 5 years old could not meet her except once in a month. This restriction on interviews was imposed by the Prison Authorities by virtue of Clause 3 (b) Sub-clauses (i) and (ii)[5] of the Conditions of

---

(ii) abetting the smuggling of goods, or

(iii) engaging in transporting or concealing or keeping smuggled goods, or

(iv) dealing in, smuggled goods otherwise than by engaging in transporting or concealing or keeping smuggled goods, or

(v) harbouring persons engaged in smuggling goods or in abetting the smuggling of goods,

It is necessary so to do, make an order directing that such person be detained.

(2) When any order of detention is made by a State Government or by an officer empowered by a State Government, the State Government shall, within ten days, forward to the Central Government a report in respect of the order.

(3) For the purposes of clause (5) of Article 22 of the Constitution, the communication to a person detained in pursuance of a detention order of the grounds on which the order has been made shall be made as soon as may be after the detention, but ordinarily not later than five days, and in exceptional circumstances and for reasons to be recorded in writing not later than fifteen days, from the date of detention.

4 Habeas corpus is a Latin term which means 'have the body'. The concept of writ of habeas corpus has originated from England. This is a writ or legal action which can be used by a person to seek relief from illegal detention. The writ of habeas corpus saves a person from harm caused by an unfair action of the legal system.

5 **These two sub-clauses of Clause 3(b) provided inter alia as under:**

3. The conditions of detention in respect of classification and interviews shall be as under :-

(a) ...

(b) Interviews : Subject to the direction issued by the Administrator from time to time, permission for the grant of interviews with a detenu shall be granted by the District Magistrate, Delhi as under :-

(i) Interview with legal adviser :

Interview with legal adviser in connection with defence of a detenu in a criminal case or in regard to writ petitions and the like, may be allowed by prior appointment, in the presence of an officer of Customs/Central Excise/Enforcement to be nominated by the local Collector of Customs/Central Excise or Deputy Director of Enforcement who sponsors the case for detention.

(ii) Interview with family members :

A monthly interview may be permitted for members of the family consisting of wife, children or parents of the detenu....

Detention laid down by the Delhi Administration under an Order dated 23rd August 1975 issued in exercise of the powers conferred under Section 5 of the COFEPOSA Act[6].

Arguments by Petitioners Counsel:

It was contended on behalf of the petitioner that allowing interview with the members of the family only once in a month was discriminatory and unreasonable, particularly when undertrial prisoners were granted the facility of interview with relatives and friends twice in a week under Rule 559A and convicted prisoners were permitted to have interview with their relatives and friends once in a week under Rule 550 of the Rules set out in the Manual for the Superintendence and Management of Jails in the Punjab. The petitioner also urged that a detenu was entitled under Article 22[7] of the Constitution to consult and be defended by a legal practitioner of his choice

---

[6] **Section 5. Power to regulate place and conditions of detention.**

Every person in respect of whom a detention order has been made shall be liable -

(a) to be detained in such place and under such conditions including conditions as to maintenance, interviews or communication with the appropriate Government may, by general or special order, specify; and

(b) to be removed from one place of detention to another place of detention, whether within the same State or in another State by order of the appropriate Government: Provided that no order shall be made by a State Government under clause (b) for the removal of a person from one State to another State except with the consent of the Government of that other State.

[7] **Article 22. Protection against arrest and detention in certain cases.**

(1) No person who is arrested shall be detained in custody without being informed, as soon as may be, of the grounds for such arrest nor shall he be denied the right to consult, and to be defended by, a legal practitioner of his choice

(2) Every person who is arrested and detained in custody shall be produced before the nearest magistrate within a period of twenty four hours of such arrest excluding the time necessary for the journey from the place of arrest to the court of the magistrate and no such person shall be detained in custody beyond the said period without the authority of a magistrate

(3) Nothing in clauses (1) and (2) shall apply (a) to any person who for the time being is an enemy alien; or (b) to any person who is arrested or detained under any law providing for preventive detention

(4) No law providing for preventive detention shall authorise the detention of a person for a longer period than three months unless (a) an Advisory Board consisting of persons who are, or have been, or are qualified to be appointed as, Judges of a High Court has reported before the expiration of the said period of three months that there is in its opinion sufficient cause for such detention:

(5) When any person is detained in pursuance of an order made under any law providing for preventive detention, the authority making the order shall, as soon as may be, communicate to such person the grounds on which the order has been made and shall afford him the earliest opportunity of making a representation against the order

(6) Nothing in clause (5) shall require the authority making any such order as is referred to in that clause to disclose facts which such authority considers to be against the public interest to disclose contd/---

and she was, therefore entitled to the facility of interview with a lawyer whom he wanted to consult or appear for him in a legal proceeding and the requirement of prior appointment for interview and of the presence of a Customs or Excise Officer at the interview was arbitrary and unreasonable and therefore violative of Articles 14[8] and 21[9] of the Constitution of India.

Preventive Detention and Punitive Detention:

'Punitive detention' is intended to inflict punishment on a person, who is found by the judicial process to have committed an offence, while 'preventive detention' is not by way of punishment at all, but it is intended to pre-empt a person from indulging in conduct injurious to the society.

Court laid emphasis on *Maneka Gandhi v. Union of India*[10] and pointed to the present position as per Article 21 which requires that no one shall be deprived of his life or personal liberty except by procedure established by law and this procedure must be reasonable, fair and just and not arbitrary, whimsical or fanciful and it is for the Court to decide in the exercise of its constitutional power of judicial review whether the deprivation of life or personal liberty in a given case is by procedure, which is reasonable, fair and just or it is otherwise. The law of preventive detention has therefore now to pass the test not only of Article 22, but also of Article 21 and if the constitutional validity of any such law is challenged, the Court would have to decide whether the procedure laid down by such law for depriving a person of his personal liberty is reasonable, fair and just. Court held in *Sampat*

---

(7) Parliament may by law prescribe

(a) the circumstances under which, and the class or classes of cases in which, a person may be detained for a period longer than three months under any law providing for preventive detention without obtaining the opinion of an Advisory Board in accordance with the provisions of sub clause (a) of clause (4);

(b) the maximum period for which any person may in any class or classes of cases be detained under any law providing for preventive detention; and

(c) the procedure to be followed by an Advisory Board in an inquiry under sub clause (a) of clause (4) Right against Exploitation

[8] **Article 14 Equality before law** The State shall not deny to any person equality before the law or the equal protection of the laws within the territory of India Prohibition of discrimination on grounds of religion, race, caste, sex or place of birth

[9] **Article 21 in The Constitution Of India**

Protection of life and personal liberty No person shall be deprived of his life or personal liberty except according to procedure established by law

[10] [1979]2SCR338

Prakash v. State of Jammu and Kashmir[11] "that the restrictions placed on a person preventively detained must, consistently with the effectiveness of detention, be minimal."

"Fundamental rights do not flee the person as he enters the prison although they may suffer shrinkage necessitated by incarceration." The prisoner or detenu has all the fundamental rights and other legal rights available to a free person, save those which are incapable of enjoyment by reason of incarceration[12].

Sunil Batra v. Delhi Admn.[13] Court emphasized on the term "life" as here used something more is meant than mere animal existence. The inhibition against its deprivation extends to all those limbs and faculties by which life is enjoyed. The provision equally prohibits the mutilation of the body or amputation of an arm or leg or the putting out of an eye or the destruction of any other organ of the body through which the soul communicates with the outer world.

Decision by Supreme Court:

Court held that right to life includes the right to live with human dignity and all that goes along with it, namely, the bare necessaries of life such as adequate nutrition, clothing and shelter and facilities for reading, writing and expressing one-self in diverse forms, freely moving about and mixing and commingling with fellow human beings. There can therefore be no doubt that 'personal liberty' would include the right to socialise with members of the family and friends subject, of course, to any valid prison regulations and under Articles 14 and 21, such prison regulations must be reasonable and non-arbitrary. If any prison regulation or procedure laid down by it regulating the right to have interviews with members of the family and friends is arbitrary or unreasonable, it would be liable to be struck down as invalid as being violative of Articles 14 and 21.

Courts are therefore of view that a Sub-clause (i) of Clause 3 (b) regulating the right of a detenu to have interview with a legal adviser of his choice is

---

[11] 1969CriLJ1555

[12] State of Maharashtra v. Prabhakar Sanzgiri MANU/SC/0089/1965 : 1966CriLJ311

[13] 1980 AIR 1579

violative of Articles 14 and 21 and must be held to be unconstitutional and void. Court also held that it would be quite reasonable if a detenu were to be entitled to have interview with his legal adviser at any reasonable hour during the day after taking appointment from the Superintendent of the Jail, which appointment should be given by the Superintendent without any avoidable delay.

16

Senior Citizens held for Playing Cards[1]

Facts in Nutshell:

There is a Gymkhana situated at Andheri, Mumbai and it is known as Andheri Gymkhana which is an Association registered under the Bombay Public Trust Act and also under the Societies Registration Act. It is in existence since more than 25 years and the Petitioners are members of the said Association. The Petitioners[2] are all senior citizens. Petitioner No.1 is 78 years of age, Petitioner No.2 is 73 years of age, Petitioner No.3 is 75 years of age, Petitioner No.4 is 63 years of age, Petitioner No.5 is 65 years of age, Petitioner No.6 & 7 are 72 years of age etc. The average age of all these Petitioners is about 60 to 65 years. Two to three Petitioners are between the age group of 40 years to 50 years. There is a Card Room in the said Gymkhana and the Rules prescribe that the said Card Room is to be used only for playingBridge and Rummy. The Gymkhana files its balance sheet and audited accounts with the Office of the Charity Commissioner, Mumbai. Most of the Petitioners who have already retired use the premises of the Gymkhana for the purpose of playing Bridge and Rummy, both of which are games of skill.

According to Petitioners, they visited Gymkhana on 10th August, 2011 for the purpose of playing Bridge and Rummy and, at about 8.50 p.m., a Police Team from Andheri Police Station comprising of Respondent Nos. 5, 6 and

---

[1]   Appellants: **Jaywant Balkrishna Sail,** Indian, Adult, aged 78 years, Residing at 6, Casa Sabina, 3, Gundavali Lane, M. V. Road, Andheri (E), Mumbai 400 069 and Ors. Vs. Respondent: **State of Maharashtra,** Through Addl. Chief Secretary, Home Department Mantralaya, Mumbai and Ors.

MANU/MH/0817/2012

Hon'bleJudges: V.M. Kanade and P.D. Kode, JJ.

[2]   Someone who petitions a court for redress of a grievance or recovery of a right

8 and other male policemen entered the Card Room and started browbeating the Petitioners who were present there and accused them of gambling and asked them to remove all the articles from their pockets. According to Petitioners, they were playing Rummy and Bridge sometimes with stakes in the form of "counters" for pure amusement for last number of years. Out of the Petitioners, most of them are senior citizens and some of them were house wives. According to Petitioners, they were not allowed to make any phone calls and they were not permitted to call their family members. They were also not permitted to take their medicines for diabetes and blood pressure etc. or even to use toilet facilities.

It is further alleged that the Petitioners were illegally detained in Police Station from 9.30 p.m to 6.00 a.m. and it is also alleged that, during this time, they were not permitted to take medicines and they were constantly threatened with arrest.

By the Petition which is filed under Articles 226[3] and 227[4] of the Constitution of India read with Section 482 of the Criminal Procedure Code[5], Petitioners

---

[3] **Article 226 of the Indian Constitution, 1950**: Power of High Courts to issue certain writs.

(1) Notwithstanding anything in Article 32 every High Court shall have powers, throughout the territories in relation to which it exercise jurisdiction, to issue to any person or authority, including in appropriate cases, any Government, within those territories directions, orders or writs, including writs in the nature of habeas corpus, mandamus, prohibitions, quo warranto and certiorari, or any of them, for the enforcement of any of the rights conferred by Part III and for any other purpose.

(2) The power conferred by clause (1) to issue directions, orders or writs to any Government, authority or person may also be exercised by any High Court exercising jurisdiction in relation to the territories within which the cause of action , wholly or in part, arises for the exercise of such power, notwithstanding that the seat of such Government or authority or the residence of such person is not within those territories.

(3) Where any party against whom an interim order, whether by way of injunction or stay or in any other manner, is made on, or in any proceedings relating to, a petition under clause (1), without-

(a) furnishing to such party copies of such petition and all documents in support of the plea for such interim order; and

(b) giving such party an opportunity of being heard, makes an application to the High Court for the vacation of such order and furnishes a copy of such application to the party in whose favor such order has been made or the counsel of such party, the High Court shall dispose of the application within a period of two weeks from the date on which it is received or from the date on which the copy of such application is so furnished, whichever is later, or where the High Court is closed on the last day of that period, before the expiry of the next day afterwards on which the High Court is open; and if the application is not so disposed of, the interim order shall, on the expiry of that period, or , as the case may be, the expiry of the aid next day, stand vacated.

(4) The power conferred on a High Court by this article shall not be in derogation of the power conferred on the Supreme court by clause (2) of Article 32.

were seeking appropriate writ, order and direction for quashing the FIR which was registered against the Petitioners and others at the Andheri Police Station for the offence punishable under sections 4[6] and 5[7] of the Bombay Prevention of Gambling Act, 1887.

Arguments on behalf of the Petitioners Counsel

The learned Counsel appearing on behalf of the Petitioners submitted that the Petitioners were playing games of skill viz. Bridge and Rummy which are expressly excluded under section 13[8] from the purview of the Gambling Act and, therefore, it is contended that the Petitioners could not have been arrested and detained in the Police Station throughout the night. He submitted that the Apex Court on several occasions had held that playing Bridge or Rummy cannot be termed as gambling since both are games of skill and fall outside the purview of the provisions of the Gambling Act. The Apex Court have consistently held that a card game of skill would not constitute an offence of gambling and that if such card game is played in a club the said club would not fall under the definition of "Common-gaming house".

---

[4] **Article 227 in The Constitution Of India**

Power of superintendence over all courts by the High Court

(1) Every High Court shall have superintendence over all courts and tribunals throughout the territories interrelation to which it exercises jurisdiction

(2) Without prejudice to the generality of the foregoing provisions, the High Court may

(a) call for returns from such courts;

(b) make and issue general rules and prescribe forms for regulating the practice and proceedings of such courts; and

(c) prescribe forms in which books, entries and accounts shall be kept by the officers of any such courts

(3) The High Court may also settle tables of fees to be allowed to the sheriff and all clerks and officers of such courts and to attorneys, advocates and pleaders practising therein: Provided that any rules made, forms prescribed or tables settled under clause (2) or clause (3) shall not be inconsistent with the provision of any law for the time being in force, and shall require the previous approval of the Governor

(4) Nothing in this article shall be deemed to confer on a High Court powers of superintendence over any court or tribunal constituted by or under any law relating to the Armed Forces

[5] **Section 482 of Cr.PC, 1973:** Saving of inherent powers of High Court. Nothing in this Code shall be deemed to limit or affect the inherent powers of the High Court to make such orders as may be necessary to give effect to any order under this Code, or to prevent abuse of the process of any Court or otherwise to secure the ends of justice.

[6] Keeping Common Gaming House

[7] Gaming in Common gaming House

[8] Saving of Games of Mere skill

Judgments Cited:

The Apex Court in State of *Andhra Pradesh vs. K. Satyanarayana* [9] held that the game of Rummy is not a game entirely of chance like 'three-card' game which goes under different names such as 'flush', 'brag' etc, which is a game of pure chance. It was observed that Rummy, on the other hand, requires certain amount of skill because the fall of the cards has to be memorised and building up of Rummy requires considerable skill in holding and discarding the cards. The Apex Court further observed that chance in Rummy is of the same character as the chance in a deal at a game of Bridge.

Decision by High Court:

Court comes to the conclusion that the prosecutions need to be quashed in the interest of justice for keeping flow of administration of justice flawless and continuous and for avoiding likelihood of harassment and expenditure to such accused. Petitions pending before concerned Courts of Metropolitan Magistrate were quashed. Court also held that Respondent Nos. 5 to 8 have clearly violated provisions of section 46(4)[10], section 54[11], section 55A[12] of the Criminal Procedure Code, 1973 and, as such, the fundamental rights of the Petitioners under Article 21[13] of the Constitution of India are clearly violated by the police. No medical tests were performed after arrest of the Petitioners as is now required under the Criminal Procedure Code. State Government was directed to pay compensation of Rs 1,000/-to each of the petitioners and, in addition, to pay compensation of Rs 25,000/-each to two women viz Petitioner Nos. 8 and 9.

---

[9] MANU/SC/0081/1967 : AIR 1968 SC 825

[10] Sub-section (4) in Section 46

46 [(4) Save in exceptional circumstances, no woman shall be arrested after sunset and before sunrise, and where such exceptional circumstances exist, the woman police officer shall, by making a written report, obtain the prior permission of the Judicial Magistrate of the first class within whose local jurisdiction the offence is committed or the arrest is to be made.]

[11] Examination of Arrested person by medical practitioner at the request of the arrested person

[12] Procedure when police officer deputes subordinate to arrest without warrant

[13] **Article 21 in The Constitution Of India**

Protection of life and personal liberty No person shall be deprived of his life or personal liberty except according to procedure established by law

17

Right to life includes right to marriage[1]

Facts in Nutshell:

The petitioner a young woman, a graduate and at the relevant time was pursuing her Masters course in Hindi in the Lucknow University. Due to the sudden death of her parents she started living with her brother at LDA Colony, Lucknow where she did her intermediate in 1997 and graduation in 2000. It is alleged by the petitioner that on 2.11.2000 she left her brother's house of her own free will and got married at Arya Samaj Mandir, Delhi to one Bramha Nand Gupta who has business in Delhi and other places and they have a child out of this wedlock. Thereafter on 4.11.2000, the petitioner's brother lodged a missing person report at Sarojini Nagar Police Station, Lucknow and consequently the police arrested two sisters of the petitioner's husband along with the husband of one of the sisters and the cousin of the petitioner's husband. Petitioners brothers were also involved in destruction of property of petitioners husbands and there relatives. It was further alleged that the petitioner's brothers were furious because the petitioner underwent an **inter-caste marriage**.

Decision by Fast Track Court:

The Fast Track Court, Lucknow issued non-bailable warrants against all the four accused, and against the order of the Fast Track Court, the accused filed a petition under Section 482 Cr.P.C.[2] in the Allahabad High Court (Lucknow Bench). The High Court directed the accused to appear before

---

[1] Appellants: **Lata Singh Vs.** Respondent: **State of U.P. and Anr.**
AIR2006SC2522
Hon'ble Judges: Ashok Bhan and Markandey Katju , JJ.

[2] **Section 482 of Cr.PC, 1973:** Saving of inherent powers of High Court. Nothing in this Code shall be deemed to limit or affect the inherent powers of the High Court to make such orders as may be necessary to give effect to any order under this Code, or to prevent abuse of the process of any Court or otherwise to secure the ends of justice.

the Sessions Judge who would scrutinize whether the accused committed any offence or not.

Decision by Supreme Court:

Court held that this case reveals a shocking state of affairs. There is no dispute that the petitioner is a major and was at all relevant times a major[3]. Hence she is free to marry anyone she likes or live with anyone she likes. There is no bar to an inter-caste marriage under the Hindu Marriage Act or any other law. Hence, court was of the view that no offence was committed by the petitioner, her husband or her husband's relatives. Judges were distressed to note that instead of taking action against the petitioner's brothers for their unlawful and high-handed acts the police has instead proceeded against the petitioner's husband and his relatives.

This writ petition under Article 32 of the Constitution of India was allowed by court. The proceedings in Sessions Trial No. 1201/2001 titled State of U.P. v. Sangita Gupta and Ors. arising out of FIR No. 336/2000 registered at Police Station Sarojini Nagar, Lucknow and pending in the Fast Track Court V, Lucknow were quashed. The warrants against the accused were also quashed. Court also directed to initiate criminal proceedings against petitioners Brothers and there relatives in accordance with the law.

General Comments by Courts related to inter-caste marriages (para 12):

The caste system is a curse on the nation and the sooner it is destroyed the better. In fact, it is dividing the nation at a time when we have to be united to face the challenges before the nation unitedly. Hence, inter-caste marriages are in fact in the national interest as they will result in destroying the caste system. However, disturbing news are coming from several parts of the country that young men and women who undergo inter-caste marriage, are threatened with violence, or violence is actually committed on them. In our opinion (Courts Opinion), such acts of violence or threats or harassment are wholly illegal and those who commit them must be severely punished. This is a free and democratic country, and once a person becomes a major

---

[3] According to Section 2 (a) of the Prohibition of Child Marriage Act, 2006, a "child" means a person who, if a male, has not completed twenty-one years of age, and if female, has not completed eighteen years of age.

he or she can marry whosoever he/she likes. *If the parents of the boy or girl do not approve of such inter-caste or inter-religious marriage the maximum they can do is that they can cut off social relations with the son or the daughter, but they cannot give threats or commit or instigate acts of violence and cannot harass the person who undergoes such inter-caste or inter- religious marriage.*

Court also direct that the administration/police authorities throughout the country will see to it that if any boy or girl who is a major undergoes inter-caste or inter-religious marriage with a woman or man who is a major, the couple are not harassed by any one nor subjected to threats or acts of violence, and any one who gives such threats or harasses or commits acts of violence either himself or at his instigation, is taken to task by instituting criminal proceedings by the police against such persons and further stern action is taken against such persons as provided by law. Judges also pointed that sometimes they hear of 'honour' killings of such persons who undergo inter-caste or inter-religious marriage of their own free will. There is nothing honourable in such killings, and in fact they are nothing but barbaric and shameful acts of murder committed by brutal, feudal minded persons who deserve harsh punishment. Only in this way can we stamp out such acts of barbarism.

18

Abuse of the Process of Courts[1]

Facts in Nutshell:

The Appellant, Shri Kishore Samrite, an ex-member of legislative assembly of Madhya Pradesh, elected on the ticket of Samajwadi Party instituted a Writ Petition in the High Court of Judicature at Allahabad being Writ Petition No. 111/2011 acting as next friend of one Sukanya Devi, Balram Singh and Sumrita Devi. Address of all these three persons was given as 23-12, Medical Chowk, Sanjay Gandhi Marg, Chhatrapati Shahu Ji Mahraj Nagar, Uttar Pradesh. According to the Appellant, these three persons were kept in illegal detention by the Respondent No. 6(Shri Rahul Gandhi) and were incapacitated to file the writ petition. It was averred in the petition filed by him before the High Court that he came to know from certain websites viz., www.indybay.org, www.arizona.indymedia.org and www.intellibriefs. blogspot.com, which contained news items stating that on the night of 3rd December, 2006, while on a tour of his parliamentary constituency in Amethi, Respondent No. 6, along with six of his friends (two from Italy and four from Britain) committed rape on Sukanya Devi, daughter of Balram Singh.

The Appellant specifically averred that he had not seen all the three persons in public for a long time, particularly since 4th January, 2007, when they were last seen in Amethi. Invoking the right to life and liberty as enshrined under Article 21 of the Constitution of India[2] on behalf of the three named Petitioners in the writ petition and alleging that Respondent No. 6 would

---

[1] Appellants: **Kishore SamriteVs.** Respondent: **State of U.P. and Ors.**
MANU/SC/0892/2012

Hon'ble Judges: B.S. Chauhan and Swatanter Kumar, JJ.

[2] **Article 21 in The Constitution Of India**

Protection of life and personal liberty No person shall be deprived of his life or personal liberty except according to procedure established by law

influence any fruitful investigation, the Appellant prayed for issuance of a writ of habeas corpus[3] commanding the opposite party particularly Respondent No. 6 to produce the Petitioners before the Court and for passing any other appropriate order or direction.

Challenge in the appeal in Supreme Court is to the order dated 7th March, 2011 passed by a Division Bench of the High Court of Judicature at Allahabad (Lucknow Bench). The operative part of the order reads as under:

In view of all the aforesaid and particularly for the reasons that the writ petition No. 111 (H/C) of 2011 was filed on the instructions of Kishor Samrite (who has also sworn the affidavit in support of the writ petition) which contained wild allegations/insinuation against Shri Rahul Gandhi and questions the virtue and modesty of a young girl of 22 years Km. Kirti Singh, we dismiss this writ petition with a cost of Rs. 50,00,000/- (Fifty lacs). Out of the cost amount, Rs. 25,00,000/- (Twenty five lacs) shall be paid to Km. Kirti Singh and Rs. 20,00,000/- (Twenty lacs) to Shri Rahul Gandhi, opposite part No. 6. The cost amount shall be deposited within a period of one month with the Registrar of this Court, failing which the Registrar shall take necessary action for recovery of the amount as land revenue.

On behalf of Respondent No. 6, Shri Rahul Gandhi, it was contended that Writ Petition No. 111 of 2011 is an abuse of the process of Court and, in fact, is a motivated petition primarily based on **'political mudslinging'**. While supporting the stand of Respondent No. 1, the State of Uttar Pradesh, it is also contended that the Appellant, Shri Kishore Samrite, was a total stranger, had no knowledge of the facts and, therefore, had no right to file the petition as next friend. It was not a case of private detention and the petition filed by the Appellant was not in conformity with the rules. The petition was primarily aimed at hurting the reputation and image of Respondent No. 6 out of ulterior motives and political vendetta.

---

[3] **Habeas Corpus** is a Latin term which literally means "you should have the body". In India the power to issue a writ of Habeas Corpus is vested only in the Supreme Court and the High Court. The writ is a direction of the Court to a person who is detaining another, commanding him to bring the body of the person in his custody a specified time to a specified place for a specified purpose. The writ has only one purpose: to set at liberty a person who is confined without legal justification; to secure release from confinement of a person unlawful detained. The writ is issued not only against the State and its authorities but also to private individuals or organization, if necessary.

High Court Order:

This writ petition was treated as private habeas corpus and was listed before a Single Judge of the Allahabad High Court. Rule 1 of Chapter XXI of the Allahabad High Court Rules provided that an application under Article 226 of the Constitution[4] for a writ in the nature of habeas corpus, except against private custody, if not sent by post or telegram, shall be made to the Division Bench appointed to receive applications or on any day on which no such Bench is sitting, to the Judge appointed to receive applications in civil matters. In the latter case, the Judge shall direct that the application be laid before a Division Bench for orders. In terms of proviso to this Rule, it is provided that an application under Article 226 of the Constitution in the nature of habeas corpus directed against private custody shall be made to the Single Judge appointed by the Chief Justice to receive such an application. The clear analysis of the above Rule shows that habeas corpus against a private custody has to be placed before a Single Judge while in the case of custody other than private custody, the matter has to be placed before a Division

---

[4] **Article 226 of the Indian Constitution, 1950**: Power of High Courts to issue certain writs.

(1) Notwithstanding anything in Article 32 every High Court shall have powers, throughout the territories in relation to which it exercise jurisdiction, to issue to any person or authority, including in appropriate cases, any Government, within those territories directions, orders or writs, including writs in the nature of habeas corpus, mandamus, prohibitions, quo warranto and certiorari, or any of them, for the enforcement of any of the rights conferred by Part III and for any other purpose.

(2) The power conferred by clause (1) to issue directions, orders or writs to any Government, authority or person may also be exercised by any High Court exercising jurisdiction in relation to the territories within which the cause of action , wholly or in part, arises for the exercise of such power, notwithstanding that the seat of such Government or authority or the residence of such person is not within those territories.

(3) Where any party against whom an interim order, whether by way of injunction or stay or in any other manner, is made on, or in any proceedings relating to, a petition under clause (1), without-

(a) furnishing to such party copies of such petition and all documents in support of the plea for such interim order; and

(b) giving such party an opportunity of being heard, makes an application to the High Court for the vacation of such order and furnishes a copy of such application to the party in whose favor such order has been made or the counsel of such party, the High Court shall dispose of the application within a period of two weeks from the date on which it is received or from the date on which the copy of such application is so furnished, whichever is later, or where the High Court is closed on the last day of that period, before the expiry of the next day afterwards on which the High Court is open; and if the application is not so disposed of, the interim order shall, on the expiry of that period, or , as the case may be, the expiry of the aid next day, stand vacated.

(4) The power conferred on a High Court by this article shall not be in derogation of the power conferred on the Supreme court by clause (2) of Article 32.

Bench. It appears that on the strength of this Rule, Writ Petition No. 111/ 2011 was listed before the Single Judge of Allahabad High Court. The roster and placing of cases before different Benches of the High Court is unquestionably the prerogative of the Chief Justice of that Court. In the High Courts, which have Principal and other Benches, there is a practice and as per rules, if framed, that the senior-most Judge at the Benches, other than the Principal Bench, is normally permitted to exercise powers of the Chief Justice, as may be delegated to the senior most Judge. In absence of the Chief Justice, the senior most Judge would pass directions in regard to the roster of Judges and listing of cases. Primarily, it is the exclusive prerogative of the Chief Justice and does not admit any ambiguity or doubt in this regard. Usefully we can refer to some judgments of this Court where such position has been clearly stated by this Court. In the case of *State of Rajasthan v. Prakash Chand and Ors.*[5], a three-Judge Bench of the Court was dealing with the requirement of constitution of Benches, issuance of daily cause list and the powers of the Chief Justice in terms of the Rajasthan High Court Ordinance, 1949 read with Article 225 of the Constitution of India[6]. The Court held as under:-

A careful reading of the aforesaid provisions of the Ordinance and Rule 54 shows that the administrative control of the High Court vests in the Chief Justice of the High Court alone and that it is his prerogative to distribute business of the High Court both judicial and administrative. He alone, has the right and power to decide how the Benches of the High Court are to be constituted: which Judge is to sit alone and which cases he can and is required to hear as also as to which Judges shall constitute a Division Bench and what work those Benches shall do. In other words the Judges of the High

---

[5] (1998) 1 SCC 1

[6] **Article 225 in The Constitution Of India 1949**

225. Jurisdiction of existing High Courts Subject to the provisions of this Constitution and to the provisions of any law of the appropriate Legislature made by virtue of powers conferred on that Legislature by this Constitution, the jurisdiction of, and the law administered in, any existing High Court, and the respective powers of the Judges thereof in relation to the administration of justice in the Court, including any power to make rules of Court and to regulate the sittings of the Court and of members thereof sitting alone or in Division Courts, shall be the same as immediately before the commencement of this Constitution: Provided that any restriction to which the exercise of original jurisdiction by any of the High Courts with respect to any matter concerning the revenue or concerning any act ordered or done in the collection thereof was subject immediately before the commencement of this Constitution shall no longer apply to the exercise of such jurisdiction

Court can sit alone or in Division Benches and do such work only as may be allotted to them by an order of or in accordance with the directions of the Chief Justice. That necessarily means that it is not within the competence or domain of any Single or Division Bench of the Court to give any direction to the Registry in that behalf which will run contrary to the directions of the Chief Justice. Therefore in the scheme of things judicial discipline demands that in the event a Single Judge or a Division Bench considers that a particular case requires to be listed before it for valid reasons, it should direct the Registry to obtain appropriate orders from the Chief Justice. The puisne Judges are not expected to entertain any request from the advocates of the parties for listing of case which does not strictly fall within the determined roster. In such cases, it is appropriate to direct the counsel to make a mention before the Chief Justice and obtain appropriate orders. This is essential for smooth functioning of the Court. Though, on the judicial side the Chief Justice is only the "first amongst the equals", on the administrative side in the matter of constitution of Benches and making of roster, he alone is vested with the necessary powers.

The Court directed transfer of Writ Petition No. 111 of 2011 and directed tagging of the same with Writ Petition No. 125 of 2011, besides issuing notice to the Director General of Police, U.P. to produce the Petitioners. In Writ Petition No. 125 of 2011, the Director General of Police filed a personal affidavit. According to him, the Superintendent of Police, Chhatrapati Shahu Ji Maharaj Nagar, while noticing the allegations made in both the writ petitions reported that the address mentioned in Writ Petition No. 111 of 2011 was wrong and there was no such place in the town of Amethi with the name of Medical Chowk, Sanjay Gandhi Marg and the address mentioned in Writ Petition No. 125 of 2011 was the correct address of Shri Balram Singh who lived there in the past.

When the Writ Petition No. 125 of 2011 came up for hearing before the Court on 7th March, 2011, the Division Bench passed the detailed order. Vide order, Writ Petition No. 111 of 2011 was disposed of while Writ Petition No. 125 of 2011 was partly disposed of and, as afore-noticed, Director of CBI was directed to register a case against Shri Kishore Samrite and all other persons involved in the plot. The Court also imposed cost of Rs. 50,00,000/- which was to be distributed as per the order.

Abuse of the process of Court (Principles)[7]:

The principles that would govern the obligations of a litigant while approaching the court for redressal of any grievance and the consequences of abuse of the process of court. These are:

(i) Courts have, over the centuries, frowned upon litigants who, with intent to deceive and mislead the Courts, initiated proceedings without full disclosure of facts and came to the courts with 'unclean hands'. Courts have held that such litigants are neither entitled to be heard on the merits of the case nor entitled to any relief.

(ii) The people, who approach the Court for relief on an ex parte statement, are under a contract with the court that they would state the whole case fully and fairly to the court and where the litigant has broken such faith, the discretion of the court cannot be exercised in favour of such a litigant.

(iii) The obligation to approach the Court with clean hands is an absolute obligation and has repeatedly been reiterated by this Court.

(iv) Quests for personal gains have become so intense that those involved in litigation do not hesitate to take shelter of falsehood and misrepresent and suppress facts in the court proceedings. Materialism, opportunism and malicious intent have over-shadowed the old ethos of litigative values for small gains.

(v) A litigant who attempts to pollute the stream of justice or who touches the pure fountain of justice with tainted hands is not entitled to any relief, interim or final.

(vi) The Court must ensure that its process is not abused and in order to prevent abuse of the process the court, it would be justified even in insisting on furnishing of security and in cases of serious abuse, the Court would be duty bound to impose heavy costs.

(vii) Wherever a public interest is invoked, the Court must examine the petition carefully to ensure that there is genuine public interest

---

[7] *Dalip Singh v. State of U.P. and Ors.* (2010) 2 SCC 114

involved. The stream of justice should not be allowed to be polluted by unscrupulous litigants.

(viii) The Court, especially the Supreme Court, has to maintain strictest vigilance over the abuse of the process of court and ordinarily meddlesome bystanders should not be granted "visa". Many societal pollutants create new problems of unredressed grievances and the Court should endure to take cases where the justice of the lis well-justifies it.

Access jurisprudence[8] requires Courts to deal with the legitimate litigation whatever be its form but decline to exercise jurisdiction, if such litigation is an abuse of the process of the Court.

Judgment cited:

The party not approaching the Court with clean hands would be liable to be non-suited and such party, who has also succeeded in polluting the stream of justice by making patently false statements, cannot claim relief, especially under Article 136 of the Constitution[9]. While approaching the court, a litigant must state correct facts and come with clean hands. Where such statement of facts is based on some information, the source of such information must also be disclosed. Totally misconceived petition amounts to abuse of the process of the court and such a litigant is not required to be dealt with lightly, as a petition containing misleading and inaccurate statement, if filed, to achieve an ulterior purpose amounts to abuse of the process of the court. A litigant is bound to make "full and true disclosure of facts"[10].

---

[8] The crucial significance of access jurisprudence has been best expressed by Cappelletti:

The right of effective access to justice has emerged with the new social rights. Indeed, it is of paramount importance among these new rights since, clearly, the enjoyment of traditional as well as new social rights presupposes mechanisms for their effective protection. Such protection, moreover, is best assured be a workable remedy within the framework of the judicial system. Effective access to justice can thus be seen as the most basic requirement the most basic 'human-right' of a system which purports to guarantee legal rights.

[9] **Article 136 in The Constitution Of India 1949**
136. Special leave to appeal by the Supreme Court
(1) Notwithstanding anything in this Chapter, the Supreme Court may, in its discretion, grant special leave to appeal from any judgment, decree, determination, sentence or order in any cause or matter passed or made by any court or tribunal in the territory of India
(2) Nothing in clause (1) shall apply to any judgment, determination, sentence or order passed or made by any court or tribunal constituted by or under any law relating to the Armed Forces

[10] *Tilokchand H.B. Motichand and Ors. v. Munshi and Anr.* 1969 (1) SCC 110

The person seeking equity must do equity. It is not just the clean hands, but also clean mind, clean heart and clean objective that are the equi-fundamentals of judicious litigation. The legal maxim jure naturae aequum est neminem cum alterius detrimento et injuria fieri locupletiorem, which means that it is a law of nature that one should not be enriched by the loss or injury to another, is the percept for Courts. Wide jurisdiction of the court should not become a source of abuse of the process of law by the disgruntled litigant. Careful exercise is also necessary to ensure that the litigation is genuine, not motivated by extraneous considerations and imposes an obligation upon the litigant to disclose the true facts and approach the court with clean hands.

No litigant can play 'hide and seek' with the courts or adopt 'pick and choose'. True facts ought to be disclosed as the Court knows law, but not facts. One, who does not come with candid facts and clean breast cannot hold a writ of the court with soiled hands. Suppression or concealment of material facts is impermissible to a litigant or even as a technique of advocacy. In such cases, the Court is duty bound to discharge rule nisi and such applicant is required to be dealt with for contempt of court for abusing the process of the court[11].

Another settled canon of administration of justice is that no litigant should be permitted to misuse the judicial process by filing frivolous petitions. No litigant has a right to unlimited drought upon the court time and public money in order to get his affairs settled in the manner as he wishes. Easy access to justice should not be used as a licence to file misconceived and frivolous petitions[12].

Decision by Supreme Court:

Court held that there is definite contradiction and falsehood in the stand taken by the Petitioner in the writ petition and in the affidavit filed before the Court. This clearly indicates the falsehood in the averments made and the intention of the Appellant to misguide the courts by filing such frivolous petitions. No details, whatsoever, have been furnished to state as to how he verified the alleged website news of the incident of 3rd December, 2006

---

[11] *K.D. Sharma v. Steel Authority of India Ltd. and Ors.* (2008) 12 SCC 481

[12] *Buddhi Kota Subbarao (Dr.) v. K. Parasaran,* (1996) 5 SCC 530).

and from whom. Strangely, he did not even know the Petitioners and could not even identify them. The prayer in the writ petition was for issuance of a direction in the nature of habeas corpus to Respondent No. 6(Shri Rahul Ganhi) to produce the Petitioners. and lastly, the writ petition is full of irresponsible allegations which, as now appears, were not true to the knowledge of the Petitioner, as he claimed to have acted as next friend of the Petitioners while he was no relation, friend or even a person known to the Petitioners. His acting as the next friend of the Petitioners smacks of malice, ulterior motive and misuse of judicial process. The alleged website provides that the girl was missing. It was not reported there that she and her parents were in illegal detention of the Respondent No. 6. So by no means, it could not be a case of habeas corpus.

Respondent No. 8(Shri Gajender Pal Singh) has, thus, for obvious and with ulterior motive abused the process of the court and filed a petition based on falsehood, came to the Court with unclean hands and even attempted to circumvent the process of law by making motivated and untenable prayers. The petitioner (Respondent No. 8) also made irresponsible allegations stating that Kishore Samrite, Petitioner in Writ Petition No. 111 of 2011, was a mentally challenged person.nIt was clear that both the Petitioners(Shri Kishore Samrite and Shri Gajender Pal Singh) have approached the Court with falsehood, unclean hands and have misled the courts by showing urgency and exigencies in relation to an incident of 3rd December, 2006 which, in fact, according to the three Petitioners and the police was false, have thus abused the process of the court and misused the judicial process. Thus, while dismissing the petition(Writ petition No. 111/2011), court impose exemplary costs of Rs. 5 lacs upon the next friend, costs being payable to Respondent No. 6. Court also dismissed Writ petition No. 125/2011 with exemplary cost of Rs. 5 Lakhs.

19

De-criminalisation of consensual - same - sex acts [1]

Facts in Nutshell:

This writ petition has been preferred by Naz Foundation, a Non Governmental Organisation (NGO) as a Public Interest Litigation to challenge the constitutional validity of Section 377 of the Indian Penal Code, 1860 (IPC)[2], which criminally penalizes what is described as "unnatural offences", to the extent the said provision criminalises consensual sexual acts between adults in private. The challenge is founded on the plea that Section 377 IPC, on account of it covering sexual acts between consenting adults in private infringes the fundamental rights guaranteed under Articles 14,[3] 15[4], 19[5]

---

[1] Appellants: **Naz Foundation** vs. Respondent: **Government of NCT and Ors.**
2010CriLJ94

Hon'ble Judges: Ajit Prakash Shah, C.J. and S. Muralidhar, J.

[2] **Section 377 IPC Unnatural Offences** - Whoever voluntarily has carnal intercourse against the order of nature with any man, woman or animal, shall be punished with imprisonment for life, or with imprisonment of either description for a term which may extend to ten years, and shall also be liable to fine.

Explanation - Penetration is sufficient to constitute the carnal intercourse necessary to the offence described in this section.

[3] **Article 14 in The Constitution Of India 1949**

14. Equality before law The State shall not deny to any person equality before the law or the equal protection of the laws within the territory of India Prohibition of discrimination on grounds of religion, race, caste, sex or place of birth

[4] **Article 15 in The Constitution Of India 1949**

15. Prohibition of discrimination on grounds of religion, race, caste, sex or place of birth

(1) The State shall not discriminate against any citizen on grounds only of religion, race, caste, sex, place of birth or any of them

(2) No citizen shall, on grounds only of religion, race, caste, sex, place of birth or any of them, be subject to any disability, liability, restriction or condition with regard to

(a) access to shops, public restaurants, hotels and palaces of public entertainment; or

(b) the use of wells, tanks, bathing ghats, roads and places of public resort maintained wholly

& 21[6] of the Constitution of India. Limiting their plea, the petitioners submit that Section 377 IPC should apply only to non-consensual penile non-vaginal sex and penile non- vaginal sex involving minors. The Union of India is impleaded as respondent No. 5 through Ministry of Home Affairs and Ministry of Health & Family Welfare. Respondent No. 4 is the National Aids Control Organisation (hereinafter referred to as "NACO") a body formed under the aegis of Ministry of Health & Family Welfare, Government of India. NACO is charged with formulating and implementing policies for the prevention of HIV/AIDS in India. Respondent No. 3 is the Delhi State Aids Control Society. Respondent No. 2 is the Commissioner of Police, Delhi. Respondents No. 6 to 8 are individuals and NGOs, who were permitted to intervene on their request. The writ petition was dismissed by Court in 2004 on the ground that there is no cause of action in favour of the petitioner and that such a petition cannot be entertained to examine the academic challenge to the constitutionality of the legislation. The Supreme Court vide order dated 03.02.2006 in Civil Appeal No. 952/2006 set aside the said order of the Court observing that the matter does require consideration and is not of a nature which could have been dismissed on the aforesaid ground. The matter was remitted to the Court for fresh decision.

---

or partly out of State funds or dedicated to the use of the general public

(3) Nothing in this article shall prevent the State from making any special provision for women and children

(4) Nothing in this article or in clause (2) of Article 29 shall prevent the State from making any special provision for the advancement of any socially and educationally backward classes of citizens or for the Scheduled Castes and the Scheduled Tribes

[5] **19. Protection of certain rights regarding freedom of speech etc**

(1) All citizens shall have the right

(a) to freedom of speech and expression;

(b) to assemble peaceably and without arms;

(c) to form associations or unions;

(d) to move freely throughout the territory of India;

(e) to reside and settle in any part of the territory of India; and

(f) omitted

(g) to practise any profession, or to carry on any occupation, trade or business

[6] **Article 21 in The Constitution Of India 1949**

21. Protection of life and personal liberty No person shall be deprived of his life or personal liberty except according to procedure established by law

History of the Legislation

The legislative history of the subject indicates that the first records of sodomy as a crime at Common Law in England were chronicled in the Fleta, 1290, and later in the Britton, 1300. Both texts prescribed that sodomites should be burnt alive. Acts of sodomy later became penalized by hanging under the Buggery Act of 1533 which was re-enacted in 1563 by Queen Elizabeth I, after which it became the charter for the subsequent criminalisation of sodomy in the British Colonies. Oral- genital sexual acts were later removed from the definition of buggery in 1817. And in 1861, the death penalty for buggery was formally abolished in England and Wales. However, sodomy or buggery remained as a crime "not to be mentioned by Christians."

Indian Penal Code was drafted by Lord Macaulay and introduced in 1861 in British India. Section 377 IPC is contained in Chapter XVI of the IPC titled "Of Offences Affecting the Human Body". Within this Chapter Section 377 IPC is categorised under the sub-chapter titled "Of Unnatural Offences" and reads as follows:

377. Unnatural Offences - Whoever voluntarily has carnal intercourse against the order of nature with any man, woman or animal, shall be punished with imprisonment for life, or with imprisonment of either description for a term which may extend to ten years, and shall also be liable to fine.

Explanation - Penetration is sufficient to constitute the carnal intercourse necessary to the offence described in this section.

Judicial Interpretation

The marginal note refers to the acts proscribed as "unnatural offences". This expression, however, is not used in the text of Section 377 IPC. The expression "carnal intercourse" is used in Section 377 IPC as distinct from the expression "sexual intercourse", which appears in Sections 375 and 497 IPC. According to the Concise Oxford Dictionary (ninth edition, 1995), the term "carnal" means "of the body or flesh; worldly" and "sensual, sexual". Consent is no defence to an offence under Section 377 IPC and no distinction regarding age is made in the section. In *Khanu v. Emperor* [7], Kennedy A.J.C. held that "section 377 IPC punishes certain persons who

---

[7] AIR 1925 Sind 286

have carnal intercourse against the order of nature with inter alia human beings.... [if the oral sex committed in this case is carnal intercourse], it is clearly against the order of nature, because the natural object of carnal intercourse is that there should be the possibility of conception of human beings, which in the case of coitus per os is impossible."[page 286] . In *Lohana Vasantlal Devchand v. State*,[8] the issue was whether oral sex amounted to an offence under Section 377IPC. It was held that the "orifice of the mouth is not, according to nature, meant for sexual or carnal intercourse." In *Calvin Francis v. Orissa*[9] relying on Lohana, it was held that oral sex fell within the ambit of Section 377 IPC. The Court used the references to the Corpus Juris Secundum relating to sexual perversity and abnormal sexual satisfaction as the guiding criteria. In *Fazal Rab Choudhary v. State of Bihar*[10] , it was observed that Section 377 IPC implied "sexual perversity". It is evident that the tests for attracting the penal provisions have changed from the non-procreative to imitative to sexual perversity.

The Challenge

The petitioner NGO has been working in the field of HIV/AIDS Intervention and prevention. This necessarily involves interaction with such sections of society as are vulnerable to contracting HIV/AIDS and which include gay community or individuals described as "men who have sex with men" (MSM). For sake of convenient reference, they would hereinafter be referred to as "homosexuals" or "gay" persons or gay community. Homosexuals, according to the petitioner, represent a population segment that is extremely vulnerable to HIV/AIDS infection. The petitioner claims to have been impelled to bring this litigation in public interest on the ground that HIV/AIDS prevention efforts were found to be severely impaired by discriminatory attitudes exhibited by state agencies towards gay community, MSM or trans-gendered individuals, under the cover of enforcement of Section 377 IPC, as a result of which basic fundamental human rights of such individuals/ groups (in minority) stood denied and they were subjected to abuse, harassment, assault from public and public authorities.

---

[8] AIR 1968 Guj 252
[9] 1992 (2) Crimes 455
[10] 1983CriLJ632

Submission on Behalf of Petitioner

1. According to the petitioner, Section 377 IPC is based upon traditional Judeo-Christian moral and ethical standards, which conceive of sex in purely functional terms, i.e., for the purpose of procreation only. Any non-procreative sexual activity is thus viewed as being "against the order of nature". The submission is that the legislation criminalising consensual oral and anal sex is outdated and has no place in modern society. In fact, studies of Section 377IPC jurisprudence reveal that lately it has generally been employed in cases of child sexual assault and abuse. By criminalising private, consensual same-sex conduct, Section 377 IPC serves as the weapon for police abuse; detaining and questioning, extortion, harassment, forced sex, payment of hush money; and perpetuates negative and discriminatory beliefs towards same-sex relations and sexuality minorities; which consequently drive the activities of gay men and MSM, as well as sexuality minorities underground thereby crippling HIV/AIDS prevention efforts. Section 377 IPC thus creates a class of vulnerable people that is continually victimised and directly affected by the provision. It has been submitted that the fields of psychiatry and psychology no longer treat homosexuality as a disease and regard sexual orientation to be a deeply held, core part of the identities of individuals.

2. The petitioner also submitted that while right to privacy is implicit in the right to life and liberty and guaranteed to the citizens, in order to be meaningful, the pursuit of happiness encompassed within the concepts of privacy, human dignity, individual autonomy and the human need for an intimate personal sphere require that privacy - dignity claim concerning private, consensual, sexual relations are also afforded protection within the ambit of the said fundamental right to life and liberty given under Article 21. It is averred that no aspect of one's life may be said to be more private or intimate than that of sexual relations, and since private, consensual, sexual relations or sexual preferences figure prominently within an individual's personality and lie easily at the core of the "private space", they are an inalienable component of the right of life. Based on this line

of reasoning, a case has been made to the effect that the prohibition of certain private, consensual sexual relations (homosexual) provided by Section 377 IPC unreasonably abridges the right of privacy and dignity within the ambit of right to life and liberty under Article 21. The petitioner argues that fundamental right to privacy under Article 21 can be abridged only for a compelling state interest which, in its submission, is amiss here. Also based on the fundamental right to life under Article 21 is the further submission that Section 377 IPC has a damaging impact upon the lives of homosexuals inasmuch as it not only perpetuates social stigma and police/public abuse but also drives homosexual activity underground thereby jeopardizing HIV/AIDS prevention efforts and, thus, rendering gay men and MSM increasingly vulnerable to contracting HIV/AIDS.

3. Further, it has been submitted on behalf of the petitioner that Section 377 IPC's legislative objective of penalizing "unnatural sexual acts" has no rational nexus to the classification created between procreative and non- procreative sexual acts, and is thus violative of Article 14 of the Constitution of India. Section 377's legislative objective is based upon stereotypes and misunderstanding that are outmoded and enjoys no historical or logical rationale which render it arbitrary and unreasonable. It is further the case of the petitioner that the expression "sex" as used in Article 15 cannot be read restrictive to "gender" but includes "sexual orientation" and, thus read, equality on the basis of sexual orientation is implied in the said fundamental right against discrimination. The petitioner argues that criminalization of predominantly homosexual activity through Section 377 IPC is discriminatory on the basis of sexual orientation and, therefore, violative of Article 15. It is further the case of the petitioner that the prohibition against homosexuality in Section 377IPC curtails or infringes the basic freedoms guaranteed under Article 19(1)(a)(b)(c) & (d); in that, an individual's ability to make personal statement about one's sexual preferences, right of association/assembly and right to move freely so as to engage in homosexual conduct are restricted and curtailed.

Reply by Union of India- Contradictory stands of Ministry of Home Affairs and Ministry of Health & Family Welfare

A rather peculiar feature of the case is that completely contradictory affidavits have been filed by two wings of Union of India. The Ministry of Home Affairs (MHA) sought to justify the retention of Section 377 IPC, whereas the Ministry of Health & Family Welfare insisted that continuance of Section 377IPC has hampered the HIV/AIDS prevention efforts.

The Director (Judicial) in the Ministry of Home Affairs, Government of India, in his affidavit, justify the retention of Section 377 IPC on the statute book broadly on the reason that it has been generally invoked in cases of allegation of child sexual abuse and for complementing lacunae in the rape laws and not mere homosexuality. This penal clause has been used particularly in cases of assault where bodily harm is intended and/or caused. It has been submitted that the impugned provision is necessary since the deletion thereof would well open flood gates of delinquent behaviour and can possibly be misconstrued as providing unfettered licence for homosexuality.

Reference has been made to 42nd report of the Commission wherein it was observed that Indian society by and large disapproved of homosexuality, which disapproval was strong enough to justify it being treated as a criminal offence even where the adults indulge in it in private. Union of India submitted that law cannot run separately from the society since it only reflects the perception of the society. It claims that at the time of initial enactment, Section 377 IPC was responding to the values and morals of the time in the Indian society. It has been submitted that in fact in any parliamentary secular democracy, the legal conception of crime depends upon political as well as moral considerations notwithstanding considerable overlap existing between legal and safety conception of crime i.e. moral factors.

Affidavit of Narco/Ministry of Health & Family Welfare

In the reply affidavit filed on behalf of NACO, it has been submitted that the report of the Expert Group on Size Estimation of Population with High Risk Behaviour for NACPIII Planning, January 2006 estimated that there are about 25 lakh MSM (Men having sex with men). The National Sentinel

Surveillance Data 2005 shows that more than 8% of the population of MSM is infected by HIV while the HIV prevalence among the general population is estimated to be lesser than 1%. Given the high vulnerability of MSM to HIV infection, NACO has developed programmes for undertaking targeted interventions among them. These projects are implemented by NGOs with financial support from NACO. Presently 1,46,397 MSM (6%) are being covered through 30 targeted interventions. Under the targeted intervention projects, the objectives are to:

a. reduce number of partners and by bringing about a change in their behaviour;

b. reduce their level of risk by informing them about and providing access to condoms;

c. providing access to STD services.

According to the submissions of NACO, those in the High Risk Group are mostly reluctant to reveal same sex behaviour due to the fear of law enforcement agencies, keeping a large section invisible and unreachable and thereby pushing the cases of infection underground making it very difficult for the public health workers to even access them. It illustrates this point by referring to the data reflected in the National Baseline Behaviour Surveillance Survey (NBBSS of 2002) which indicates that while 68.6% MSM population is aware about the methods of preventing infection, only 36% of them actually use condoms.

NACO has further submitted that enforcement of Section 377 IPC against homosexual groups renders risky sexual practices to go unnoticed and unaddressed inasmuch as the fear of harassment by law enforcement agencies leads to sex being hurried, particularly because these groups lack 'safe place', utilise public places for their indulgence and do not have the option to consider or negotiate safer sex practices. It is stated that the very hidden nature of such groups constantly inhibits/impedes interventions under the National AIDS Control Programme aimed at prevention. Thus NACO reinforces the plea raised by the petitioner for the need to have an enabling environment where the people involved in risky behaviour are encouraged not to conceal information so that they can be provided total access to the services of such preventive efforts.

Response of Other Respondents

'Voices against Section 377 IPC' (hereinafter referred to as "respondent No. 8") is a coalition of 12 organisations that represent child rights, women's rights, human rights, health concerns as well as the rights of same sex desiring people including those who identify as Lesbian, Gay, Bisexual, Transgenders, Hijra and Kothi persons (which are referred to in the affidavit as "LGBT"). It has been submitted on its behalf that organisations that constitute respondent No. 8 are involved in diverse areas of public and social importance and that in the course of their work they have repeatedly come across gross violation of basic human rights of "LGBT" persons, both as a direct and indirect consequence of the enforcement of Section 377 IPC.

Respondent No. 8 supports the cause espoused by the petitioner in this PIL and avers that Section 377 IPC, which criminalises 'carnal intercourse against the order of the nature', is an unconstitutional and arbitrary law based on archaic moral and religious notions of sex only for procreation. It asserts that criminalisation of adult consensual sex under Section 377 IPC does not serve any beneficial public purpose or legitimate state interest. On the contrary, according to respondent No. 8, Section 377 IPC by criminalising the aforementioned kinds of sexual acts has created an association of criminality towards people with same sex desires. It pleads that the continued existence of this provision on the statute book creates and fosters a climate of fundamental rights violations of the gay community, to the extent of bolstering their extreme social ostracism.

Reference was made to a judgment of the High Court of Madras reported as *Jayalakshmi v. The State of Tamil Nadu[11]*, in which an eunuch had committed suicide due to the harassment and torture at the hands of the police officers after he had been picked up on the allegation of involvement in a case of theft. There was evidence indicating that during police custody he was subjected to torture by a wooden stick being inserted into his anus and some police personnel forcing him to have oral sex. The person in question immolated himself inside the police station on 12.6.2006 and later succumbed to burn injuries on 29.6.2006. The compensation of Rs. 5,00,000/- was awarded to the family of the victim.

---

[11] (2007)4MLJ849

Submission by Additional Solicitor General of India

Learned ASG submitted that there is no fundamental right to engage in the same sex activities. In our country, homosexuality is abhorrent and can be criminalised by imposing proportional limits on the citizens' right to privacy and equality. Learned ASG submitted that right to privacy is not absolute and can be restricted for compelling state interest. Article 19(2)[12] expressly permits imposition of restrictions in the interest of decency and morality. Social and sexual mores in foreign countries cannot justify de-criminalisation of homosexuality in India. According to him, in the western societies the morality standards are not as high as in India. Learned ASG further submitted that Section 377 IPC is not discriminatory as it is gender neutral. If Section 377 IPC is struck down there will be no way the State can prosecute any crime of nonconsensual carnal intercourse against the order of nature or gross male indecency.

Article 21, The Right to Life and Protection of a Person's Dignity, Autonomy and Privacy

Dignity

In *Francis Coralie Mullin v. Administrator, Union Territory of Delhi and Ors.*[13], Justice P.N. Bhagwati explained the concept of right to dignity in the following terms:

...We think that the right to life includes the right to live with human dignity and all that goes along with it, namely, the bare necessaries of life such as adequate nutrition, clothing and shelter and facilities for reading, writing and expressing oneself in diverse forms, freely moving about and mixing and commingling with fellow human beings. Every act which offends against or impairs human dignity would constitute deprivation pro tanto of this right to live and it would have to be in accordance with reasonable, fair and just

---

[12] **Article 19(2) in The Constitution Of India 1949**

(2) Nothing in sub clause (a) of clause (1) shall affect the operation of any existing law, or prevent the State from making any law, in so far as such law imposes reasonable restrictions on the exercise of the right conferred by the said sub clause in the interests of the sovereignty and integrity of India, the security of the State, friendly relations with foreign States, public order, decency or morality or in relation to contempt of court, defamation or incitement to an offence

[13] 1981CriLJ306 .

procedure established by law which stands the test of other fundamental rights. [para 8 of SCC]

Privacy

Article 12 of the Universal Declaration of Human Rights (1948) refers to privacy and it states:

No one shall be subjected to arbitrary interference with his privacy, family, home or correspondence nor to attacks upon his honour and reputation. Everyone has the right to the protection of the law against such interference or attacks.

Article 17 of the International Covenant of Civil and Political Rights (to which India is a party), refers to privacy and states that:

No one shall be subjected to arbitrary or unlawful interference with his privacy, family, home and correspondence, nor to unlawful attacks on his honour and reputation.

A two-Judge Bench in *R. Rajagopal v. State of T.N.* [14], held the right to privacy to be implicit in the right to life and liberty guaranteed to the citizens of India by Article 21. "It is the right to be left alone". A citizen has a right to safeguard the privacy of his own, his family, marriage, procreation, motherhood, child bearing and education among many other matters.

"Aravanis (hijras) are discriminated by the society and remain isolated" following directions were issued:

In 2006, the State of Tamil Nadu recognising that "aravanis (hijras) are discriminated by the society and remain isolated" issued directions thus:

I.   counseling be given to children who may feel different from other individuals in terms of their gender identity.

II.   Family counseling by the teachers with the help of NGOs sensitized in that area should be made mandatory so that such children are not disowned by their families. The C.E.O.s, D.E.O.s, District Social Welfare Officers and Officers of Social Defence are requested to

---

[14] AIR1995SC264

arrange compulsory counseling with the help of teachers and NGOs in the Districts wherever it is required.

III. Admission in School and Colleges should not be denied based on their sex identity. If any report is received of denying admission of aravani's suitable disciplinary action should be taken by the authorities concerned.

Law Commission's 172nd Report

In the 172nd report, the Law Commission has recommended deletion of Section 377 IPC, though in its earlier reports it had recommended the retention of the provision. In the 172nd report, the Law Commission of India, focused on the need to review the sexual offences laws in the light of increased incidents of custodial rape and crime of sexual abuse against youngsters, and inter alia, recommended deleting the Section 377 IPC by effecting the recommended amendments in Sections 375 to 376E of IPC. The Commission discussed various provisions related to sexual offences and was of considered opinion to amend provisions in the Indian Penal Code, 1860; the Code of Criminal Procedure, 1973; and Indian Evidence Act, 1872. In the Indian penal Code, recasting of 375 IPC has been recommended by redefining it under the head of 'Sexual Assault' encompassing all ranges of non consensual sexual offences/assaults, which in particular penalize not only the sexual intercourse with a woman as in accordance with the current 'Rape Laws'; but any non-consensual or non-willing penetration with bodily part or object manipulated by the another person except carried out for proper hygienic or medicinal purposes.

The recommended provision to substitute the existing Section 375 IPC reads thus:

375.Sexual Assault: Sexual assault means -

(a) penetrating the vagina (which term shall include the labia majora), the anus or urethra of any person with -

i) any part of the body of another person or

ii) an object manipulated by another person

except where such penetration is carried out for proper hygienic or medical purposes;

(b) manipulating any part of the body of another person so as to cause penetration of the vagina (which term shall include the labia majora), the anus or the urethra of the offender by any part of the other person's body;

(c) introducing any part of the penis of a person into the mouth of another person;

(d) engaging in cunnilingus or fellatio; or

(e) continuing sexual assault as defined in clauses (a) to (d) above in circumstances falling under any of the six following descriptions:

First- Against the other person's will.

Secondly- Without the other person's consent.

Thirdly- With the other person's consent when such consent has been obtained by putting such other person or any person in whom such other person is interested, in fear of death or hurt.

Fourthly- Where the other person is a female, with her consent, when the man knows that he is not the husband of such other person and that her consent is given because she believes that the offender is another man to whom she is or believes herself to be lawfully married.

Fifthly- With the consent of the other person, when, at the time of giving such consent, by reason of unsoundness of mind or intoxication or the administration by the offender personally or through another of any stupefying or unwholesome substance, the other person is unable to understand the nature and consequences of that to which such other person gives consent.

Sixthly- With or without the other person's consent, when such other person is under sixteen years of age.

Explanation: Penetration to any extent is penetration for the purposes of this section.

Exception: Sexual intercourse by a man with his own wife, the wife not being under sixteen years of age, is not sexual assault.

Pertinently, the major thrust of the recommendation is on the word 'Person' which makes the sexual offences gender neutral unlike gender specific as under the 'Rape Laws' which is the current position in statute book. Amendments in Section 376A, 376B, 376C, 376D have been recommended on the same lines with enhanced punishments. An added explanation defining sexual intercourse is sought to be introduced governing Section 376B, 376C, 376D. Insertion of new Section 376E has been recommended to penalize non consensual, direct or indirect, intentional unlawful sexual contact with part of body or with an object, any part of body of another person. This section specifically penalizes the person committing unlawful sexual contact who is in a position of trust or authority towards a young person (below the age of sixteen years), thereby protecting children. Conclusively the Section 377 IPC in the opinion of the Commission, deserves to be deleted in the light of recommended amendments. However persons, having carnal intercourse with any animal, were to be left to their just deserts. Though the Law Commission report would not expressly say so, it is implicit in the suggested amendments that elements of "will" and "consent" will become relevant to determine if the sexual contact (homosexual for the purpose at hand) constitute an offence or not.

Whether Section 377 IPC Violates Constitutional Guarantee of Equality Uuder Article 14 of the Constitution

The scope, content and meaning of Article 14 of the Constitution has been the subject matter of intensive examination by the Supreme Court in a catena of decisions. The decisions lay down that though Article 14 forbids class legislation, it does not forbid reasonable classification for the purpose of legislation. In order, however, to pass the test of permissible classification, two conditions must be fulfilled, namely, (i) that the classification must be founded on an intelligible differentia which distinguishes persons or things that are grouped together from those that are left out of the group; and (ii) that the differentia must have a rational relation to the objective sought to be achieved by the statute in question. The classification may be founded on differential basis according to objects sought to be achieved but what is implicit in it is that there ought to be a nexus, i.e., causal connection between the basis of classification and object of the statute under consideration[15]. In considering reasonableness from the point of view of Article 14, the Court has also to consider the objective for such classification. If the objective be illogical, unfair and unjust, necessarily the classification will have to be held as unreasonable[16].

Section 377 IPC Targets Homosexuals as a Class

Section 377 IPC is facially neutral and it apparently targets not identities but acts, but in its operation it does end up unfairly targeting a particular community. The fact is that these sexual acts which are criminalised are associated more closely with one class of persons, namely, the homosexuals as a class. Section 377 IPC has the effect of viewing all gay men as criminals. When everything associated with homosexuality is treated as bent, queer, repugnant, the whole gay and lesbian community is marked with deviance and perversity. They are subject to extensive prejudice because what they are or what they are perceived to be, not because of what they do. The result is that a significant group of the population is, because of its sexual nonconformity, persecuted, marginalised and turned in on itself[17].

The inevitable conclusion is that the discrimination caused to MSM and gay community is unfair and unreasonable and, therefore, in breach of Article 14 of the Constitution of India.

Infringement of Article 15- Whether 'Sexual Orientation' is a Ground Analogous to 'Sex'

Article 15 is an instance and particular application of the right of equality which is generally stated in Article 14. Article 14 is genus while Article 15 along with Article 16[18] are species although all of them occupy same field and the doctrine of "equality" embodied in these Articles has

---

[15] *Budhan Choudhry v. State of Bihar*, 1955CriLJ374.

[16] *Deepak Sibal v. Punjab University* , [1989]1SCR689

[17] [Sachs, J. in The National Coalition for Gay and Lesbian Equality v. The Minister of Justice, para 108].

[18] **Article 16 in The Constitution Of India 1949**

16. Equality of opportunity in matters of public employment

(1) There shall be equality of opportunity for all citizens in matters relating to employment or appointment to any office under the State

(2) No citizen shall, on grounds only of religion, race, caste, sex, descent, place of birth, residence or any of them, be ineligible for, or discriminated against in respect or, any employment or office under the State

many facets. Article 15 prohibits discrimination on several enumerated grounds, which include 'sex'. The argument of the petitioner is that 'sex' in Article 15(1) must be read expansively to include a prohibition of discrimination on the ground of sexual orientation as the prohibited ground of sex- discrimination cannot be read as applying to gender simpliciter. The purpose underlying the fundamental right against sex discrimination is to prevent behaviour that treats people differently for reason of not being in conformity with generalization concerning "normal" or "natural" gender roles. Discrimination on the basis of sexual orientation is itself grounded in stereotypical judgments and generalization about the conduct of either sex. This is stated to be the legal position in International Law and comparative jurisprudence.

Court hold that sexual orientation is a ground analogous to sex and that discrimination on the basis of sexual orientation is not permitted by Article 15. Further, Article 15(2) incorporates the notion of horizontal application of rights. In other words, it even prohibits discrimination of one citizen by another in matters of access to public spaces. In courts view, discrimination on the ground of sexual orientation is impermissible even on the horizontal application of the right enshrined under Article 15."

Supreme Court in *Anuj Garg v. Hotel Association of India*[19] , constitutional validity of Section 30 of the Punjab Excise Act, 1914 prohibiting employment of "any man under the age of 25 years" or "any woman" in any part of such premises in which liquor or intoxicating drug is consumed by the public was challenged before the High Court of Delhi. The High Court declared Section 30 of the Act as ultra vires Articles 19(1) (g)[20], 14and 15 of the Constitution of India to the extent it prohibits

---

(3) Nothing in this article shall prevent Parliament from making any law prescribing, in regard to a class or classes of employment or appointment to an office under the Government of, or any local or other authority within, a State or Union territory, any requirement as to residence within that State or Union territory prior to such employment or appointment

(4) Nothing in this article shall prevent the State from making any provision for the reservation of appointments or posts in favor of any backward class of citizens which, in the opinion of the State, is not adequately represented in the services under the State

(5) Nothing in this article shall affect the operation of any law which provides that the incumbent of an office in connection with the affairs of any religious or denominational institution or any member of the governing body thereof shall be a person professing a particular religion or belonging to a particular denomination

[19] AIR2008SC663

[20] **Article 19(1)(g) in The Constitution Of India 1949**

(g) to practise any profession, or to carry on any occupation, trade or business

employment of any woman in any part of such premises, in which liquor or intoxicating drugs are consumed by the public. National Capital Territory of Delhi accepted the said judgment but an appeal was filed by few citizens of Delhi. The appeal was ultimately dismissed by the Supreme Court, but the principles laid down by the Court relating to the scope of the right to equality enunciated in Articles 14and 15 are material for the purpose of the present case. At the outset, the Court observed that the Act in question is a pre-constitutional legislation and although it is saved in terms of Article 372 of the Constitution[21], challenge to its validity on the touchstone of Articles 14, 15 and 19 of the Constitution of India, is permissible in law. There is thus no presumption of constitutionality of a colonial legislation. Therefore, though the statute could have been held to be a valid piece of legislation keeping in view the societal condition of those times, but with the changes occurring therein both in the domestic as also international arena, such a law can also be declared invalid.

In Anuj Garg, the Court, however, clarified that the heightened review standard does not make sex a proscribed classification, "...sex classifications" may be used to compensate women "for particular economic disabilities (they have) suffered", "to promote equal employment opportunity", to advance full development of the talent and capacities of our nation's people. Such classifications may not be used, as they once were, to create or perpetuate the legal, social, and economic inferiority of women."

As held in Anuj Garg, if a law discriminates on any of the prohibited grounds, it needs to be tested not merely against "reasonableness" under Article14 but be subject to "strict scrutiny". The impugned provision in Section 377 IPC criminalises the acts of sexual minorities particularly men who have sex with men and gay men. It disproportionately impacts them solely on the basis of their sexual orientation. The provision runs counter to

---

[21] **Article 352 in The Constitution Of India 1949**

352. Proclamation of Emergency

(1) If the President is satisfied that a grave emergency exists whereby the security of India or of any part of the territory thereof is threatened, whether by war or external aggression or armed rebellion, he may, by Proclamation, made a declaration to that effect in respect of the whole of India or of such part of the territory thereof as may be specified in the Proclamation Explanation A Proclamation of Emergency declaring that the security of India or any part of the territory thereof is threatened by war or by external aggression or by armed rebellion may be made before the actual occurrence of war or of any such aggression or rebellion, if the President is satisfied that there is imminent danger thereof

the constitutional values and the notion of human dignity which is considered to be the cornerstone of our Constitution. Section 377 IPC in its application to sexual acts of consenting adults in privacy discriminates a section of people solely on the ground of their sexual orientation which is analogous to prohibited ground of sex. A provision of law branding one section of people as criminal based wholly on the State's moral disapproval of that class goes counter to the equality guaranteed under Articles 14 and 15 under any standard of review.

Grounds on which Act of the legislature can be held to invalid

There is one and only one ground for declaring an Act of the legislature (or a provision in the Act) to be invalid, and that is if it clearly violates some provision of the Constitution in so evident a manner as to leave no manner of doubt. This violation can, of course, be in different ways, e.g. if a State legislature makes a law which only the Parliamnet can make under List I to the Seventh Schedule, in which case it will violate Article 246(1) of the Constitution[22], or the law violates some specific provision of the Constitution (other than the directive principles). But before declaring the statute to be unconstitutional, the Court must be absolutely sure that there can be no manner of doubt that it violates a provision of the Constitution. If two views are possible, one making the statute constitutional and the other making it unconstitutional, the former view must always be preferred. Also, the Court must make every effort to uphold the constitutional validity of a statute, even if that requries giving a strained construction or narrowing down its scope [23] Also, it is none of the concern of the Court whether the legislation in its opinion is wise or unwise.

Decision of the Court

Court declared that Section 377 IPC, insofar it criminalises consensual sexual acts of adults in private, is violative of Articles 21, 14 and 15 of the Constitution. The provisions of Section 377 IPC will continue to govern non-consensual penile non-vaginal sex and penile non-vaginal sex involving

---

[22] **Article 246(1) in The Constitution Of India 1949**

(1) Notwithstanding anything in clauses (2) and (3), Parliament has exclusive power to make laws with respect to any of the matters enumerated in List I in the Seventh Schedule (in this Constitution referred to as the Union List)

[23] *Mark Netto v. State of Kerala and Ors.* [1979]1SCR609

minors. By 'adult' court mean everyone who is 18 years of age and above. A person below 18 would be presumed not to be able to consent to a sexual act. This clarification will hold till, of course, Parliament chooses to amend the law to effectuate the recommendation of the Law Commission of India in its 172nd Report which court believe removes a great deal of confusion. Secondly, court clarified that there judgment will not result in the re-opening of criminal cases involving Section 377 IPC that have already attained finality.

20

Duty of driver in case of accident and injury to a person[1]

Ratio Decidendi[2]— *"Prosecution shall be proved his case beyond all reasonable doubt."*

Question before the Court:

Whether Respondent accused deserves to be held guilty of commission of offence under Section 304 Part II of the Indian Penal Code (for short Indian Penal Code)[3] or the conviction and sentence awarded to him by the High Court of Delhi, under Section 304 A of the Indian Penal Code[4] should be held to be good and legally tenable.

---

[1] Appellants: **State Tr. P.S. Lodhi Colony New Delhi Vs.** Respondent: **Sanjeev Nanda** (2012)8SCC450

Hon'bleJudges: Deepak Verma and K.S. Panicker Radhakrishnan, JJ.

[2] **Meaning of Ratio Decidendi**

Ratio decidendi is a Latin phrase meaning "the reason" or "the rationale for the decision." The *ratio decidendi* is "[t]he point in a case which determines the judgment" or "the principle which the case establishes."

[3] Indian Penal Code (IPC) Section 304. Punishment for culpable homicide not amounting to murder

Whoever commits culpable homicide not amounting to murder shall be punished with [1][imprisonment for life], or imprisonment of either description for a term which may extend to ten years, and shall also be liable to fine, if the act by which the death is caused is done with the intention of causing death, or of causing such bodily injury as is likely to cause death,

or with imprisonment of either description for a term which may extend to ten years, or with fine, or with both, if the act is done with the knowledge that it is likely to cause death, but without any intention to cause death, or to cause such bodily injury as is likely to cause death.

[4] Indian Penal Code (IPC) Section 304A. Causing death by negligence

[304A. Causing death by negligence.—Whoever causes the death of any person by doing any rash or negligent act not amounting to culpable homicide, shall be punished with imprisonment of either description for a term which may extend to two years, or with fine, or with both.]

Facts in Nutshell:

An unfortunate motor accident took place involving BMW Car No. M-312 LYP. At the relevant point of time, it was not in dispute that offending vehicle BMW was being driven by Respondent. As per prosecution story, the said vehicle was coming from Nizamuddin side and was proceeding towards Lodhi Road. Just at the corner from where Lodhi Road starts, seven persons were standing on the road at about 4.00 a.m. In the said car, Manik Kapur and Sidharth Gupta (since discharged) were also sitting.

As per prosecution story, Manoj Malik (P.W. 2) had started from his house to leave friends Nasir, Mehendi Hasan and his friend Gulab at Nizamudin Railway Station on foot. When they reached the petrol pump of Lodhi Road, three police officials of checking squad, Constables Rajan, Ram Raj and Peru Lal, stopped them and started checking. In the meantime, BMW car driven rashly and negligently came from Nizamuddin side at a high speed and dashed violently against them. The impact was so great and severe, that they flew in the air and fell on the bonnet and wind screen of the car. Some of them rolled down and came beneath the car. On account of this, accused lost control of the vehicle which swerved to right side of the road and ultimately hit the central verge. The persons who had come under the car were dragged up to that point. Manoj (P.W. 2) who had fallen on the bonnet fell down at some distance but did not come under the wheels. After hitting the central verge, car finally stopped at some distance, Respondent came out from the car and inspected the gruesome site. It is said that co-passenger Manik Kapur asked the accused to rush from the scene of occurrence. Injured persons were shouting and crying for help. But ignoring them, he drove away the car at high speed towards Dayal Singh College, even though there were still some persons beneath the car. In the said accident ultimately six of them were killed and Manoj (P.W. 2) was injured. Accused then took the car to his friend Sidharth Gupta's house at 50, Golf Links, New Delhi. Prosecution further told that there another accused Rajeev Gupta, father of Sidharth Gupta with the help of two servants, accused Shyam and Bhola washed the car and destroyed the material evidence.

Decision of Trail Court:

The trial court found Respondent guilty of commission of offence under Section 304 Part II of the Indian Penal Code and awarded him a jail sentence of five years. He was acquitted of other charges. However, accused Rajeev Gupta, Shyam Singh and Bhola Nath were convicted under Section 201 Indian Penal Code[5]. Rajeev Gupta was sentenced to undergo a sentence of one year and Bhola Nath and Shyam Singh to undergo a sentence of six months each. Feeling aggrieved by the said judgment and order of conviction, Respondent filed Criminal Appeal in the High Court of Delhi at New Delhi.

Decision by High Court:

The learned Single Judge considered the matter at great length and thereafter found the accused Sanjeev Nanda guilty of commission of offence under Section 304 A of the Indian Penal Code and reduced the sentence to two years. While converting the conviction of said accused from Section 304 Part II to 304 A, the High Court has disbelieved the testimony of Sunil Kulkarni which was the basis for the trial court to come to a conclusion that the case fell under Section 304 Part II. The High Court has also held that though the act of accused amounted to rashness and negligence endangering the lives of others, since there was no intention or knowledge of causing death, no case for conviction of accused under Section 304 Part II was made out.

Other accused Rajeev Gupta, Shyam and Bhola were found guilty of commission of offence under Section 201 of the Indian Penal Code and were awarded six months' and three months' RI respectively.

---

[5] **Section 201 in The Indian Penal Code, 1860**

201. Causing disappearance of evidence of offence, or giving false information to screen offender.— Whoever, knowing or having reason to believe that an offence has been committed, causes any evidence of the commission of that offence to disappear, with the intention of screening the offender from legal punishment, or with that intention gives any information respecting the offence which he knows or believes to be false, if a capital offence; if a capital offence.— shall, if the offence which he knows or believes to have been committed is punishable with death, be punished with imprisonment of either description for a term which may extend to seven years, and shall also be liable to fine; if punishable with imprisonment for life; if punishable with imprisonment for life.— and if the offence is punishable with 1[imprisonment for life], or with imprisonment which may extend to ten years, shall be punished with imprisonment of either description for a term which may extend to three years, and shall also be liable to fine; if punishable with less than ten years' imprisonment. if punishable with less than ten years' imprisonment.— and if the offence is punishable with imprisonment for any term not extending to ten years, shall be punished with imprisonment of the description provided for the offence, for a term which may extend to one- fourth part of the longest term of the imprisonment provided for the offence, or with fine, or with both.

Arguments on behalf of learned Additional Solicitor General:

a) Admittedly Respondent was not holding any valid Indian licence to drive a vehicle in India.

b) He was driving a powerful machine like BMW in excessive speed in a rash and negligent manner and certainly beyond reasonable control over it.

c) His negligence coupled with intoxication would lead to culpable homicide with knowledge.

d) He knew that persons have been crushed and some of them were underneath his car, yet he continued to drive the vehicle till all the injured were disentangled from the vehicle.

e) He fled away from the scene of crime, did not render any help to the injured. Not only this, he did not report the matter to the police and tried to obliterate the evidence available.

f) Even if intention may not be attributed to him but at least he had knowledge of what he had done, thus ingredients mandated under Section 304 Part II Indian Penal Code were fully met.

g) Thus, High Court committed grave error in interfering with a well reasoned order of the Trial Court. Respondent should thus be held guilty of commission of offence under Section 304 Part II Indian Penal Code and sentence be awarded accordingly.

Cases referred by Additional Solicitor General:

Dalbir Singh v. State of Haryana[6], has been cited to show that as far back as in the year 2000, drunken driving was heavily criticized and a warning was issued to all those who may be in the habit, to be more careful and cautious. It further went on to say that no benefit to the accused found guilty, can be granted under the Probation of Offenders Act, 1958.

State of Maharashtra v. Salman Salim Khan[7] was cited to show that in identical circumstances where the accused was not holding a valid motor

---

[6] (2000) 5 SCC 82

[7] (2004) 1 SCC 525

driving licence and was under influence of alcohol, he would be held to have committed offence under Section 304 Part II of the Indian Penal Code.

Arguments on behalf of Respondent Counsel:

a) Offence was said to have been committed in the year 1999, almost 13 years back.

b) Respondent was aged 21 years at that time, and was prosecuting his course in foreign country. He had come to India on a short holiday.

c) He has already undergone the sentence of two years awarded by High Court and only thereafter, after the period of limitation of filing the appeal had expired, he got married to his long time love, now they are blessed with a daughter.

d) His behaviour and conduct in jail was extremely good, which is evident from the two affidavits filed in support of the Respondent by two NGOs.

e) Fact cannot be given a go-by that it was a cold wintry night of 9/ 10th January, 1999, thus possibility cannot be ruled out that visibility must have been poor due to fog.

f) He had neither any previous criminal record nor has been involved in any criminal activity ever since then.

g) It was contended that Respondent has already learnt sufficient lesson at young age and no useful purpose would be served, if he is sent to jail again.

h) The victim and/or families of deceased have been paid handsome amount of compensation of Rs. 65 lacs, in the year 1999 itself, i.e. Rs. 10 lacs each to the families of the deceased and Rs. 5 lacs to the injured.

i) It would not only be humiliating but great embarrassment to the Respondent, if he is again sent to jail for little more period, over and above the period of two years awarded and undergone.

j) He had neither intention nor knowledge of the ultimate consequences of the offence said to have been committed.

Court Observed (Para 32) :

Respondent, instead of rendering helping hand to the injured, ran away from the scene, thus adding further to the miseries of the victims. It is not a good trend to run away after causing motor road accidents. An attempt should be made to render all possible help, including medical assistance, if required. Human touch to the same has to be given

Meaning of Accident:

'Accident' has been defined by Black's Law Dictionary as under:

Accident: An unintended and unforeseen injurious occurrence; something that does not occur in the usual course of events or that could not be reasonably anticipated.

Thus, it means, if the injury/death is caused by an accident, that itself cannot be attributed to an intention. If intention is proved and death is caused, then it would amount to culpable homicide.

Again appeal was filed by the State contending that the High Court has committed an error in converting the conviction from Section 304(II) to Section 304A of the Indian Penal Code considering the seriousness of charges proved and the gravity of the offence. Counsel for the state also submitted that the accused deserves harsher punishment, as rightly held by the trial court considering the fact that he was driving the vehicle in an inebriated state, without licence and that he had left the scene of occurrence without extending any helping hand to the victims either by taking them to the hospital or reporting the accident to the police at the earliest point of time.

(Driving by a drunken person or by a person under the influence of drugs, Section 185 of the M.V. Act):

Section 185 - Driving by a drunken person or by a person under the influence of drugs

Whoever, while Driving, or attempting to drive, a motor vehicle,-

   (a) has, in his blood, alcohol exceeding 30 mg. per 100 ml. of blood detected in a test by a breath analyser, or

(b) is under this influence of a drug to such an extent as to be incapable of exercising proper control over the vehicle, shall be punishable for the first offence with imprisonment for a term which may extend to six months, or with fine which may extend to two thousand rupees, or with both; and for a second or subsequent offence, if committed within three years of the commission of the previous similar offence, with imprisonment for a term which may extend to two years, or with fine which may extend to three thousand rupees, or with both.

(Duty of driver in case of accident and injury to a person, Section 134 of M.V. Act, 1988)

134. Duty of driver in case of accident and injury to a person. - When any person is injured or any property of a third party is damaged, as a result of an accident in which a motor vehicle is involved, the driver of the vehicle or other person in charge of the vehicle shall -

(a) unless it is not practicable to do so on account of mob fury or any other reason beyond his control, take all reasonable steps to secure medical attention for the injured person, by conveying him to the nearest medical practitioner or hospital, and it shall be the duty of every registered medical practitioner or the doctor on the duty in the hospital immediately to attend to the injured person and render medical aid or treatment without waiting for any procedural formalities, unless the injured person or his guardian, in case he is a minor, desired otherwise;

(b) give on demand by a police officer any information required by him or, if no police officer is present, report the circumstances of the occurrence, including the circumstances, if any, or not taking reasonable steps to secure medical attention as required under Clause (a), at the nearest police station as soon as possible, and in any case within twenty-four hours of the occurrence;

(c) give the following information in writing to the insurer, who has issued the certificates of insurance, about the occurrence of the accident, namely:

(i) insurance policy number and period of its validity;

(ii) date, time and place of accident;

(iii) particulars of the persons injured or killed in the accident;

(iv) name of the driver and the particulars of his driving licence.

Explanation. - For the purposes of this section, the expression "driver" includes the owner of the vehicle.

Duty of every citizen to help motor Accident Victim

In *Pt. Parmanand Katara v. Union of India (UOI) and Ors*[8] it was pointed out that it is the duty of every citizen to help a motor accident victim, more so when one is the cause of the accident, or is involved in that particular accident. Situations may be there, in a highly charged atmosphere or due to mob fury, the driver may flee from the place, if there is a real danger to his life, but he cannot shirk his responsibility of informing the police or other authorized persons or good samaritans forthwith, so that human lives could be saved.

Passengers who are in the vehicle which met with an accident, have also a duty to arrange proper medical attention for the victims. Further they have equal responsibility to inform the police about the factum of the accident, in case of failure to do so they are aiding the crime and screening the offender from legal punishment. No legal obligation as such is cast on a bystander either under the Motor Vehicle Act or any other legislation in India. But greater responsibility is cast on them, because they are people at the scene of the occurrence, and immediate and prompt medical attention and care may help the victims and their dear ones from unexpected catastrophe. Private hospitals and government hospitals, especially situated near the Highway, where traffic is high, should be equipped with all facilities to meet with such emergency situations. Ambulance with all medical facilities including doctors and supporting staff should be ready, so that, in case of emergency, prompt and immediate medical attention could be given.

Decision of Supreme Court:

Court Ordered Accused to pay an amount of Rs. 50 lakh (Rupees Fifty lakh) to the Union of India within six months, which will be utilized for providing compensation to the victim of motor accidents, where the vehicle

---

[8] (1989) 4 SCC 286)

owner, driver etc. could not be traced, like victims of hit and run cases. On default, he will have to undergo simple imprisonment for one year. This amount be kept in a different head to be used for the aforesaid purpose only. The accused would do community service for two years which will be arranged by the Ministry of Social Justice and Empowerment within two months. On default, he will have to undergo simple imprisonment for two years.

The judgment and order of conviction passed by Delhi High Court under Section 304A of the Indian Penal Code (Indian Penal Code) is set aside and the order of conviction of Trial Court under Part II of the Indian Penal Code is restored and upheld. However, court deem it appropriate to maintain the sentence awarded by the High Court, which the accused has already undergone.

21

Methods of Executing Death Sentence[1]

Facts in Nutshell:

Writ Petitions were filed by Petitioners who were sentenced to death for the offence of murder Under Section 302 of the Penal Code[2]. They have nothing in common except that they committed murders and have been sentenced to death. The sentence of death imposed upon them has become final in the sense that the Special Leave Petitions[3], Appeals, Review Petitions and Mercy Petitions filed by them have been dismissed, some of these more than once.

Section 354(5) of the CrPC provides that:

When any person is sentenced to death, the sentence shall direct that he be hanged by the neck till he is dead.

The petitioners challenge the constitutional validity of this provision on the ground that hanging a convict by rope is a cruel and barbarous method of executing a death sentence, which is violative of Article 21 of the Constitution.[4]

---

[1] Appellants **Deena alias Deen Dayal and Ors. Vs.** Respondent: **Union of India(UOI) and Ors.**

AIR1983SC1155

Hon'ble Judges: Y. V. Chandrachud, C.J., R. S. Pathak and Sabyasachi Mukherjee, JJ.

[2] Section 302 I.P.C 1860

Punishment for murder: Whoever commits murder shall be punished with death or [imprisonment for life] and shall also be liable to fine.

[3] Article 136 Constitution of India

Special Leave to appeal by the Supreme Court

(1) Notwithstanding anything in this Chapter, the Supreme Court may, in its discretion, grant special leave to appeal from any judgment, decree, determination, sentence or order in any cause or matter passed or made by any court or tribunal in the territory of India.

(2) Nothing in clause (1) shall apply to any judgment, determination, sentence or order passed or made by any court or tribunal constituted by or under any law relating to the Armed Forces.

[4] Article 21- No person shall be deprived of his life or personal liberty except according to procedure established by law.

Question before the Court:

The main question which has been raised by the petitioners in writ petitions relates to the validity of the mode of execution of the death Sentence.

Rarest of rare cases (Death Sentence):

The validity of Death Sentence which Section 302 prescribes for the offence of murder was upheld by Court in Bachan Singh.[5] The ratio of that decision is that the normal sentence for murder is life imprisonment and that the sentence of death can be imposed in a very exceptional class of cases, described in that judgment as the 'rarest of rare cases'. Which kind of cases would precisely fall within that category is in the very nature of things difficult to define and even to describe. The question that, in the circumstances mentioned in Bachan Singh, it is permissible to impose the sentence of death must be treated as concluded and not any longer open to argument. There has to be finality to litigation, criminal as much as civil, if law is not to lose its credibility.

Justice Sarkaria who spoke for the majority concludes: Under the successive Criminal Procedure Code which have been in force for about 100 years, a sentence of death is to be carried out by hanging. In view of the aforesaid constitutional postulates, by no stretch of imagination can it be said that the death penalty Under Section 302, Penal Code, either per se or because of its execution by hanging, constitutes an unreasonable, cruel or unusual punishment. By reason of the same constitutional postulates, it cannot be said that the framers of the Constitution considered death sentence for murder or the prescribed traditional mode of its execution as a degrading punishment which would defile "the dignity of the individual" within the contemplation of the Preamble to the Constitution.

Bhagwati, J. who dissented from the majority considered the question of the constitutional validity of the death sentence, both from the substantive and the procedural points of view. The learned Judge says that "the worst' time for most of the condemned prisoners would be the last few hours when all certainty is gone and the moment of death is known". After extracting quotation from Dostoyevsky and Canns which bear upon the

---

[5] 1980CriLJ636

execution of death sentence, the learned Judge observes : "There can be no stronger words to describe the utter depravity and inhumanity of death sentence". After making this observation Bhagwati, J., proceeds thus :

The physical pain and suffering which the execution of the sentence of death involves is also no less cruel and inhuman. In India, the method of execution followed is hanging by the rope. Electrocution or application of lethal gas has not yet taken its place as in some of the western countries. It is no doubt true that the Royal Commission on Capital Punishment 1949-53 found that hanging is the most humane method of execution and so also in *Ichikawa v. Japan*, the Japanese Supreme Court held that execution by hanging does not correspond to cruel punishment inhibited by Article 36 of the Japanese Constitution. But whether amongst all the methods of execution, hanging is the most humane or in view of the Japanese Supreme Court, hanging is not cruel punishment within the meaning of Article 36, one thing is clear that hanging is undoubtedly unaccompanied by intense physical torture and pain."

Contention of the Petitioners against section 354(5) CrPC

1. It is impermissible to take human life even under the decree of a Court since it is inhuman to take life under any circumstances ;

2. By reason of the provision contained in Article 21, it is impermissible to cause pain or suffering of any kind whatsoever in the execution of any senetence, much more while executing a death senetence;

3. The method of hanging prescribed by Section 354(5) for executing the death sentence is barbarous, inhuman and degrading; and

4. It is the constitutional obligation of the State to provide for humane and dignified, method for executing the death sentence, which does not involve torture of any kind. If the method prescribed by Section 354(5) does not meet this requirement, no death senetence can be executed since, no other method for executing that senetence is prescribed by or is permissible under the law.

Reply of Attorney General:

Learned Attorney General contended that a sentence lawfully imposed by a Court can and has to be executed, though by causing the least pain arid suffering and by avoiding torture of degradation of any kind; that the method prescribed by Section 354(5) for executing the death sentence is a humane and dignified method which involves the least amount of pain and cruelty; that no other method of executing the death sentence is quicker or less painful; that Article 21 does not postulate that no pain or suffering whatsoever shall be caused in the execution of a sentence lawfully imposed by a Court, including the sentence of death; and that, since the method of hanging prescribed by Section 354(5) does not suffer from any constitutional infirmity, the question of the Court substituting that method by any other method does not arise for consideration.

New dimensions were added to these arguments by the other learned Counsel. For example, Shri Salman Khurshid advocated that instead of putting out life for ever by executing the death sentence, persons sentenced to death should be deprived of their eye sight by blinding them so that, if and when they are reformed, they could be given back their sight by transplantation or by whatever method medicine may discover for restoring the eye sight.

Royal Commission Report:

In the year 1949 the Government of United Kingdom appointed a Commission to report upon the various facets of the capital punishment. The Commission submitted its report in September 1953 after extensive research into the questions referred to it and after interviewing experts, visiting jails and examining the merits and demerits of hanging as a method for executing the death senetence. Chapter 13 of the Royal Commission's Report deals with the "methods of execution".

In paragraph 709, the Commission refers to five methods of execution of the death sentence which were then in vogue in the different parts of the world. Electrocution was in vogue in 23 States of U.S.A.; Guillotine in France and Belgium; Hanging in England, Scotland, the Commonwealth countries and 10 States of U.S.A.; and lethal gas in 8 States of U.S.A. Shooting was in vogue in the State of Utah in America which allowed a choice between hanging and shooting. Besides, shooting was used in almost every country as a method of execution of persons sentenced to death for offences against the Military Code. Rejecting Guillotine and shooting as methods for executing the death sentence for the reason that the former produces mutilation and the latter is inefficient, uncertain and unacceptable as a standard mthod of civil executions.

The Commission observes in paragraph 724 that the requirements of humanity are essentially two : (1) that the preliminaries to the acts of execution should be as quick and as simple as possible, and free from anything that unnecessarily sharpens the poignancy of the prisoner's apprehension, and (2) that the act of execution should produce immediate unconsciousness passing quickly in into death.

The Commission records its final conclusion in paragraph 734 of the Report by saying that after weighing all the factors carefully and bearing in mind that the onus of proof was on the advocates of change, it could not recommend that either electrocution or gas chamber should replace hanging as a method of judicial execution : In the matter of humanity and certainty, the advantage lay with the system of hanging; in regard to one aspect of the requirement of decency the other two methods were preferable; But, according to the Commission, that advantage could not be regarded as enough to turn the scale.

35th Report of the Law Commission:

The 35th Report of the Law Commission of India on Capital Punishment, dated September 30, 1967 deals with "Execution of Sentences" in Chapter XV. The Commission observes in paragraph 1097 of the Report that though hanging continued to be the most prevalent method ofr executing the death sentence, the course of events showed that it was being slowly abandoned. Thus, while, in 1930, 17 States in U.S.A. used to employ that method, only 6 retained it in 1967. Again, while it was in force in Yugoslavia before 1950, it was replaced by the firing squad in that year. In other words, the recommendation of the Commission was that death sentence should be executed, by the method of hanging prescribed in Section 354(5) of the Criminal Procedure Code, since there were no circumstances justifying its substitution by any other method and since, no other method was shown to be more satisfactory.

In February 1978, Dr, Hira Singh, Prison Adviser to the National Institute of Social Defence, submitted his opinion to the Ministry of Home Affairs, Government of India, as follows :

In ancient days the execution of death sentence was often attended by cruel forms of torture and suffering inflicted on the offender. With the passage of time, however, the methods of execution have undergone various changes. The old practices such as beheading, drawing, stoning, impaling, precipitation from a height, etc., have been gradually replaced in all civilised countries by new methods of hanging, electrocution, gas chamber and shooting. These changes have occurred mainly on the premise that death penalty means simply the deprivation of life and as such should be made as quicker and less painful as possible. The old methods were considered inhuman. Dr. Hira Singh. concludes:' The question of introducing electric chair in place of hanging as a mode of execution may be examined from the administrative as well as humanitarian view-points. It is often argued that death by hanging takes lesser time to execute than the other modes, though it may not be invariably true. In any case electric chair has in no way proved to be more efficient in reducing pain or suffering inflicted on the offender. In hanging the body is liable to be disfigured but in electrocution also the leg is sometimes slightly burnt. Above all electrocution involves much costlier equipment and operational preciseness than hanging. In view of such considerations there seems to be no particular advantage in switching over to the electric chair in the execution of death sentence even if Such a system may outwardly look to be more sophisticated.

Idea of Death by Electric Chair in India:

Power seldom fails in countries like America, U.S.S.R., and Japan. Even then, the failure of electrical energy supplied by commercial undertakings has been considered in America as an impediment in the use of the electric chair. With frequent failures of electrical power in our country, the electric chair will become an instrument of torture. One can well imagine the consequences of the use of the electric chair in the city of Kolkata or, for the matter of that, in the capital City of Delhi. For technical reasons, even the Supreme Court complex is not spared from frequent load-shedding during working hours. Lawyers, litigants and Judges have now trained themselves to suffer the inconvenience arising from failure of electricity. But, it would be most unfair to expect a prisoner condemned to death to get into the electric chair twice or thrice, for the reason that the electric current failed during the process of electrocution. It is not court intention to blame anyone for the power crisis because it would seem that it is partly due to natural causes and is not man-made. But facts are facts and facts must be faced.

Decision of Court:

Court held that neither electrocution, nor lethal gas, nor shooting, nor even the lethal injection has any distinct or demonstrable advantage over the system of hanging. Therefore, court held that it is impossible to record the conclusion with any degree of certainty that the method of hanging should be replaced by any of these methods.

Also the method of hanging prescribed by Section 354(5) of the CrPC does not violate the guarantee contained in Article 21 of the Constitution. The method is a quick and certain means of executing the extreme penalty of law. It eliminates the possibility of a lingering death.

Court held that the challenge to the constitutionality of Section 354(5) of the CrPC fails and the writ petitions were dismissed.

22

Every doctor has professional duty to protect human life[1]

Facts in Nutshell:

The petitioner who claims himself to be a 'small human right activist and fighting for the good causes for the general public interest' filed application under Article 32 of the Constitution[2] asking for a direction to the Union of India that every injured citizen brought for treatment should instantaneously be given medical aid to preserve life and thereafter the procedural criminal law should be allowed to operate in order to avoid negligent death and in the event of breach of such direction, apart from any action that may be taken for negligence, appropriate compensation should be admissible. He appended to the writ petition a report entitled 'Law helps the injured to die' published in the Hindustan Times. In the said publication it was alleged that a scooterist was knocked down by a speeding car. Seeing the profusely bleeding scooterist, a person who was on the road picked up the injured and took him to the nearest hospital. The doctors refused to attend on the injured and told the man that he should take the patient to a named different hospital located

---

[1] Appellants:**Pt. Parmanand Katara Vs.** Respondent:**Union of India (UOI) and Ors.**
AIR1989SC2039

Hon'ble Judges: G. L. Oza and Ranganath Misra, JJ.

[2] **Article 32. Remedies for enforcement of rights conferred by this Part**

(1) The right to move the Supreme Court by appropriate proceedings for the enforcement of the rights conferred by this Part is guaranteed

(2) The Supreme Court shall have power to issue directions or orders or writs, including writs in the nature of habeas corpus, mandamus, prohibition, quo warranto and certiorari, whichever may be appropriate, for the enforcement of any of the rights conferred by this Part

(3) Without prejudice to the powers conferred on the Supreme Court by clause (1) and (2), Parliament may by law empower any other court to exercise within the local limits of its jurisdiction all or any of the powers exercisable by the Supreme Court under clause (2)

(4) The right guaranteed by this article shall not be suspended except as otherwise provided for by this Constitution

some 20 kilometres away authorised to handle medico-legal cases. The Samaritan carried the victim, lost no time to approach the other hospital but before he could reach, the victim succumbed to his injuries.

Code of Medical Ethics:

The Secretary of the Medical Council of India in his affidavit referred to clauses 10 and 13 of the Code of Medical Ethics drawn up with the approval of the Central Government under Section 33 of the Act by the Council, wherein it had been said:

10. Obligations to the sick:

Though a physician is not bound to treat each and every one asking his services except in emergencies for the sake of humanity and the noble traditions of the profession, he should not only be ever ready to respond to the calls of the sick and the injured, but should be mindful of the high character of his mission and the responsibility he incurs in the discharge of his ministrations, he should never forget that the health and the lives of those entrusted to his care depend on his skill and attention. A physician should endeavour to add to the comfort of the sick by making his visits at the hour indicated to the patients.

13. The patient must not be neglected:

A physician is free to choose whom he will serve. He should, however, respond to any request for his assistance in an emergency or whenever temperate public opinion expects the service. Once having undertaken a case, the physician should not neglect the patient, nor should he withdraw from the case without giving notice to the patient, his relatives or his responsible friends sufficiently long in advance of his withdrawal to allow them to secure another medical attendant. No provisionally or fully registered medical practitioner shall wilfully commit an act of negligence that may deprive his patient or patients from necessary medical care.

The affidavit further stated :

The Medical Council of India therefore expects that all medical practitioners must attend to sick and injured immediately and it is the duty of the medical practitioners to make immediate and timely medical care available to every injured person whether he is injured in accident or otherwise. It is also submitted that the formalities under the Criminal Procedure Code or any other local laws should not stand in the way of the medical practitioners attending an injured person. It should be the duty of a doctor in each and every casualty department of, the hospital to attend such person first and thereafter take care of the formalities under the Criminal Procedure Code. The life of a person is far more important than the legal formalities. In view of this, the deponent feels that it is in the interest of general human life and welfare that the Government should immediately make such provisions in law and amendments in the existing laws, if required, so that immediate medical relief and care to injured persons and/or serious patients are available without any delay and without waiting for legal formalities to be completed in the presence of the police officers. The doctors attending such patients should be indemnified under law from any action by the Government/police authorities/any person for not waiting for legal formalities before giving relief as a doctor would be doing his : professional duty; for which he has taken oath as medical practitioner.

It was further submitted that it is for the Government of India to take necessary and immediate steps to amend various provisions of law which come in the way of Government Doctors as well as other doctors in private hospitals or public hospitals to attend the injured/serious persons immediately without waiting for the police report or completion of police formalities. They should be free from fear that they would be unnecessarily harassed or prosecuted for doing their duty without first complying with the police formalities. It was further submitted that a doctor should not feel himself handicapped in extending immediate help in such cases fearing that he would be harassed by the police or dragged to Court in such a case. It was submitted that Evidence Act should also be so amended as to provide that the Doctor's diary maintained in regular course by him in respect of the accident cases would be accepted by the Courts in evidence without insisting the doctors being present to prove the same or subject himself to cross-examination/harassment for long period of time.

Director-General of Health Services decisions:

1.   Whenever any medico-legal case attends the hospital, the medical officer on duty should inform the Duty Constable, name, age, sex of the

patient and place and time of occurrence of the incident, and should start the required treatment of the patient. It will be the duty of the Constable on duty to inform the concerned Police Station or higher police functionaries for further action.

Full medical report should be prepared and given to the Police, as soon as examination and treatment of the patient is over. The treatment of the patient would not wait for the arrival of the Police or completing the legal formalities.

2.   Zonalisation as has been worked out for the hospitals to deal with medico-legal cases will only apply to those cases brought by the Police. The medico-legal cases coming to hospital of their own (even if the incident has occurred in the zone of other hospital) will not be denied the treatment by the hospital where the case reports, nor the case will be referred to other hospital because the incident has occurred in the area which belongs to the zone of any other hospital. The same police formalities as given in para 1 above will be followed in these cases.

All Government Hospitals, Medical Institutes should be asked to provide the immediate medical aid to all the cases irrespective of the fact whether they are medico-legal cases or otherwise. The practice of certain Government institutions to refuse even the primary medical aid to the patient and referring them to other hospitals simply because they are medico-legal cases is not desirable. However, after providing the primary medical aid to the patient, patient can be referred to the hospital if the expertise facilities required for the treatment are not available in that Institution.

Decision of the Court

Article 21 of the Constitution[3] casts the obligation on the State to preserve life. A doctor at the Government hospital positioned to meet this State obligation is, therefore, duty-bound to extend medical assistance for preserving life. Every doctor whether at a Government hospital or otherwise has the professional obligation to extend his services with due expertise for protecting life. No law or State action can intervene to avoid/delay the

---

[3] **Article 21 in The Constitution Of India**

Protection of life and personal liberty No person shall be deprived of his life or personal liberty except according to procedure established by law

discharge of the paramount obligation cast upon members of the medical profession. The obligation being total, absolute and paramount, laws of procedure whether in statutes or otherwise which would interfere with the discharge of this obligation cannot be sustained and must, therefore, give way.

Observation of Court:

Whenever on such occasions (accident cases) a man of the medical profession is approached and if he finds that whatever assistance he could give is not sufficient really to save the life of the person but some better assistance is necessary it is also the duty of the man in the medical profession so approached to render all the help which he could and also see that the person reaches the proper expert as early as possible.

23

Arresting a woman in night in absence of lady police[1]

Facts in Nutshell:

Some of the policemen on duty in the Crime Branch Office of Nagpur City took into custody one Junious Adam Illamatti, a resident of Ajini Railway Colony on 23.6.1993. While he was in Police custody, it was stated he was found dead. It is also alleged that when his wife Jarina Adam went to the Police Station to enquire about her husband, she was also locked up by the said Police and molested. On 26.6.1993 a criminal case was registered for offences under Sections 302,[2] 342,[3] 330,[4] 354[5] read with 34[6]against 10 Police

---

[1] Appellants: **State of Maharashtra Vs.** Respondent: **Christian Community Welfare Council of India and Anr.**
AIR2004SC7
Hon'ble Judges: N. Santosh Hedge and B. P. Singh, JJ.

[2] **Section 302, IPC Punishment for murder**
Whoever commits murder shall be punished with death, or [imprisonment for life], and shall also be liable to fine.

[3] **Section 342, IPC Punishment for wrongful confinement**
Whoever wrongfully confines any person shall be punished with imprisonment of either description for a term which may extend to one year, or with fine which may extend to one thousand rupees, or with both.

[4] **Section 330, IPC Voluntarily causing hurt to extort confession, or to compel restoration of property**
Whoever voluntarily causes hurt for the purpose of extorting from the sufferer or from any person interested in the sufferer, any confession or any information which may lead to the detection of an offence or misconduct, or for the purpose of constraining the sufferer or any person interested in the sufferer to restore or to cause the restoration of any property or valuable security or to satisfy any claim or demand, or to give information which may lead to the restoration of any property or valuable security, shall be punished with imprisonment of either description for a term which may extend to seven years, and shall also be liable to fine.

[5] **Section 354. Assault or criminal force to woman with intent to outrage her modesty.**
Whoever assaults or uses criminal force to any woman, intending to outrage or knowing it to be likely that he will thereby outrage her modesty, shall be punished with imprisonment of either description for a term which may extend to two years, or with fine, or with both.

[6] **Section 34 IPC Acts done by several persons in furtherance of common intention**
When a criminal act is done by several persons in furtherance of the common intention of all, each of such persons is liable for that act in the same manner as if it were done by him alone.

Officers. The Additional Sessions Judge, Nagpur, ordered that 10 Police Officers were acquitted of the charge under Section 302 IPC, a punishment of 3 years' RI (Rigorous Imprisonment) with fine for the principal offence was awarded by said Sessions Judge to the 10 Police Officers. A criminal appeal against the said judgment and conviction is pending before the High Court. In that case High court has directed the State Government to issue instructions in the following terms :

"(vii) The State Government should issue instructions immediately in unequivocal and unambiguous terms to all concerned *that no female persons shall be detained or arrested without the presence of lady constable and in no case, after sunset and before sun-rise*;"

The mandate issued by the High Court prevents the Police from arresting a lady without the presence of a lady constable. Said direction also prohibits the arrest of a lady after sunset and before sunrise under any circumstances.

Decision of the Supreme Court:

While it is necessary to protect the female sought to be arrested by the Police from Police misdeeds, it may not be always possible and practical to have the presence of a lady constable when the necessity for such arrest arises, therefore, Court thought that the direction issued requires some modification without disturbing the object behind the same. Court thought that the object will be served if a direction is issued to the arresting authority that while arresting a female person, all efforts should be made to keep a lady constable present but in circumstances where the arresting officers is reasonably satisfied that such presence of a lady constable is not available or possible and/or the delay in arresting caused by securing the presence of a lady constable would impede the course of investigation such arresting officer for reasons to be recorded either before the arrest or immediately after the arrest be permitted to arrest a female person for lawful reasons at any time of the day or night depending on the circumstances of the case even that without the presence of a lady constable.

24

Phone Tapping[1]

Facts in Nutshell:

Jagdishprasad Ramnarayan Khandelwal was admitted to the nursing home of a Gynaecologist Dr. Adatia on 3 May, 1964. Dr. Adatia, diagnosed the case as acute appendicitis. Dr. Adatia kept the patient under observation. After 24 hours the condition of the patient became serious. Dr. Adatia performed the operation. The patient developed paralysis of the ileum. He was removed to Bombay Hospital on 10 May, 1964 to be under the treatment of Dr. Motwani. The patient died on 13 May, 1964. The Hospital issued a Death Intimation Card as "paralytic ileus and peritonitis following an operation for acute appendicitis".

The disposal of the dead body was allowed without ordering post-mortem. There was however a request for an inquest[2] from the Police Station. The cause for the inquest was that his was a case of post operation death in a hospital.

It was alleged that Dr. Adatia had been told a few days earlier that though he might have operated satisfactorily the cause of death given by the hospital would give rise to a presumption of negligence on his part. Dr. Adatia was asked to meet Dr. Motwani, to resolve the technical difficulties. The appellant (R.M Malkani) told Dr. Motwani that Dr. Adatia was at fault but he might be cleared of the charge in the inquest. The appellant asked for a sum of Rs. 20,000. Dr. Motwani said that he would consult Dr. Adatia. Dr. Motwani conveyed the proposal to Dr. Adatia. The latter refused to pay any illegal

---

[1] Appellants: **R.M. Malkani Vs.** Respondent: **State of Maharashtra**
AIR1973SC157

Hon'ble Judges: A. N. Ray and I. D. Dua, JJ.

[2] A judicial inquiry into a matter usually held before a jury, especially an inquiry into the cause of a death.

gratification. Dr. Motwani intimated the same to the appellant. The appellant then reduced the demand to Rs. 10,000. Dr. Adatia also refused to pay the same. On 4 October the appellant got in touch with Dr. Jadhav. Superintendent of the Bombay Hospital to find out if the cause of death given in the Hospital Card could be substantiated. Dr. Motwani told Dr. Jadhav on the same day that incorrect cause of death was shown and great injustice was done to Dr. Adatia. Dr. Jadhav said that he would send an amended deposition to the Coroner[3], the appellant.

On 5 October, 1964 Dr. Motwani and Dr Adatia decided to lodge a complaint with the Anti Corruption Bureau. The appellant asked Dr. Motwani to intimate by 10 a.m. on 7 October whether Dr. Adatia was willing to pay Rs. 10,000. Dr. Motwani rang up Mugwe, Director of the Anti Corruption Branch and complained that a higher Government official was demanding a heavy bribe from a Doctor. Mugwe men arranged for the tape recording equipment to be attached to the telephone of Dr. Motwani. Dr. Motwani was asked by Mugwe to ring up the appellant in the presence of Mugwe and other Police Officers about the appellant's demand for the money. The conversation between Dr. Motwani and the appellant and the conversation between Dr. Motwani and Dr. Adatia are all recorded on the tape.

Dr. Adatia paid Rs. 15,000 to Dr. Motwani. Dr. Motwani took the amount to his house. Dr. Motwani informed the appellant on the telephone that he had received the money from Dr. Adatia. The appellant asked Dr. Motwani to keep it. Mugwe then ordered an open investigation into the case. The appellant was charged Under Sections 161[4], 385[5] and 420[6] read

---

[3] A public officer whose primary function is to investigate by inquest any death thought to be of other than natural causes.

[4] Indian Penal Code (IPC) Section 161-165A. Repealed

[Rep. by the Prevention of Corruption Act, 1988 (49 or 1988), sec. 31.]

[5] **Indian Penal Code (IPC) Section 385. Putting person in fear of injury in order to commit extortion**

Whoever, in order to the committing of extortion, puts any person in fear, or attempts to put any person in fear, of any injury, shall be punished with imprisonment of either description for a term which may extend to two years, or with fine, or with both.

[6] **Indian Penal Code (IPC) Section 420. Cheating and dishonestly inducing delivery of property**

Whoever cheats and thereby dishonestly induces the person deceived any property to any person, or to make, alter or destroy the whole or any part of a valuable security, or anything which is signed or sealed, and which is capable of being converted into a valuable security, shall be punished with imprisonment of either description for a term which may extend to seven years, and shall also be liable to fine.

with Section 511[7] of the Indian Penal Code. Broadly stated, the charges against the appellant were these. He attempted to obtain from Dr. Adatia through Dr. Motwani a sum of Rs. 20,000 which was later reduced to Rs. 10,000 and which was then raised to Rs. 15,000 as gratification for doing or forbearing to do official acts. He put Dr. Adatia in fear of injury in body, mind, reputation and attempted dishonestly to induce Dr. Adatia and Dr. Motwani to pay the sum of money. The appellant was also charged with cheating for having falsely represented to Dr. Adatia and Dr. Motwani that Rs. 5,000 out of the amount of Rs. 10,000 was required to be paid to the Police Surgeon for obtaining his favourable opinion.

Questions raised before the Court:

The evidence was illegally obtained in contravention of Section25 of the Indian Telegraph Act[8] and therefore the evidence was inadmissible. Secondly, the conversation between Dr. Motwani and the appellant which was recorded on the tape took place during investigation inasmuch as Mugwe, (Director of the Anti Corruption Branch) asked Dr. Motwani to talk and therefore the conversation was not admissible Under Section 162 of the CrPC[9]. The third contention was that the appellant did not attempt to obtain gratification.

---

[7] **Indian Penal Code (IPC) Section 511. Punishment for attempting to commit offences punishable with imprisonment for life or other imprisonment**

Whoever attempts to commit an offence punishable by this Code with1[imprisonment for life] or imprisonment, or to cause such an offence to be committed, and in such attempts does any act towards the commission of the offence, shall, where no express provision is made by this Code for the punishment of such attempt, be punished with 2[imprisonment of any description provided for the offence, for a term which may extend to one-half of the imprisonment for life or, as the case may be, one-half of the longest term of imprisonment provided for that offence], or with such fine as is provided for the offence, or with both.

[8] **Section 25 of the Indian Telegraph Act 1885** states that if any person intending (b) to intercept or to acquaint himself with the contents of any message damages, removes, tampers with or touches any battery, machinery, telegraph line, post or other thin whatever, being part of or used in or about any telegraph or in the working thereof he shall be punished with imprisonment for a term which may extend to three years, or with fine, or with both. "Telegraph" is defined in the Indian Telegraph Act in Section 3 to mean any appliance, instrument, material or apparatus used or capable of use for transmission or reception of signs, signals, writing, images and sounds or intelligence of any nature by wire, visual or other electro-magnetic emissions, radio waves or Hertzian waves, galvanie, electric or magnetic means.

[9] **The Code of Criminal Procedure, 1973 (CrPc) 162. Statements to police not to be signed: Use of statements in evidence.**

(1) No statement made by any person to a police officer in the course of' an investigation under this Chapter, shall, if reduced to writing, be signed by the person making it, nor shall any such statement or any record thereof, whether in a police diary or otherwise, or any part of

Fourthly, it was said that the sentence of six months imprisonment should be interfered with because the appellant has already paid Rs. 10,000 as fine. The appellant suffered heart attacks and therefore the sentence should be modified.

Arguments by appellant counsel

This tape recorded conversation is challenged by counsel for the appellant to be inadmissible because it infringes Articles 20(3)[10] and 21 of the Constitution[11] and is an offence Under Section 25 of the Indian Telegraph Act[12].

Counsel for the appellant submitted that attaching the tape recording instrument to the telephone instrument, of Dr. Motwani was an offence Under Section 25 of the Indian Telegraph Act. It was also said that if a Police Officer intending to acquaint himself with the contents of any message touched machinery or other thing whatever used in or about or telegraph or in the working thereof he was guilty of an offence under the Telegraph Act. Reliance was placed on rule 149 of the Telegraph Rules which states that it

---

such statement or record, be used for any purpose, save as hereinafter provided, at any inquiry or trial in respect of any offence under investigation at the time when such statement was made:

Provided that when any witness is called for the prosecution in such inquiry or trial whose statement has been reduced into writing as aforesaid, any part of his statement, if duly proved, may be used by the accused, and with the permission of the Court, by the prosecution, to contradict such witness in the manner provided by section 145 of the Indian Evidence Act, 1872 (1 of 1872) and when any part of such statement is so used, any part thereof may also be used in the re-examination of such witness, but for the purpose only of explaining any matter referred to in his cross-examination.

(2) Nothing in this section shall be deemed to apply to any statement failling within the provisions of clause (1) of section 32 of the Indian Evidence Act, 1872 (1 of 1872), or to affect the provisions of section 27 of that Act.

[10] **Article 20(3) in The Constitution Of India 1949**

(3) No person accused of any offence shall be compelled to be a witness against himself

[11] **Article 21 in The Constitution Of India 1949**

21. Protection of life and personal liberty No person shall be deprived of his life or personal liberty except according to procedure established by law

[12] Section 25 of the Indian Telegraph Act, 1885

25. Intentionally damaging or tampering with telegraphs If any person, intending

a) to prevent or obstruct the transmission or delivery of any message, or

b) to intercept or to acquaint himself with the contents of any message, or

c) to commit mischief,

damages, removes, tampers with or touches any battery, machinery, telegraph line, post or other thing whatever, being part of or used in or about any telegraph or in the working thereof, he shall be punished with imprisonment for a term which may extend to three years, or with fine or with both.

Shall be lawful for the Telegraph Authority to monitor or intercept a message or messages transmitted through telephone, for the purpose of verification of any violation of these rules or for the maintenance of the equipment. This Rule was referred to for establishing that Only the Telegraph Authorities could intercept message under the Act and Rules and a Police Officer could not.

Points in favour of police officer

The Police Officer in the present case fixed the tape recording instrument to the telephone instrument with the authority of Dr. Motwani. The Police Officer could not be said to intercept any message or damage or tamper or remove or touch any machinery within the meaning of Section 25 of the Indian Telegraph Act. The reason is that the Police Officer instead of hearing directly the oral conversation between Dr. Motwani and the appellant recorded the conversation with the device of the tape recorder. The substance of the offence Under Section 25 of the Indian Telegraph Act is damaging, removing, tampering, touching machinery battery line or post for interception or acquainting oneself with the contents of any message. Where a person talking on the telephone allows another person to record it or to hear it it can-not be said that the other person who is allowed to do so is damaging, removing, tampering, touching machinery battery line or post for intercepting or acquainting himself with the contents of any message. There was no element of coercion or compulsion in attaching the tape recorder to the telephone. There was no violation of the Indian Telegraph Act.

Decision of High court

In the present case the High Court held that the telephone call put by Dr. Motwani to the appellant was tapped by the Police Officers, and, therefore, there was violation of Section 25 of the Indian Telegraph Act. But the High Court held that the tape recorded conversation was admissible in evidence in spite of the violation of the Telegraph Act.

Case Referred

This Court in *Shri N. Sri Rama Reddy etc.* v. *Shri V. V. Giri* [13] accepted conversation or dialogue recorded on a tape recording machine as admissible evidence.

---

[13] [1971]1SCR399

Decision by Supreme Court

Court held that there was no scope for holding that the appellant was made to incriminate[14] himself. At the time of the conversation there was no case against the appellant. He was not compelled to speak or confess. Article21 was invoked by submitting that the privacy of the appellant's conversation was invaded. Article 21contemplates procedure established by law with regard to deprivation of life or personal liberty. The telephonic conversation of an innocent citizen will be protected by Courts against wrongful or high handed interference by tapping the conversation. The protection is not for the guilty citizen against the efforts of the police to vindicate the law and prevent corruption of public servants. It must not be understood that the. Courts will tolerate safeguards for the protection of the.citizen to be imperriled by permitting the police to proceed by unlawful or irregular methods. Court held that in the present case there is no unlawful or irregular method in obtaining the tape recording of the conversation. Court also held that appellant will surrender to his bail and serve out the sentence.

---

[14] **Meaning of Incriminate:**

1. To accuse of a crime or other wrongful act.

2. To cause to appear guilty of a crime or fault;

25

Guidelines regarding Ragging[1]

Facts in Nutshell:

The public interest litigation highlights a menace pervading the educational institutions of the country which in spite of efforts made by the Central Government, the University Grants Commission, State Governments and some of the educational institutions is unfortunately showing an upwards trend. The Petitioner seeks directions of this Court so as to curb the menace of ragging.

Guidelines of the Court regarding Ragging:

In exercise of the jurisdiction conferred by Article 32[2] and Article 142 of the Constitution[3], court issued the following guidelines:

---

[1] Appellants: **Vishwa Jagriti Mission through President Vs.** Respondent: **Central Government through Cabinet Secretary and Ors.**

2001 3 AWC2276SC

Hon'ble Judges: Dr. A. S. Anand , C.J.I.,R. C. Lahoti and K. G. Balakrishnan, JJ.

[2] **Article 32 in The Constitution Of India 1949**

32. Remedies for enforcement of rights conferred by this Part

(1) The right to move the Supreme Court by appropriate proceedings for the enforcement of the rights conferred by this Part is guaranteed

(2) The Supreme Court shall have power to issue directions or orders or writs, including writs in the nature of habeas corpus, mandamus, prohibition, quo warranto and certiorari, whichever may be appropriate, for the enforcement of any of the rights conferred by this Part

(3) Without prejudice to the powers conferred on the Supreme Court by clause (1) and (2), Parliament may by law empower any other court to exercise within the local limits of its jurisdiction all or any of the powers exercisable by the Supreme Court under clause (2)

(4) The right guaranteed by this article shall not be suspended except as otherwise provided for by this Constitution

[3] **Article 142 in The Constitution Of India 1949**

142. Enforcement of decrees and orders of Supreme Court and unless as to discovery, etc

(1) The Supreme Court in the exercise of its jurisdiction may pass such decree or make such order as is necessary for doing complete justice in any cause or matter pending before it, and any decree so passed or orders so made shall be enforceable throughout the territory of India

(i) The Court viewed with concern the increase in the number of incidents of ragging in educational institutions. Some of the reported incidents have crossed the limits of decency, morality and humanity. Some of the States have acted by enacting legislations and making ragging as defined therein a cognizable and punishable offence. However, Court felt that ragging cannot be cured merely by making it a cognizable, criminal offence. Moreover, Court also felt that the acts of indiscipline and misbehaviour on the part of the students must primarily be dealt with within the institution and by exercise of the disciplinary authority of the teachers over the students and of the management of the institutions over the teachers and students. Students ought not ordinarily be subjected to police action unless it be unavoidable. The students going to educational institutions for learning should not remain under constant fear of being dealt with by police and sent to jail and face the Courts. The faith in the teachers for the purpose of maintaining discipline should be restored and the responsibility fixed by emphasising the same.

(ii) Broadly speaking, ragging is: Any disorderly conduct whether by words spoken or written or by an act which has the effect of teasing, treating or handling with rudeness any other student, indulging in rowdy or indisciplined activities which causes or is likely to cause annoyance, hardship or psychological harm or to raise fear or apprehension thereof in a fresher or a junior student or asking the student to do any act or perform something which such student will not do in the ordinary course and which has the effect of causing or generating a sense of shame or embarrassment so as to adversely affect the physique or psyche of a fresher or a junior student.

(iii) The cause of indulging in ragging is deriving a sadistic pleasure or showing off power, authority or superiority by the seniors over their juniors or freshers.

(iv) Ragging can be stopped by creating awareness amongst the students, teachers and parents that ragging is a reprehensible act which does no good to any one and by simultaneously generating an atmosphere of discipline by sending a clear message that no act of ragging shall be tolerated and any

in such manner as may be prescribed by or under any law made by Parliament and, until provision in that behalf is so made, in such manner as the President may by order prescribe

(2) Subject to the provisions of any law made in this behalf by Parliament, the Supreme Court shall, as respects the whole of the territory of India, have all and every power to make any order for the purpose of securing the attendance of any person, the discovery or production of any documents, or the investigation or punishment of any contempt of itself

act of ragging shall not go unnoticed and unpunished.

(v) Anti-ragging movement should be initiated by the institutions right from the time of advertisement for admissions. The prospectus, the form for admission and/or any other literature issued to aspirants for admission must clearly mention that ragging is banned in the institution and any one indulging in ragging is likely to be punished appropriately which punishment may include expulsion from the institution, suspension from the institution or classes for a limited period or fine with a public apology. The punishment may also take the shape of: (i) withholding scholarships or other benefits, (ii) debarring from representation in events, (iii) withholding results and (iv) suspension or expulsion from hostel or mess, and the like. If there be any legislation governing ragging or any provisions in the statute/ordinances they should be brought to the notice of the students/parents seeking admissions.

(vi) The application form for admission/enrolment shall have a printed undertaking to be filled up and signed by the candidate to the effect that he/ she is aware of the institution's approach towards ragging and the punishments to which he or she shall be liable if found guilty of ragging. A similar undertaking shall be obtained from the parent/guardian of the applicant.

(vii) Such of the institutions as are introducing such a system for the first time shall ensure undertakings being obtained from the students and their parents/guardians already studying in the institutions before the commencement of the next educational year/session.

(viii) A printed leaflet detailing when and to whom one has to turn for information, help and guidance for various purposes, keeping in view the needs of new entrants in the institution, along with the addresses and telephone numbers of such persons, should be given to freshers at the time of admissions so that the freshers need not look up to the seniors for help in such matters and feel indebted to or obliged by them.

(ix) The management, the principal, the teaching staff should interact with freshers and take them in confidence by apprising them of their rights as well as obligation to fight against ragging and to generate confidence in their mind that any instance of ragging to which they are subjected or which comes in their knowledge should forthwith be brought to their knowledge and shall be promptly dealt with while protecting the complainants from any harassment by perpetrators of ragging. It would be better if the head of the institution or a person high in authority addresses meetings of teachers, parents and students collectively or in groups in this behalf.

(x) At the commencement of the academic session, the institution should constitute a proctorial committee consisting of senior faculty members and hostel authorities like wardens and a few responsible senior students:

(i) to keep a continuous watch and vigil over ragging so as to prevent its occurrence and recurrence, and

(ii) to promptly deal with the incidents of ragging brought to its notice and summarily punish the guilty either by itself or by putting-forth its finding/recommendation/sugg estions before the authority competent to take decision.

All vulnerable locations shall be identified and specially watched.

(xi) The local community and the students in particular must be made aware of dehumanising effect of ragging inherent in its perversity. Posters, notice boards and sign-boards-wherever necessary, may be used for the purpose.

(xii) Failure to prevent ragging shall be construed as an act of negligence in maintaining discipline in the institution on the part of the management, the principal and the persons in authority of the institution. Similar responsibility shall be liable to be fixed on hostel wardenes/superintendents.

(xiii) The hostels/accommodations where freshers are accommodated shall be carefully guarded, if necessary by posting security personnel and placed incharge of a warden/superintendent who should himself/herself reside thereat, and wherein the entry of seniors and outsiders shall be prohibited after specified hour of night and before except under the permission of the person incharge. Entry at other times may also be regulated.

(xiv) If the individuals committing or abetting ragging are not identified collective punishment could be resorted to act as a deterrent punishment and to ensure collective pressure on the potential raggers.

(xv) Migration certificate issued by the institution should have an entry apart from that of general conduct and behaviour whether the student had participated in and in particular was punished for ragging.

(xvi) If an institution fails to curb ragging, the U.G.C./Funding Agency may consider stoppage of financial assistance to such an institution till such time as it achieves the same. A University may consider disaffiliating a college or institution failing to curb ragging.

(xvii) The Universities and the institutions shall at a reasonable time before the commencement of an academic year, and therefore, at such frequent intervals as may be expedient deliberate over and devise such positive and constructive activities to be arranged by involving the students generally so that the seniors and juniors, and the existing students and the freshers, interact with each other in a healthy atmosphere and develop a friendly, relationship so as to behave like members of a family in an institution. Seniors or juniors should be encouraged to exhibit their talents in such events so as to shed their complexes.

Observation by Court:

Ragging, if it becomes unmanageable or amounts to a cognizable offence[4], the same may be reported to the police. However, the police should be called in or allowed entry in the campus at the instance of the head of the institution or the person in charge. Police should also deal with such incidents when brought to its notice for action by keeping in mind that they are dealing with students and not criminals. The action of the police should never be violent and be always guided by a correctional attitude. The U.G.C. shall bring these guidelines to the notice of all educational institutions. Publicity may also be given by issuing press notes in public interest by U.G.C. and Central Government.

---

[4] **Sectio 2 (c) of The Code of Criminal Procedure, 1973 (CrPc)**

(c) "cognizable offence" means an offence for which, and "cognizable case" means a case in which, a police officer may, in accordance with the First Schedule or under and other law for the time being in force, arrest without warrant

26

People Charged for Minor Offences Languishing in Jails[1]

Facts in Nutshell:

This petition[2] for a writ of habeas corpus[3] discloses a shocking state of affairs in regard to administration of justice in the State of Bihar. An alarmingly large number of men and women, children including, are behind prison bars for years awaiting trial in courts of law. The offences with which some of them are charged are trivial, which, even if proved, would not warrant punishment for more than a few months, perhaps for a year or two, and yet these unfortunate forgotten specimens of humanity are in jail, deprived of their freedom, for periods ranging from three to ten years without even as much as their trial having commenced. It is a crying shame on the judicial system which permits incarceration of men and women for such long periods of time without trial.

Some of the under-trial prisoners whose names are given in the newspaper cuttings have been in jail for as many as 5, 7 or 9 years and a few of them, even more than 10 years, without their trial having begun. What faith can these lost souls have in the judicial system which denies them a bare trial for so many years and keeps them behind bars, not because they are guilty, but because they are too poor to afford bail and the courts have no time to try

---

[1] Appellants: **Hussainara Khatoon and Ors. Vs. Respondent: Home Secretary, State of Bihar, Patna**

AIR1979SC1360

Hon'ble Judges: A. D. Koshal, P. N. Bhagwati and R. S. Pathak, JJ.

[2] A formal written application requesting a court for a specific judicial action

[3] *Habeas corpus* is a writ which requires a person under arrest to be brought before a judge or into court. This ensures that a prisoner can be released from unlawful detention—that is, detention lacking sufficient cause or evidence. The remedy can be sought by the prisoner or by another person coming to the prisoner's aid.

them. It is a travesty of justice that many poor accused, 'little Indians, are forced into long cellular servitude for little offences' because the bail procedure is beyond their meager means and trials don't commence and even if they do, they never conclude.

Unsatisfactory bail system

Now, one reason why our legal and judicial system continually denies justice to the poor by keeping them for long years in pretrial detention is our highly unsatisfactory bail system. It suffers from a property oriented approach which seems to proceed on the erroneous assumption that risk of monetary loss is the only deterrent against fleeing from justice. The CrPC, even after its re-enactment, continues to adopt the same antiquated approach as the earlier Code enacted towards the end of the last century, and where an accused is to be released' on his personal bond, it insists that the bond should contain a monetary obligation requiring the accused to pay a sum of money in case he fails to appear at the trial. Moreover, as if this were not sufficient deterrent to the poor the courts mechanically and as a matter of course insist that the accused should produce sureties who will stand bail for him and these sureties must again establish their solvency to be able to pay up the amount of the bail in case the accused fails to appear to answer the charge. This system of bails operates very harshly against the poor and it is only the non-poor who are able to take advantage of it by getting themselves released on bail. The poor find it difficult to furnish bail even without sureties because very often the amount of the bail fixed by the courts is so un-realistically excessive that in a majority of cases the poor are unable to satisfy the police or the Magistrate about their solvency for the amount of the bail and where the bail is with sureties, as is usually the case, it becomes an almost impossible task for the poor to find persons sufficiently solvent to stand as sure-ties. The result is that either they are fleeced by the police and revenue officials or by touts and professional sureties and sometimes they have even to incur debts for securing their release or, being unable to obtain release, they have to remain in jail until such time as the court is able to take up their cases for trial, leading to grave consequences, namely, (1) though presumed innocent, they are subjected to psychological and physical privations of jail life, (2) they are prevented from contributing to the preparation of their defence and (3) they lose their job, if they have one, and are deprived of an opportunity to work to support themselves and their family members with the result that the burden of their detention almost invariably falls heavily on the innocent members of the family. It is here that the poor find our legal and judicial system oppressive and heavily weighed against them and a feeling of frustration and despair occurs upon them as they find that they are helplessly in a position of inequality with the non-poor.

Moreover, the bail system causes discrimination against the poor since the poor would not be able to furnish bail on account of their poverty while the wealthier persons otherwise similarly situate would be able to secure their freedom because they can afford to furnish bail. This discrimination arises even if the amount of the bail as fixed by the Magistrate is not high, for a large majority of those who are brought before the Courts in criminal cases are so poor that they would find it difficult to furnish bail even in a small amount.

The discriminatory nature of the bail system becomes all the more acute by reason of the mechanical way in which it is customarily operated. It is no doubt true that theoretically the Magistrate has broad discretion in fixing the amount of bail but in practice it seems that the amount of bail depends almost always on the seriousness of the offence. It is fixed according to a schedule related to the nature of the charge. Little weight is given either to the probability that the accused will attempt to flee before his trial or to his individual financial circumstances, the very factors which seem most relevant if the purpose of bail is to assure the appearance of the accused at the trial. The result of ignoring these factors and fixing the amount of bail mechanically having regard only to the seriousness of the offence is to discriminate against the poor who are not in the same position as the rich as regards capacity to furnish bail. The Courts by ignoring the differential capacity of the rich and the poor to furnish bail and treating them equally produce inequality between the rich and the poor; the rich who is charged with the same offence in the same circumstances is able to secure his release while the poor is unable to do so on account of his poverty. These are some of the major defects in the bail system as it is operated today.

The bail system, as it operates today, is a source of great hardship to the poor and if we really want to eliminate the evil effects of poverty and assure a fair and just treatment to the poor in the administration of justice, it is imperative that the bail system should be thoroughly reformed so that it should be possible for the poor, as easily as the rich, to obtain pretrial release without jeopardizing the interest of justice.

Speedy Trail[4]

Speedy trial is essence of criminal justice and there can be no doubt that delay in trial by itself constitutes denial of justice. It is interesting to note that in the United States, speedy trial is one of the constitutionally guaranteed rights. The Sixth Amendment to the Constitution provides that,

In all criminal prosecutions, the accused shall enjoy the right to a speedy and public trial.

Also Article 3 of the European Convention, on Human Rights provides that,

Every one arrested or detained—shall be entitled to trial within a reasonable time or to release pending trial.

Decision of the Court:

Court directed that all women and children who are in the jails in the State of Bihar under 'protective custody'[5] or who are in jail because their presence is required for giving evidence or who are victims of offence should be released and taken forthwith to welfare homes or rescue homes and should be kept there and properly looked after. Court also directed the Government of Bihar to scrutinise the cases of under-trial prisoners charged with offences which are punishable with fine only or punishable with imprisonment for a term not exceeding one year or punishable with imprisonment for a term exceeding one year but not exceeding three years and release such of them who are not liable to be proceeded against by reason of the period of limitation[6] having expired.

---

[4] Speedy trial means a trial conducted according to fixed rules, regulations, and proceedings of law, free from vexatious, capricious, and oppressive delays.

[5] **Protective Custody**: An arrangement whereby a person is safeguarded by law enforcement authorities in a location other than the person's home because his or her safety is seriously threatened.

[6] **Limitation Period**: The period established by law for protecting a violated right (limitation of actions) and the period upon whose expiration, provided that certain conditions established by law have been met, a person is relieved of criminal responsibility (limitation on instituting criminal proceedings) or it becomes impossible to carry out the appointed punishment (limitation on execution of a judgment of guilty).

27

Right against Self Incrimination[1]

Ratio Decidendi[2]:

"Compulsory involuntary administration of the Narcoanalysis, polygraph examination and the Brain Electrical Activation Profile (BEAP) violates the `right against self-incrimination' enumerated in Article 20(3) of the Constitution as the subject does not exercise conscious control over the responses during the administration of the test."

"Article 20(3) not only a trial right but its protection extends to the stage of investigation also."

"Provisions of Section 27 of the Evidence Act are not within the prohibition under Article 20(3) unless compulsion has been used in obtaining the information and any information or material that is subsequently discovered with the help of voluntary administered test results to be admitted."

Facts in Nutshell:

The legal questions relates to the involuntary administration of certain scientific techniques, namely narcoanalysis, polygraph examination and the Brain Electrical Activation Profile (BEAP) test for the purpose of improving investigation efforts in criminal cases. This issue has received considerable attention since it involves tensions between the desirability of efficient

---

[1] Appellants: **Smt. Selvi and Ors.Vs.**Respondent: **State of Karnataka**
AIR2010SC1974

Hon'ble Judges: K. G. Balakrishnan, C.J.,R. V. Raveendran and J. M. Panchal, JJ.

[2] **Meaning of Ratio Decidendi**

Ratio decidendi is a Latin phrase meaning "the reason" or "the rationale for the decision." The *ratio decidendi* is "[t]he point in a case which determines the judgment" or "the principle which the case establishes."

investigation and the preservation of individual liberties. The case is not an ordinary dispute between private parties. It raises pertinent questions about the meaning and scope of fundamental rights[3] which are available to all citizens.

The involuntary administration of the impugned techniques prompts questions about the protective scope of the 'right against self-incrimination' which finds place in Article 20(3) of our Constitution[4]. In one of the judgments, it has been held that the information extracted through methods such as 'polygraph examination' and the 'Brain Electrical Activation Profile (BEAP) test' cannot be equated with 'testimonial compulsion' because the test subject is not required to give verbal answers, thereby falling outside the protective scope of Article 20(3). It was further ruled that the verbal revelations made during a narcoanalysis test do not attract the bar of Article 20(3) since the inculpatory or exculpatory nature of these revelations is not known at the time of conducting the test.

Questions before the Court:

I.   Whether the involuntary administration of the impugned techniques violates the 'right against self-incrimination' enumerated in Article 20(3) of the Constitution?

II. I-A. Whether the investigative use of the impugned techniques creates a likelihood of incrimination for the subject?

I-B. Whether the results derived from the impugned techniques amount to 'testimonial compulsion' thereby attracting the bar of Article 20(3)?

II. Whether the involuntary administration of the impugned techniques is a reasonable restriction on 'personal liberty' as understood in the context of Article 21 of the Constitution[5]?

---

[3] http://en.wikisource.org/wiki/Constitution_of_India/Part_III

[4] **Article 20(3) in The Constitution Of India 1949**

(3) No person accused of any offence shall be compelled to be a witness against himself

[5] **Article 21 in The Constitution Of India**

Protection of life and personal liberty No person shall be deprived of his life or personal liberty except according to procedure established by law

Description of Tests - Uses, Limitations and Precedents

Polygraph Examination

The origins of polygraph examination have been traced back to the efforts of Lombroso, a criminologist who experimented with a machine that measured blood pressure and pulse to assess the honesty of persons suspected of criminal conduct. His device was called a hydrosphygmograph.

The theory behind polygraph tests is that when a subject is lying in response to a question, he/she will produce physiological responses that are different from those that arise in the normal course. During the polygraph examination, several instruments are attached to the subject for measuring and recording the physiological responses. The examiner then reads these results, analyzes them and proceeds to gauge the credibility of the subject's answers. Instruments such as cardiographs, pneumographs, cardio-cuffs and sensitive electrodes are used in the course of polygraph examinations. They measure changes in aspects such as respiration, blood pressure, blood flow, pulse and galvanic skin resistance. The truthfulness or falsity on part of the subject is assessed by relying on the records of the physiological responses. [6]

There are three prominent polygraph examination techniques:

    i. The relevant-irrelevant (R-I) technique

    ii. The control question (CQ) technique

    iii. Directed Lie-Control (DLC) technique

Each of these techniques includes a pre-test interview during which the subject is acquainted with the test procedure and the examiner gathers the information which is needed to finalize the questions that are to be asked. An important objective of this exercise is to mitigate the possibility of a feeling of surprise on part of the subject which could be triggered by unexpected questions. Needless to say, the polygraph examiner should be familiar with the details of the ongoing investigation. To meet this end the investigators are required to share copies of documents such as the First

---

[6] [See:*Laboratory Procedure Manual - Polygraph Examination* (Directorate of Forensic Science, Ministry of Home Affairs, Government of India, New Delhi - 2005)]

Information Report (FIR), Medico-Legal Reports (MLR) and Post-Mortem Reports (PMR) depending on the nature of the facts being investigated.

The control-question (CQ) technique is the most commonly used. The test consists of control questions and relevant questions. The control questions are irrelevant to the facts being investigated but they are intended to provoke distinct physiological responses, as well as false denials. These responses are compared with the responses triggered by the relevant questions. In other words, a guilty subject is more likely to be concerned with lying about the relevant facts as opposed to lying about other facts in general. An innocent subject will have no trouble in truthfully answering the relevant questions but will have trouble in giving false answers to control questions. The scoring of the tests is done by assigning a numerical value, positive or negative, to each response given by the subject. After accounting for all the numbers, the result is compared to a standard numerical value to indicate the overall level of deception. The net conclusion may indicate truth, deception or uncertainty.

The errors associated with polygraph tests are broadly grouped into two categories, i.e., 'false positives' and 'false negatives'. A 'false positive' occurs when the results indicate that a person has been deceitful even though he/she answered truthfully. Conversely a 'false negative' occurs when a set of deceptive responses is reported as truthful. On account of such inherent complexities, the qualifications and competence of the polygraph examiner are of the utmost importance. The examiner needs to be thorough in preparing the questionnaire and must also have the expertise to account for extraneous conditions that could lead to erroneous inferences.

Narcoanalysis technique

This test involves the intravenous administration of a drug that causes the subject to enter into a hypnotic trance and become less inhibited. The drug-induced hypnotic stage is useful for investigators since it makes the subject more likely to divulge information. The drug used for this test is sodium pentothal, higher quantities of which are routinely used for inducing general anaesthesia in surgical procedures. This drug is also used in the field of psychiatry since the revelations can enable the diagnosis of mental disorders. The use of 'truth-serums' and hypnosis is not a recent development. Earlier versions of the narcoanalysis technique utilised substances such as scopolamine and sodium amytal.

In recent years, the debate over the use of 'truth-serums' has been revived with demands for their use on persons suspected of involvement in terrorist activities. Coming to the test procedure, when the drug (sodium pentothal) is administered intravenously, the subject ordinarily descends into anaesthesia in four stages, namely:

(i) Awake stage

(ii) Hypnotic stage

(iii) Sedative stage

(iv) Anaesthetic stage

A relatively lighter dose of sodium pentothal is injected to induce the 'hypnotic stage' and the questioning is conducted during the same. The hypnotic stage is maintained for the required period by controlling the rate of administration of the drug.

The personnel involved in conducting a 'narcoanalysis' interview include a forensic psychologist, an anaesthesiologist, a psychiatrist, a general physician or other medical staff and a language interpreter if needed. Additionally a videographer is required to create video-recordings of the test for subsequent scrutiny. In India, this technique has been administered either inside forensic science laboratories or in the operation theatres of recognised hospitals. While a psychiatrist and general physician perform the preliminary function of gauging whether the subject is mentally and physically fit to undergo the test, the anaesthesiologist supervises the intravenous administration of the drug. It is the forensic psychologist who actually conducts the questioning. Since the tests are meant to aid investigation efforts, the forensic psychologist needs to closely co-operate with the investigators in order to frame appropriate questions.

Brain Electrical Activation Profile (BEAP) test

The third technique in question is the 'Brain Electrical Activation Profile test', also known as the 'P300 Waves test'. It is a process of detecting whether an individual is familiar with certain information by way of measuring activity in the brain that is triggered by exposure to selected stimuli. This test consists of examining and measuring 'event-related potentials' (ERP) i.e. electrical wave forms emitted by the brain after it has absorbed an external event. An ERP measurement is the recognition of specific patterns of electrical brain activity in a subject that are indicative of certain cognitive mental activities that occur when a person is exposed to a stimulus in the form of an image or a concept expressed in words. The measurement of the cognitive brain activity allows the examiner to ascertain whether the subject recognised stimuli to which he/she was exposed[7]

Historical origins of the 'right against self-incrimination'

The right of refusal to answer questions that may incriminate a person is a procedural safeguard which has gradually evolved in common law and bears a close relation to the 'right to fair trial'. There are competing versions about the historical origins of this concept. Some scholars have identified the origins of this right in the medieval period. In that account, it was a response to the procedure followed by English judicial bodies such as the Star Chamber and High Commissions which required defendants and suspects to take ex officio oaths. These bodies mainly decided cases involving religious non-conformism in a Protestant dominated society, as well as offences like treason and sedition. Under an ex officio oath the defendant was required to answer all questions posed by the judges and prosecutors during the trial and the failure to do so would attract punishments that often involved physical torture. It was the resistance to this practice of compelling the accused to speak which led to demands for a 'right to silence'.

The practice of requiring the accused persons to narrate or contest the facts on their own corresponds to a prominent feature of an inquisitorial system, i.e. the testimony of the accused is viewed as the 'best evidence' that can be gathered. The premise behind this is that innocent persons should not be reluctant to testify on their own behalf. This approach was followed in the inquisitional procedure of the ecclesiastical courts and had thus been followed in other courts as well. The obvious problem with compelling the accused to testify on his own behalf is that an ordinary

---

[7] [Cited from: Andre A Moenssens, 'Brain Fingerprinting - Can it be used to detect the innocence of persons charged with a crime?' 70 *University of Missouri at Kansas City Law Review* 891-920 (Summer 2002) at p. 893]

person lacks the legal training to effectively respond to suggestive and misleading questioning, which could come from the prosecutor or the judge. Furthermore, even an innocent person is at an inherent disadvantage in an environment where there may be unintentional irregularities in the testimony. Most importantly the burden of proving innocence by refuting the charges was placed on the defendant himself. In the present day, the inquisitorial conception of the defendant being the best source of evidence has long been displaced with the evolution of adversarial procedure in the common law tradition. Criminal defendants have been given protections such as the presumption of innocence, right to counsel, the right to be informed of charges, the right of compulsory process and the standard of proving guilt beyond reasonable doubt among others. It can hence be stated that it was only with the subsequent emergence of the 'right to counsel' that the accused's 'right to silence' became meaningful. With the consolidation of the role of defence lawyers in criminal trials, a clear segregation emerged between the testimonial function performed by the accused and the defensive function performed by the lawyer. This segregation between the testimonial and defensive functions is now accepted as an essential feature of a fair trial so as to ensure a level-playing field between the prosecution and the defence. In addition to a defendant's 'right to silence' during the trial stage, the protections were extended to the stage of pre-trial inquiry as well. With the enactment of the Sir John Jervis Act of 1848, provisions were made to advise the accused that he might decline to answer questions put to him in the pre-trial inquiry and to caution him that his answers to pre-trial interrogation might be used as evidence against him during the trial stage.

The 'right against self-incrimination' protects persons who have been formally accused as well as those who are examined as suspects in criminal cases.

What constitutes 'incrimination' for the purpose of Article 20(3)?

Various circumstances that could 'expose a person to criminal charges'. The scenario under consideration is one where a person in custody is compelled to reveal information which aids the investigation efforts. The information so revealed can prove to be incriminatory in the following ways:

- The statements made in custody could be directly relied upon by the prosecution to strengthen their case. However, if it is shown that such statements were made under circumstances of compulsion, they will be excluded from the evidence.

- Another possibility is that of 'derivative use', i.e. when information revealed during questioning leads to the discovery of independent materials, thereby furnishing a link in the chain of evidence gathered by the investigators.

- Yet another possibility is that of 'transactional use', i.e. when the information revealed can prove to be helpful for the investigation and prosecution in cases other than the one being investigated.

- A common practice is that of extracting materials or information, which are then compared with materials that are already in the possession of the investigators. For instance, handwriting samples and specimen signatures are routinely obtained for the purpose of identification or corroboration.

Settled principle with regard to Confession:

The crucial question is whether such derivative use of information extracted in a custodial environment is compatible with Article 20(3). It is a settled principle that statements made in custody are considered to be unreliable unless they have been subjected to cross- examination or judicial scrutiny. The scheme created by the Code of Criminal Procedure and the Indian Evidence Act also mandates that confessions made before police officers are ordinarily not admissible as evidence and it is only the statements made in the presence of a judicial magistrate which can be given weightage. The doctrine of excluding the 'fruits of a poisonous tree' has been incorporated in Sections 24, 25 and 26 of the Indian Evidence Act, 1872 which read as follows:

24. Confession caused by inducement, threat or promise, when irrelevant in criminal proceeding. - A confession made by an accused person is irrelevant in a criminal proceeding, if the making of the confession appears to the Court to have been caused by any inducement, threat or promise, having reference to the charge against the accused person, proceeding from a person in authority and sufficient, in the opinion of the Court, to give the accused person grounds, which would appear to him reasonable, for supposing that by making it he would gain any advantage or avoid any evil of a temporal nature in reference to the proceedings against him.

25. Confession to police officer not proved. - No confession made to a police officer shall be proved as against a person accused of any offence.

26. Confession by accused while in custody of police not to be proved against him. - No confession made by any person whilst he is in the custody of a police officer, unless it be made in the immediate presence of a Magistrate, shall be proved as against such person.

However, Section 27 of the Evidence Act incorporates the 'theory of confirmation by subsequent facts' - i.e. statements made in custody are admissible to the extent that they can be proved by the subsequent discovery of facts. It is quite possible that the content of the custodial statements could directly lead to the subsequent discovery of relevant facts rather than their discovery through independent means. Hence such statements could also be described as those which 'furnish a link in the chain of evidence' needed for a successful prosecution. This provision reads as follows:

27. How much of information received from accused may be proved. - Provided that, when any fact is deposed to as discovered in consequence of information received from a person accused of any offence, in the custody of a police officer, so much of such information, whether it amounts to a confession or not, as relates distinctly to the fact thereby discovered, may be proved.

Law Commission Report:

The *180ᵗʰ Report* of the Law Commission of India (May 2002) dealt with this very issue. It considered arguments for diluting the 'rule against adverse inferences from silence'. Apart from surveying several foreign statutes and decisions, the report took note of the fact that Section 342(2) of the erstwhile Code of Criminal Procedure, 1898 permitted the trial judge to draw an inference from the silence of the accused. However, this position was changed with the enactment of the new Code of Criminal Procedure in

1973, thereby prohibiting the making of comments as well as the drawing of inferences from the fact of an accused's silence. In light of this, the report concluded:

...We have reviewed the law in other countries as well as in India for the purpose of examining whether any amendments are necessary in the Code of Criminal Procedure, 1973. On a review, we find that no changes in the law relating to silence of the accused are necessary and if made, they will be ultra vires of Article 20(3) and Article 21 of the Constitution of India. We recommend accordingly.

Law on 'medical examination'

The Code of Criminal Procedure in 1973. Sections 53[8] and 54 of the CrPC[9] contemplate the medical examination of a person who has been arrested, either at the instance of the investigating officer or even the arrested person himself. The same can also be done at the direction of the jurisdictional

---

[8] The Code of Criminal Procedure, 1973 (CrPc)

53. Examination of accused by medical practitioner at the request of police officer.

(1) When a person is arrested on a charge of committing an offence of such a nature and alleged to have been committed under such circumstances that there are reasonable grounds for believing that an examination of his person will afford evidence as to the commission of an offence, it shall be lawful for a registered medical practitioner, acting, at the request of a police officer not below the rank of sub-inspector, and for- any person acting in good faith in his aid and -under his direction, to make such all examination of the person arrested as is reasonably necessary in order to ascertain the facts which may afford such evidence, and to use such force as is reasonably necessary for that purpose.

(2) Whenever the person of a female is to be examined under this section, the examination shall be made only by, or under the supervision of, a female registered medical practitioner.

[9] The Code of Criminal Procedure, 1973 (CrPc)

54. Examination of arrested person by medical practitioner at the request of the arrested person.

[(1)] When a person who is arrested, whether on a charge or otherwise, alleges, at the time when he is produced before a Magistrate or at any time during the period of his detention in custody that the examination of his body will afford evidence which will disprove the commission by him of any offence or which will establish the commission by any other person of any offence against his body, the Magistrate shall, if requested by the arrested person so to do direct the examination of the body of such person by a registered medical practitioner unless the Magistrate considers that the request is made for the purpose of vexation or delay or for defeating the ends of justice.

[(2) Where an examination is made under sub-section (1), a copy of the report of such examination shall be furnished by the registered medical practitioner to the arrested person or the person nominated by such arrested person.]

CrPc (Amendment) Act, 2005 (Notes on Clauses)

Section 54 has been amended to provide that a copy of the report of the medical examination of the arrested person should also be furnished by the registered medical practitioner to the arrested person or his nominee, after his medical examination has been conducted.

court.

A similar conclusion was arrived at by Tarkunde, Judge in ***Deomam Shamji Patel*** v. ***State of Maharashtra*** [10], who held that a person suspected or accused of having committed an offence cannot be forcibly subjected to a medical examination. It was also held that if police officers use force for this purpose, then a person can lawfully exercise the right of private defence to offer resistance.

Decision of the Court:

Court held that the compulsory administration of the techniques violates the 'right against self- incrimination'. This is because the underlying rationale of the said right is to ensure the reliability as well as voluntariness of statements that are admitted as evidence. Court has recognised that the protective scope of Article 20(3) extends to the investigative stage in criminal cases and when read with Section 161(2) of the Code of Criminal Procedure, 1973[11] it protects accused persons, suspects as well as witnesses who are examined during an investigation. The test results cannot be admitted in evidence if they have been obtained through the use of compulsion. Article 20(3) protects an individual's choice between speaking and remaining silent, irrespective of whether the subsequent testimony proves to be inculpatory or exculpatory. Article 20(3) aims to prevent the forcible 'conveyance of personal knowledge that is relevant to the facts in issue'. The results obtained from each of the impugned tests bear a 'testimonial' character and they cannot be categorised as material evidence.

Court was also of the view that forcing an individual to undergo any of the impugned techniques violates the standard of 'substantive due process' which is required for restraining personal liberty. Such a violation will occur irrespective of whether these techniques are forcibly administered during the course of an investigation or for any other purpose since the test results could also expose a person to adverse consequences of a non-penal nature.

---

[10] AIR 1959 Bom 284

[11] **Section 161(2) in The Code Of Criminal Procedure, 1973**

(2) Such person shall be bound to answer truly all questions relating to such case put to him by such officer, other than questions the answers to which would have a tendency to expose him to a criminal charge or to a penalty or forfeiture.

Court also held that no individual should be forcibly subjected to any of the techniques in question, whether in the context of investigation in criminal cases or otherwise. Doing so would amount to an unwarranted intrusion into personal liberty. However, there is room for the voluntary administration of the impugned techniques in the context of criminal justice, provided that certain safeguards are in place. Even when the subject has given consent to undergo any of these tests, the test results by themselves cannot be admitted as evidence because the subject does not exercise conscious control over the responses during the administration of the test. However, any information or material that is subsequently discovered with the help of voluntary administered test results can be admitted, in accordance with Section 27 of the Evidence Act[12], 1872. The National Human Rights Commission had published *'Guidelines for the Administration of Polygraph Test (Lie Detector Test) on an Accused'* in 2000. These guidelines should be strictly adhered to and similar safeguards should be adopted for conducting the 'Narcoanalysis technique' and the 'Brain Electrical Activation Profile' test. The text of these guidelines has been reproduced below:

(i) No Lie Detector Tests should be administered except on the basis of consent of the accused. An option should be given to the accused whether he wishes to avail such test.

(ii) If the accused volunteers for a Lie Detector Test, he should be given access to a lawyer and the physical, emotional and legal implication of such a test should be explained to him by the police and his lawyer.

(iii) The consent should be recorded before a Judicial Magistrate.

(iv) During the hearing before the Magistrate, the person alleged to have agreed should be duly represented by a lawyer.

(v) At the hearing, the person in question should also be told in clear terms that the statement that is made shall not be a 'confessional'

---

[12] **Section 27 of the Evidence Act**: How much of information received from accused may be proved.- Provided that, when any fact is deposed to as discovered in consequence of information received from a person accused of any ffence, in the custody of a police- officer, so much of such information, whether it amounts to a confession or not, as relates distinctly to the fact thereby discovered, may be proved.

statement to the Magistrate but will have the status of a statement made to the police.

(vi) The Magistrate shall consider all factors relating to the detention including the length of detention and the nature of the interrogation.

(vii) The actual recording of the Lie Detector Test shall be done by an independent agency (such as a hospital) and conducted in the presence of a lawyer.

(viii) A full medical and factual narration of the manner of the information received must be taken on record.

28

Duty of Care by 5 Star Hotels[1]

Facts in Nutshell:

Klaus Mittelbachert, the plaintiff, a German national was a co-pilot in Lufthansa. He landed at Delhi and was scheduled to continue the flight to Frankfurt on 14th August, 1972. For the intervening time, designated in the air-line terminology as lay- over-period, he checked into and stayed at the Hotel Oberoi Intercontinental. Hotel Oberoi Intercontinental, defendant No.3 (hereinafter, the said Hotel) is a five star hotel located at Dr. Zakir Hussein Marg, New Delhi. It is owned by the defendant No.1. The defendant No.4 was its Chairman and it was allegedly being managed by defendant No.2 at the material time. The Hotel had a swimming pool equipped with a diving board.

In the afternoon of August 13, 1972 the plaintiff visited the swimming pool. While diving the plaintiff met with an accident. He had hit his head on the bottom of the swimming pool. He was taken out bleeding from right ear and appearing to have paralysed in the arms and the legs. He was taken to Holy Family Hospital, situated nearby, where he remained admitted and under treatment until August, 21, 1972 on which date he was flown to Germany under medical escort. On 11.8.75, the suit has been filed for recovery of an amount of Rs.50 lacs by way of damages with interest calculated @ 12% from the date of the filing of the suit until payment and costs.

---

[1] Appellants: **Klaus Mittel bachertVs.** Respondent: **East India Hotels Ltd.**
AIR1997Delhi201
Hon'ble Judges: R.C. Lahoti, J.

Contention of Plaintiff[2]:

According to the plaintiff, the accident was caused by what in the circumstances amounted to a trap. The diving board placed at the swimming pool suggested a proper depth of water into which a swimmer could dive. The defendant hotel owed the plaintiff a duty to take care and ensure his safety. Having failed therein the defendants are guilty of negligence[3] and are, Therefore, liable to compensate the plaintiff for the consequences flowing from the accident.

Contention of Defendants[4]:

The defendants in their written statements have taken the plea that the plaintiff was in the pool ever since 2.30 p.m. on 13.8.72. He had taken some drinks and was diving in the pool repeatedly till the evening right from the afternoon. He was performing acrobatics, dangerous in tendency, and many a times he was warned by the hotel staff not to do such dangerous acts from the diving board. Diving at a continuous stretch for about one-and-a-half hour, the plaintiff was virtually exhausted. There was a notice also at the foot of the diving board reading—"dive at your own risk".

The last act performed by the plaintiff was a naggers dive taking a long sprint and high jump from the diving board without stretching his hands over the head with the result that the plaintiff hit his head on the bottom of the pool. This was the result of the plaintiff's own negligence. It was also pleaded in the written statement that the plaintiff was suffering from meaning IT is and it was quite possible that he got an attack of epilepsy while diving which prevented him from diving with accuracy and putting his hands above his head and regulate and guide his course of movement after plunge into the water coupled with his drunken state and physical exhaustion resulted into injuries to the plaintiff for which the hotel cannot be held liable. The plea of the defendants that the attack of epilepsy might have been the case for plaintiff's accident is based on mere surmises having no material in the record available to sustain the same. It was rejected by court.

---

[2] **Meaning of Plaintiff:** The party who initiates a lawsuit by filing a complaint with the clerk of the court against the defendant(s) demanding damages

[3] 'Negligence' is failure to observe, for the protection of the interests of another person, the degree of care, precaution and vigilance which the circumstances justly demand, whereby such other person suffers injury.

[4] **Meaning of Defendant:** The party against which an action is brought.

Decision of High Court:

A five star hotel charging a high or fancy price from its guests owes a high degree of care to its guests as regards quality and safety of its structure and services it offers and makes available. Any latent defect in its structure or service, which is hazardous to guests, would attract strict liability to compensate for consequences flowing from its breach of duty to take care. The five star price tag hanging on its service pack attracts and casts an obligation to pay exemplary damages if an occasion may arise for the purpose. A five star hotel can not be heard to say that its structure and services satisfied the standards of safety of the time when it was built or introduced. It has to update itself with the latest and advanced standard of safety.

A person received in a hotel as a guest enjoys an implied assurance from the hotel' that the proprietor by himself and through his servants, agents would take proper care of the safety of the customer. Not only the building structure but the services offered thereat have to be safe and immune from any danger inherent or otherwise. A hotel owner holds himself out as willing and also as capable to accommodate and entertain the guests. The quality and safety of the services offered increases with the quantum of the price paid for being guest at the hotel. *Higher the charges, higher the degree to take care.*

A swimming pool in a hotel is an open invitation to the guests to swim in the pool either subject to payment of extra charges or if it be without any charges then an im-pliedly announcement that the charges were included in the overall charges for staying in the hotel. Presence of a diving board at the head of the swimming pool is an invitation for the guests to use it and dive in the swimming pool. In a hotel, the swimming pool filled with water carries an implied warranty as to safety- that the swimming pool is structurally and from architectural point of view so designed as to be safe, that the water is free from infection, that the depth of the water is safe for swimming. In the absence of a specific warning to the contrary, the swimming pool is an invitation not only to those who have learnt the art of swimming but also to amateurs who may like to take a plunge into water just for the pleasure of that. Availability of a diving board over the swimming pool is an invitation to the guests to take dives into the swimming pool with an implied warranty that the height and protrusion of the diving board or the spring board (as the case may be) are safe; and that the depth of water at the plummet point has been so maintained that any one taking a plunge into the water is not likely to suffer an injury.

Having arrived at a finding that the design of the swimming pool was defective, the conclusion which necessarily emerges is that the swimming pool of the defendant's hotel was a trap. It was a 'hazardous premises' in the sense in which the term is used in the law of torts. The liability of the defendants for adverse consequences flowing from the use of the swimming pool- an hazardous premises - would be absolute.

Reiterating the view taken in *Indian Council for Environ-Legal Action vs Union of India*[5]

"Once the activity carried on is hazardous or inherently dangerous, the person carrying on such activity is liable to make good the loss caused to any other person by his activity irrespective of the fact whether he took reasonable care while carrying on his activity."

Court ordered recovery of Rs. 50 lakhs from Defendants.

---

[5] [1996]2SCR503

29

Do's and Don't's under Armed Forces Special Powers Act, 1958[1]

Facts in Nutshell:

The Writ Petition was filed under Article 32 of the Constitution[2] and the validity of the Armed Forces (Special Powers) Act, 1958 have been challenged. In writ petition[3] allegations have been made regarding infringement of human rights by personnel of armed forces in exercise of the powers conferred by the Armed Forces Act, 1958. The writ petition raise question relating to the validity of the Armed Forces (Special Powers) Act, 1958 (as amended). The Central Act was enacted in 1958 to enable certain special powers to be conferred upon the members of the armed forces in the disturbed areas[4] in the State of Assam and the Union Territory of Manipur.

---

[1] Appellants: **Naga People's Movement of Human Rights Vs.** Respondent: **Union of India (UOI)**

AIR1998SC465

Hon'ble Judges: J. S. Verma, C.J., M. M. Punchhi, S. C. Agrawal, Dr. A. S. Anand and S. P. Bharucha, JJ.

[2] **Article 32. Remedies for enforcement of rights conferred by this Part**

(1) The right to move the Supreme Court by appropriate proceedings for the enforcement of the rights conferred by this Part is guaranteed

(2) The Supreme Court shall have power to issue directions or orders or writs, including writs in the nature of habeas corpus, mandamus, prohibition, quo warranto and certiorari, whichever may be appropriate, for the enforcement of any of the rights conferred by this Part

(3) Without prejudice to the powers conferred on the Supreme Court by clause (1) and (2), Parliament may by law empower any other court to exercise within the local limits of its jurisdiction all or any of the powers exercisable by the Supreme Court under clause (2)

(4) The right guaranteed by this article shall not be suspended except as otherwise provided for by this Constitution

[3] A writ petition is a right endowed by the law for a person to seek speedy trial before an appellate court after a trial court's judgment on his case. The petitioner seeks to rush his case to prevent irreparable harm

Section 4 of Armed Forces Act, 1958

Special powers of the armed forces- Any Commissioned Officer, Warrant Officer, Non-Commissioned Officer or any other person of equivalent rank in the armed forces may, in a disturbed area,-

(a) if he is of opinion that it is necessary so to do for the maintenance of public order, after giving such due warning as he may consider necessary fire upon or otherwise use force, even to the causing of death, against any person who is acting in contravention of any law or order for the time being in force in the disturbed area prohibiting the assembly of five or more persons or the carrying of weapons or of things capable of being used as weapons or of fire-arms, ammunition or explosive substances;

(b) if he is of opinion that it is necessary so to do, destroy any arms dump, prepared or fortified position or shelter from which armed attacks are made or are likely to be made or are attempted to be made, or any structure used as training camp for armed volunteers or utilised as a hide-out by armed gangs or absconders wanted for any offence;

(c) arrest, without warrant[5], any person who has committed a cognizable

---

[4] **Section 2(b) of Act, 1958:** "**Disturbed area**" means an area which is for the time being declared by notification under Section 3 to be a disturbed area;

Section 3 of Act, 1958: Power to declare areas to be disturbed areas,- If, in relation to any State or Union Territory to which this Act extends, the Governor of that State or the Administrator of that Union Territory or the Central Government, in either case, is of the opinion that the whole or any part of such State or Union Territory, as the case may be, is in such a disturbed or dangerous condition that the use of armed forces in aid of the civil power is necessary, the Governor of that State or the Administrator of the Union Territory or the Central Government, as the case may be, may, by notification in the Official Gazette, declare the whole or such part of such State or Union Territory to be a disturbed area.

[5] An **arrest without warrant** or a warrantless arrest is an arrest of an individual without the use of an arrest warrant

ARREST WITHOUT WARRANT

A Police Officer can arrest a person without warrant in the following circumstances:-

1. When the person has been concerned in any congnizable offence, or when a reasonable complaint or a credible information has been received by the Police Officer about the commission of a non-cognizable offence by that person or when the police officer has the reasonable suspicion about the offence committed by the person.

2. When a person commits the offence of house breaking.

3. When a person is proclaimed as an offender by the competent authority.

4. When a person is suspected to be in possession of stolen property and is suspected of having committed an offence concerning the property in his possession.

5. When one obstructs a police officer while he executes his duty or when one has escaped or attempts to escape from lawful custody.

offence[6] or against whom a reasonable suspicion exists that he has committed or is about to commit a cognizable offence and may use such force as may be necessary to effect the arrest;

(d) enter and search without warrant any premises to make any such arrest as aforesaid or to recover any person believed to be wrongfully restrained or confined or any property reasonably suspected to be stolen property or any arms, ammunition or explosive substances believed to be unlawfully kept in such premises, and may for that purpose use such force as may be necessary.

"List of Do's and Don'ts While Acting Under Armed Forces Special Powers Act, 1958

Do's.

I. Action before Operation.

(a) Act only in the area declared 'Disturbed Area' under Section 3 of the Act.

(b) Power to open fire using force or arrest is to be exercised under this Act only by an officer/JCO/WO and NCO.

(c) Before launching any raid/search, definite information about the activity to be obtained from the local civil authorities.

(d) As far as possible co-opt representative of local civil administration during the raid.

2. Action during Operation.

(a) In case of necessity of opening fire and using any force against the suspect or any person acting in contravention to law and order, ascertain first that it is essential for maintenance of public order.

---

contd/-

6. When there is a reasonable suspicion of being a desert from any armed forces of the Union.

7. When a person has committed any act out of India and it is punishable in India and that he is liable to be extradited or detained in custody in India.

8. When a released convict commits a breach of any rule that he has to abide under the law.

[6] The Code of Criminal Procedure, 1973 (CrPc)

Section 2 (C) "cognizable offence" means an offence for which, and "cognizable case" means a case in which, a police officer may, in accordance with the First Schedule or under and other law for the time being in force, arrest without warrant.

Open fire only after due warning.

(b) Arrest only those who have committed cognizable offence or who are about to commit cognizable offence or against whom a reasonable ground exists to prove that they have committed or are about to commit cognizable offence.

(c) Ensure that troops under command do not harass innocent people destory property of the public or unnecessarily enter into the house/dwelling of people not connected with any unlawful activities.

(d) Ensure that women are not searched/arrested without the presence of female police. In fact women should be searched by female police only.

3. Action after Operation.

(a) After arrest prepare a list of the persons so arrested.

(b) Handover the arrested persons to the nearest Police Station with least possible delay.

(c) While handing over to the police a report should accompany with detailed circumstances occasioning the arrest.

(d) Every delay in handing over the suspects to the police must be justified and should be reasonable depending upon the place, time of arrest and the terrain in which such person has been arrested. Least possible delay may be 2-3 hours extendable to 24 hours or so depending upon a particular case.

(e) After raid make out a list of all arms, ammunition or any other incriminating material/document taken into possession.

(f) All such arms, ammunition, stores etc. should be handed over to the Police Station alongwith the seizure memo.

(g) Obtain receipt of persons and arms/ammunition, stores etc. so handed over to the police.

(h) Make record of the area where operation is launched having the date and time and the persons participating in such raid.

(i) Make a record of the commander and other officer/JCOs/NCOs forming part of such force.

(k) Ensure medical relief to any person injured during the encounter, if any person dies in the encounter his dead body be handed over immediately to the police alongwith the details leading to such death.

4. Dealing with Civil Court.

(a) Directions of the High Court/Supreme Court should be promptly attended to.

(b) Whenever summoned by the courts, decorum of the court must be maintained and proper respect paid.

(c) Answer questions of the court politely and with dignity.

(d) Maintain detailed record of the entire operation correctly and explicitly.

Don'ts

1. Do not keep a person under custody for any period longer than the bare necessity for handing over to the nearest Police Station.

2. Do not use any force after having arrested a person except when he is trying to escape.

3. Do not use third degree methods to extract information or to extract confession or other involvement in unlawful activities.

4. After arrest of a person by the member of the Armed forces, he shall not be interrogated by the member of the Armed forces.

5. Do not release the person directly after apprehending on your own. If any person is to be released, he must be released through civil authorities.

6. Do not temper with official records.

7. The Armed Forces shall not take back a person after he is handed over to civil police."

"List of Do's and Dont's While Providing Aid to Civil Authority.

Do's

1. Act in closest possible communication with civil authorities throughout.

2. Maintain inter-communication if possible by telephone/radio.

3. Get the permission/requisition from the Magistrate when present.

4. Use the little force and do as little injury to person and property as may be consistent with attainment of objective in view.

5. In case you decide to open fire :-

   (a) Give warning in local language that fire will be effective.

   (b) Attract attention before firing by bugle or other means.

   (c) Distribute your men in fire units with specified Commanders.

   (d) Control fire by issuing personal orders.

   (e) Note number of rounds fired.

   (f) Aim at the front of crowd actually rioting or inciting to riot or at conspicuous ring leaders, i.e., do not fire into the thick of the crowd at the back.

   (g) Aim low and short for effect.

   (h) Keep Light Machine Gun and Medium Gun in reserve.

   (i) Cease firing immediately once the object has been attained,

   (j) Take immediate steps to secure wounded.

6. Maintain cordial relations with civilian authorities and Para Military Forces.

7. Ensure high standard of discipline.

Don'ts

8. Do not use excessive force.

9. Do not get involved in hand to hand struggle with the mob.

10. Do not ill treat any one, in particular, women and children.

11. No harassment of civilians.

12. No torture.

13. No communal bias while dealing with civilians.

14. No meddling in civilian administration affairs.

15. No military disgrace by loss/surrender of weapons.

16. Do not accept presents, donations and rewards.

17. Avoid indiscriminate firing."

Decision of the Supreme Court

Court held that the powers conferred under Clauses (a) to (d) of Section 4 (powers as mentioned above) of the Armed Forces Act, 1958 on the officers of the armed forces, including a Non-Commissioned Officer are not arbitrary and unreasonable and are not violative of the provisions of Articles 14[7], 19[8] or 21[9] of the Constitution.

---

[7] **Article 14 in The Constitution Of India 1949**

14. Equality before law The State shall not deny to any person equality before the law or the equal protection of the laws within the territory of India Prohibition of discrimination on grounds of religion, race, caste, sex or place of birth

[8] **Article 19 in The Constitution Of India 1949**

19. Protection of certain rights regarding freedom of speech etc

(1) All citizens shall have the right

(a) to freedom of speech and expression;

(b) to assemble peaceably and without arms;

(c) to form associations or unions;

(d) to move freely throughout the territory of India;

(e) to reside and settle in any part of the territory of India; and

(f) omitted

(g) to practise any profession, or to carry on any occupation, trade or business

[9] **Article 21 in The Constitution Of India**

Protection of life and personal liberty No person shall be deprived of his life or personal liberty except according to procedure established by law

30

Impounding of Passport[1]

Ratio Decidendi[2]:

Where there is a special Act dealing with specific subject, resort should be had to that Act instead of general Act providing for the matter connected with the specific Act.

Facts in Nutshell:

The appellant[3] claimed to be a non-resident Indian settled in United Kingdom for the last 23 years. The passport of the appellant as well as other documents were seized by the respondent[4] when the appellant was on a visit to India. The passport seized during the search was retained by the C.B.I. officials. An application was moved by the appellant before the Special Judge, C.B.I., New Delhi praying for release of his passport so that he can travel abroad to London and Ducal for a period of 15 days. The learned Special Judge directed the release of the passport to the appellant by imposing upon him certain conditions. Aggrieved against the order passed by the Special Judge, C.B.I., respondent preferred a Criminal Revision before the High Court, The High Court reversed the order of the learned Special Judge and refused to release the passport to the appellant. Aggrieved against the order of the

---

[1] Appellants: **Suresh Nanda** Vs. Respondent: **C.B.I.**
     AIR2008SC1414
     Hon'ble Judges: P. P. Naolekar and Markandey Katju , JJ.

[2] Meaning of **Ratio Decidendi**
     Ratio decidendi is a Latin phrase meaning "the reason" or "the rationale for the decision. " The ratio decidendi is "[t]he point in a case which determines the judgment" or "the principle which the case establishes."

[3] One who appeals, or asks for a rehearing or review of a cause by a higher tribunal.

[4] A person against whom a petition or complaint is filed in a court.

High Court appellant filed appeal by special leave[5]

Submission on Behalf of Counsel for Appellant

Learned counsel for the appellant submitted that the power and jurisdiction to impound the passport of any individual has to be exercised under the Passports Act, 1967. He specifically referred to Sub-section (3)(e) of the Passport Act, 1967 which reads as under:

(3) The passport authority may impound or cause to be impounded or revoke a passport or travel document -

(e) if proceedings in respect of an offence alleged to have been committed by the holder of the passport or travel document are pending before a criminal court in India

Counsel also referred to the case of *Satwant Singh Sawhney v. D. Rajnarathnam, Asstt. Passport Officer*[6] wherein it was held as under:

It follows that under Article 21 of the Constitution[7] no person can be deprived of his right to travel except according to procedure established by law. It is not disputed that no law was trade by the State regulating or depriving persons of such a right. Thus, no person can be deprived of his right to go abroad unless there is a law made by the State prescribing the procedure for so depriving him and the deprivation is effected strictly in accordance with such procedure....

Decision of the Court:

Court held that the passport of the appellant cannot be impounded except by the Passport Authority in accordance with law. The retention of the

---

[5] **Article 136 Constitution of India**

Special Leave to appeal by the Supreme Court

(1) Notwithstanding anything in this Chapter, the Supreme Court may, in its discretion, grant special leave to appeal from any judgment, decree, determination, sentence or order in any cause or matter passed or made by any court or tribunal in the territory of India.

(2) Nothing in clause (1) shall apply to any judgment, determination, sentence or order passed or made by any court or tribunal constituted by or under any law relating to the Armed Forces.

[6] [1967]3SCR525

[7] **Article 21 of the Constitution of India, 1950**: Protection of Life and Personal Liberty

No person shall be deprived of his life or personal liberty except according to procedure established by law.

passport by the respondent (CBI) has not been done in conformity with the provisions of law as there is no order of the passport authorities to impound the passport.

Court also held that while the police may have the power to seize a passport under Section 102(1) Cr.P.C[8], it does not have the power to impound the same[9]. Impounding of a passport can only be done by the passport authority under Section 10(3) of the Passports Act, 1967[10]. It is thereafter the passport authority to decide whether to impound the passport or not. Since impounding

---

[8] **The Code of Criminal Procedure, 1973 (CrPc)**
102. Power of police officer to seize certain property.
(1) Any police officer may seize any property which may be alleged or suspected to have been stolen, or which may be found under circumstances, which create suspicion of the Commission of any offence.

[9] It may be mentioned that there is a difference between seizing of a document and impounding a document. a seizure is made e at a particular moment when a person or authority taxes into his possession some property which was earlier not in his possession. Thus, seizure is done at a particular moment of time. However, if after seizing of a property or document the said property or document is retained for some period of time, then such retention amounts to impounding of the property/or document. In the Law Lexicon by P. Ramanatha Aiyar (2nd Edition), the word "impound" has been defined to mean *"to take possession of a document or thing for being held in custody in accordance with law"*. Thus, the word 'impounding" really means retention of possession of a good or a document which has been seized.

[10] **Section 10(3) in The Passports Act, 1967**
(3) The passport authority may impound or cause to be impounded or revoke a passport or travel document,-
(a) if the passport authority is satisfied that the holder of the passport or travel document is in wrongful possession thereof;
(b) if the passport or travel document was obtained by the suppression of material information or on the basis of wrong information provided by the holder of the passport or travel document or any other person on his behalf; 1[Provided that if the holder of such passport obtains another passport, the passport authority shall also impound or cause to be impounded or revoke such other passport.]
(c) if the passport authority deems it necessary so to do in the interests of the sovereignty and integrity of India, the security of India, friendly relations of India with any foreign country, or in the interests of the general public;
(d) if the holder of the passport or travel document has, at any time after the issue of the passport or travel document, been convicted by a court in India for any offence involving moral turpitude and sentenced in respect thereof to imprisonment for not less than two years;
(e) if proceedings in respect of an offence alleged to have been committed by the holder of the passport or travel document are pending before a criminal court in India;
(f) if any of the conditions of the passport or travel document has been contravened;
(g) if the holder of the passport or travel document has failed to comply with a notice under sub- section (1) requiring him to deliver up the same;
(h) if it is brought to the notice of the passport authority that a warrant or summons for the appearance, or a warrant for the arrest, of the holder of the passport or travel document has been issued by a court under any law for the time being in force or if an order prohibiting the departure from India of the holder of the passport or other travel document has been made by any such court and the passport authority is satisfied that a warrant or summons has been so issued or an order has been so made.

of a passport has civil consequences, the passport authority must give an opportunity of hearing to the person concerned before impounding his passport. It is well settled that any order which has civil consequences must be passed after giving opportunity of hearing to a party.[11] Court also held that possession of passport by CBI (respondent) is illegal. . Under Section 10A of the Act, 1967 retention of the passport by the Central Government can only be for four weeks. Thereafter it can only be retained by an order of the Passport authority under Section 10(3) act, 1967. Court also held that impounding of a passport cannot be done by the Court under Section 104 Cr.P C.[12] though it can impound any other document or thing.

---

[11] *State of Orissa v. Binapani Dei* , (1967)IILLJ266SC

[12] **The Code of Criminal Procedure, 1973 (CrPc)**

 Section 104. Power to impound document, etc., produced.

 Any court may, if it thinks fit impound any document or thing produced before it under this Code.

31

Parents will Pay if Minor Causes Accident[1]

Ratio Decidendi: Minor and inconsequential deviations with regard to licensing conditions not constitute sufficient ground to deny benefit of coverage of insurance to third parties.

Facts in Nutshell: One Balwant Singh filed an application claiming a sum of Rs. 10,00,000/- (Rupees Ten Lakhs) by way of compensation for death of his son Virender Singh in an accident which took place on 5.2.1997. The owner of the vehicle contested the said claim. United India Insurance Co. Ltd. (Appellant) raised a contention before the Tribunal that the driver of the vehicle, namely, Karan Arora was a **minor** on the date of the accident and was not holding a valid and effective driving licence and thus it was not liable to reimburse the owner of the vehicle.

Decision by Tribunal: While determining the said issue the learned Tribunal opined that the Insurance Company was not liable for payment of the amount of compensation to the claimants, stating: The Driver Karan Arora appearing as respondent 1, was aged about 15 years[2], he does not know driving; he was born on 7.8.1983 and that he is not having any driving license till 25.7.1998, when his statement was recorded. Under these circumstances, the Tribunal finds that respondent driver Karan Arora had no valid/effective driving license on the day of the accident i.e. 5.2.1997.

Decision by High Court: An appeal under Section 173 of the Motor

---

[1] Appellants: **United India Insurance Co. Ltd**. Vs. Respondent: **Rakesh Kumar Arora and Ors**. 2008ACJ2855, AIR2009SC24

Hon'ble Judges: S. B. Sinha and Cyriac Joseph, JJ.

[2] Section 4 of the Motor Vehicle Act, 1988 prohibits driving of a vehicle by any person under the age of 18 years in any public place.

Vehicles Act, 1988[3] was filed before the High court which was marked as First Appeal from Order No. 2627/1998. A learned single Judge of the said Court allowed the appeal. The division bench of the High Court dismissed the appeal.

Decision by Supreme Court: The Judgment of the Tribunal is restored. However, keeping in view the admitted fact that as no stay had been granted by the High Court the appellant has deposited the entire amount which has since been withdrawn by the claimant-respondent; the Hon'ble Judges directed that the appellant shall be entitled to recover the amount in question from the owner of the vehicle, namely, respondent No. 1 (Rakesh Kumar Arora, Father of Minor).

---

[3] **Appeals**: (1) Subject to the provisions of sub-section (2) any person aggrieved by an award of a Claims Tribunal may, within ninety days from the date of the award, prefer an appeal to the High Court:

Provided that no appeal by the person who is required to pay any amount in terms of such award shall be entertained by the High Court unless he has deposited with it twenty-five thousand rupees or fifty per cent, of the amount so awarded, whichever is less, in the manner directed by the High Court:

Provided further that the High Court may entertain the appeal after the expiry of the said period of ninety days, if it is satisfied that the appellant was prevented by sufficient cause from preferring the appeal in time.

(2) No appeal shall lie against any award of a Claims Tribunal if the amount in dispute in the appeal is less than ten thousand rupees.

CONSTITUTION LAW

Constitution Law

The Constitution of India is the Supreme Law of India. It lays down the framework defining fundamental political principles, establishes the structure, procedures, powers, and duties of government institutions, and sets out fundamental rights, directive principles, and the duties of citizens. It is the longest written constitution of any sovereign country in the world, containing 395 articles in 22 parts, 12 schedules and 118 amendments. The Constitution was adopted by the Constituent Assembly on 26 November 1949, and came into effect on 26 January 1950. The Constitution declares India to be a sovereign, socialist, secular, democratic republic, assuring its citizens of justice, equality, and liberty, and endeavours to promote fraternity among them. The words "socialist" and "secular" were added to the definition in 1976 by constitutional amendment.

Part III - Fundamental Rights' is a charter of rights contained in the Constitution of India. It guarantees civil liberties such that all Indians can lead their lives in peace and harmony as citizens of India. These include individual rights common to most liberal democracies, such as equality before law, freedom of speech and expression, and peaceful assembly, freedom to practice religion, and the right to constitutional remedies for the protection of civil rights by means of writs such as habeas corpus. Violation of these rights result in punishments as prescribed in the Indian Penal Code, subject to discretion of the judiciary. The Fundamental Rights are defined as basic human freedoms which every Indian citizen has the right to enjoy for a proper and harmonious development of personality. These rights universally apply to all citizens, irrespective of race, place of birth, religion, caste, creed, color or gender. They are enforceable by the courts, subject to certain restrictions. The Rights have their origins in many sources, including England's Bill of Rights, the United States Bill of Rights and France's Declaration of the Rights of Man.

The six fundamental rights recognised by the constitution are:

1) Right to equality, including equality before law, prohibition of discrimination on grounds of religion, race, caste, sex or place of birth, and equality of opportunity in matters of employment, abolition of untouchability and abolition of titles.

2) Right to freedom which includes speech and expression, assembly, association or union or cooperatives, movement, residence, and right to practice any profession or occupation (some of these rights are subject to security of the State, friendly relations with foreign countries, public order, decency or morality), right to life and liberty, right to education, protection in respect to conviction in offences and protection against arrest and detention in certain cases.

3) Right against exploitation, prohibiting all forms of forced labour, child labour and traffic in human beings;

4) Right to freedom of religion, including freedom of conscience and free profession, practice, and propagation of religion, freedom to manage religious affairs, freedom from certain taxes and freedom from religious instructions in certain educational institutes.

5) Cultural and Educational rights preserving Right of any section of citizens to conserve their culture, language or script, and right of minorities to establish and administer educational institutions of their choice.

6) Right to constitutional remedies for enforcement of Fundamental Rights. Fundamental rights for Indians have also been aimed at overturning the inequalities of pre-independence social practices. Specifically, they have also been used to abolish untouchability and hence prohibit discrimination on the grounds of religion, race, caste, sex, or place of birth. They also forbid trafficking of human beings and forced labour. They also protect cultural and educational rights of ethnic and religious minorities by allowing them to preserve their languages and also establish and administer their own education institutions. Right to property was originally a fundamental right, but is now a legal right.

The fundamental rights were included in the constitution because they were considered essential for the development of the personality of every individual and to preserve human dignity. The writers of the constitution regarded democracy of no avail if civil liberties, like freedom of speech and religion were not recognized and protected by the State. According to them, "democracy" is, in essence, a government by opinion and therefore, the means of formulating public opinion should be secured to the people of a democratic nation. For this purpose, the constitution guaranteed to all the citizens of India the freedom of speech and expression and various other freedoms in the form of the fundamental rights.

All people, irrespective of race, religion, caste or sex, have been given the right to move the Supreme Court and the High Courts for the enforcement of their fundamental rights. It is not necessary that the aggrieved party has to be the one to do so. Poverty stricken people may not have the means to do so and therefore, in the public interest, anyone can commence litigation in the court on their behalf. This is known as "Public interest litigation" In some cases, High Court judges have acted on their own on the basis of newspaper reports.

These fundamental rights help not only in protection but also the prevention of gross violations of human rights. They emphasize on the fundamental unity of India by guaranteeing to all citizens the access and use of the same facilities, irrespective of background. Some fundamental rights apply for persons of any nationality whereas others are available only to the citizens of India. The right to life and personal liberty is available to all people and so is the right to freedom of religion. On the other hand, freedoms of speech andexpression and freedom to reside and settle in any part of the country are reserved to citizens alone, including non-resident Indian citizens. The right to equality in matters of public employment cannot be conferred to overseas citizens of India.

Fundamental rights primarily protect individuals from any arbitrary state actions, but some rights are enforceable against individuals. For instance, the Constitution abolishes untouchability and also prohibits begar. These provisions act as a check both on state action as well as the action of private individuals. However, these rights are not absolute or uncontrolled and are subject to reasonable restrictions as necessary for the protection of general welfare. They can also be selectively curtailed. The Supreme Court has ruled that all provisions of the Constitution, including fundamental rights can be amended. However, the Parliament cannot alter the basic structure of the constitution. Features such as secularism and democracy fall under this category. Since the fundamental rights can only be altered by a constitutional amendment, their inclusion is a check not only on the executive branch, but also on the Parliament and state legislatures.

A state of national emergency has an adverse effect on these rights. Under such a state, the rights conferred by Article 19 (freedoms of speech, assembly and movement, etc.) remain suspended. Hence, in such a situation, the legislature may make laws which go against the rights given in Article 19. Also, the President may by order suspend the right to move court for the enforcement of other rights as well.

32

No School if Building Not Fire-safe[1]

Facts in Nutshell: Important Public Interest Litigation[2] relates to a fire swept through the Lord Krishna Middle School in District Kumbakonam in the city of Madras, Tamil Nadu. The fire started in the school's kitchen while cooks were preparing mid-day meal. In order to protect the rights of life and education guaranteed to all school going children under Articles 21[3] and 21A[4], the petitioner[5] prayed in Hon'ble Court to bring about **safer school conditions.**

It was alleged by Mr. Avinash Mehrotra (petitioner) that Lord Krishna Middle School is one of the thousands of private schools that have sprung up in response to drastic cuts in government spending on education. The school has more than 900 students in a crowded building, thatched-roof building with a single entrance, a narrow stairway, windowless classrooms and only one entrance and exit. It was alleged by him that the ventilation of the entire school building was extremely poor with only cement-perforated windows.

---

[1] Appellants: **Avinash Mehrotra** Vs. Respondent: **Union of India (UOI) and Ors**.
2009(5)SCALE354, (2009)6SCC398

Hon'ble Judges: Dalveer Bhandari and Lokeshwar Singh Pantaa Panta, JJ.

[2] In Indian law, public-interest litigation (PIL) is litigation for the protection of the public interest. PIL may be introduced in a court of law by the court itself (*suo moto*), rather than the aggrieved party or another third party.

[3] **Article 21 of the Constitution of India, 1950**: Protection of Life and Personal Liberty

No person shall be deprived of his life or personal liberty except according to procedure established by law.

[4] **Article 21 A of the Constitution of India, 1950:** Right to Education

The State shall provide free and compulsory education to all children of the age of six to fourteen years in such manner as the State may, by law, determine.

[5] Someone who petitions a court for redress of a grievance or recovery of a right

Rules regarding Safety in Schools: According to rules, a government-certified engineer is supposed to visit these schools once every two years and issue a "stability certificate" if the building is found to be in good condition and all safety precautions are met. The engineer can refuse to issue the certificate if he finds the safety measures inadequate, losing the school its licence to operate.

Petitioner Prayer in P.I.L:

The petitioner has prayed that he filed the petition with a specific objective that:

(1) Each and every child of this country can receive good education free from fear of safety and security,

(2) To ensure that more stringent rules and regulations are framed keeping in mind the safety of the students,

(3) To ensure that such standards of safety are at par with the highest standards set up anywhere in the world; and

(4) To ensure that such standards are in fact enforced regularly for the safety and protection of children in classrooms across the country.

Decision by Hon'ble Court:

In view of what happened in Lord Krishna Middle School in District Kumbakonam where 93 children were burnt alive and several similar incidences had happened in the past, therefore, it has become imperative to direct that safety measures as prescribed by the National Building Code of India, 2005 be implemented by all government and private schools functioning in our country.

Direction of Court:

(i) Before granting recognition or affiliation, the concerned State Governments and Union Territories are directed to ensure that the buildings are safe and secured from every angle and they are constructed according to the safety norms incorporated in the **National Building Code** of India, 2005.

(ii) All existing government and private schools shall install fire extinguishing equipments within a period of six months.

(iii) The school buildings be kept free from inflammable and toxic material. If storage is inevitable, they should be stored safely.

(iv) Evaluation of structural aspect of the school may be carried out periodically. We direct that the concerned engineers and officials must strictly follow the National Building Code.

The safety certificate be issued only after proper inspection. Dereliction in duty must attract immediate disciplinary action against the concerned officials.

(v) Necessary training be imparted to the staff and other officials of the school to use the fire extinguishing equipments.

Education Secretaries of State and Union Territories were directed to file an affidavit of compliance of this order within one month after installation of fire extinguishing equipments.

33

Caste of a person depends upon birth[1]

Ratio Decidendi[2]:

"Benefit of reservation shall not be claim by anybody on basis of Government order which is already cancelled by State."

Question before the Court:

Whether children born out of inter-caste married couple could claim the status of Scheduled Caste/Scheduled Tribe for the benefit of reservation in admission to educational institutions and in public employment on the mere fact that one of their parents belongs to Scheduled Caste/Scheduled Tribe is the question that is posed before the court.

Facts in Nutshell:

State of Kerala had extended various educational concessions to children born to inter-caste married couples. By virtue of the Government order No. J4/23203/60 dated 24.6.1960 they used to get such concessions provided their mother belonged to SC/ST and not the father. Later with a view to encourage intercaste marriage Government issued G.O.(Ms) No. 298 dated 23.6.1961 stating that children born of inter caste marriages would be allowed all educational concessions if either of the parents belongs to Scheduled Caste/Scheduled Tribe. The order dated 24.6.1960 was accordingly cancelled.

---

[1] Appellants: **Indira Vs.** Respondent: **State of Kerala**
AIR2006Ker1
Hon'ble Judges: K.S. Radhakrishnan , K.A. Abdul Gafoor and M. Ramachandran, JJ.

[2] **Meaning of Ratio Decidendi**
Ratio decidendi is a Latin phrase meaning "the reason" or "the rationale for the decision." The *ratio decidendi* is "[t]he point in a case which determines the judgment" or "the principle which the case establishes."

Later on a query made by the Kerala Public Service Commission Government clarified vide G.O.(Ms) No. 1/77/PD dt. 25.1.1977 that the Government order dated 23.3.1961 could be adopted for determining the caste of the children born out of such intercaste marriage for all purposes. Resultantly such children were treated as belonging to Scheduled Caste or Scheduled Tribe, if either of their parents belongs to SC/ST. On the strength of the above mentioned Government order, several claims were raised claiming reservation for admission to the educational institutions as well as for appointment to various posts in public services which gave rise to several litigations before Court. Claims were even raised by children whose grandparents had contracted inter-caste marriage.

Judgments Referred:

A learned single judge of the Court in *Bijumon v. Commissioner for Entrance Examination*[3] held that a combined reading of Article 366(24)[4] and 341[5] of the Constitution showed that members of the caste specified in the Presidential notification alone are entitled to be treated as Scheduled Caste and that the Parliament alone is given power to exclude any caste from the Presidential notification. Learned judge also held that Government order G.O.(Ms) 11/77/DD dated 25.1.1977[6] to the effect that all children born to parents of whom one is a member of the SC/ST have to be treated as scheduled caste cannot be accepted in toto.

---

[3] (1993 (2) KLT 1074)

[4] Article 366(24) is as follows:

"Scheduled Castes" means such castes, races or tribes or parts of or groups within such castes, races or tribes as are deemed under Article 341 to be Scheduled Castes for the purpose of this constitution."

[5] **Article 341 in The Constitution Of India 1949**

341. Scheduled Castes

(1) The President may with respect to any State or Union territory, and where it is a State after consultation with the Governor thereof, by public notification, specify the castes, races or tribes or parts of or groups within castes, races or tribes which shall for the purposes of this Constitution be deemed to be Scheduled Castes in relation to that State or Union territory, as the case may be

(2) Parliament may by law include in or exclude from the list of Scheduled Castes specified in a notification issued under clause (1) any caste, race or tribe or part of or group within any caste, race or tribe, but save as aforesaid a notification issued under the said clause shall not be varied by any subsequent notification

[6] G.O.(MS)No. 298/61/ReV. dated 23.3.1961 will be adopted for determining the caste of the children born of intercaste marriage for all purposes, according to which the children will be treated as belonging to Scheduled Caste or Scheduled Tribe community if either of the parents belongs to that community".

In *Punit Rai v. Dinesh Chaudhary* [7] case learned Judge held that the caste or tribe of the parents to be determined depended upon several factors including "customary laws". Learned Judge also held that the caste system is ingrained in the Indian's mind and a person, in the absence of any statutory law, would inherit his caste from his father and not his mother even in a case of inter caste marriage. Learned Judge in paragraph 31 of the judgment held: "If he is considered to be a member of the scheduled caste, he has to be accepted by the community". Learned Judge also held that the question as to whether a person belonged to a particular caste or not is to be determined by the statutory authorities specified therefor. Learned Judge opined in paragraph 41 of the judgment that determination of caste of a person is governed by the customary laws and a person under the customary Hindu law would be inheriting his caste from his father ("Traditionally, a person belongs to a caste in which he is born. The caste of the parents determines his caste...."). It was also ruled that the caste of an offspring of an intercaste married couple shall be determined based on the caste of its father.

The Apex Court in *Valsamma Paul v. Cochin University* [8] dealt with a case where the lady, a Syrian Catholic, married a Latin Catholic, other backward class, had applied for selection of reserved candidate. Apex Court examined whether the candidate who had the advantageous start in life being born in forward caste and had march of advantageous life but is transplanted in backward caste by adoption or marriage or conversion does not become eligible to the benefit of reservation under Article 15(4) [9] or 16(4) [10]. Contention was raised that due to marriage she has subjected herself and suffered to all family disabilities of her husband. The recognition of the appellant by the member of Latin Catholic would

---

[7] AIR2003SC4355

[8] 1996 1SCR128

[9] **Article 15(4) in The Constitution Of India 1949**

(4) Nothing in this article or in clause (2) of Article 29 shall prevent the State from making any special provision for the advancement of any socially and educationally backward classes of citizens or for the Scheduled Castes and the Scheduled Tribes

[10] **Article 16(4) in The Constitution Of India 1949**

(4) Nothing in this article shall prevent the State from making any provision for the reservation of appointments or posts in favor of any backward class of citizens which, in the opinion of the State, is not adequately represented in the services under the State

not, therefore, be relevant for the purpose of her entitlement to the reservation under Article 16(4), for the reason that she, as a member of the forward caste, had advantageous start in life and after her completing education and becoming major married a Latin Catholic, and so, she is not entitled to the facility of reservation given to the Latin Catholic, a backward class.

A caste is nothing but a social class - a socially homogeneous class. It is also an occupational grouping with its difference that its membership is hereditary. One is born into it. Its membership is involuntary.[11] A Division Bench of the Court in *Haridasan v. State of Kerala* [12] held that "the question of caste depends upon the caste in which the person is born". This court also held that "the crucial point is to ascertain the caste at the time of birth."

Decision by High Court:

All the writ petitions claiming there right to reservation under constitutional provisions were dismissed by court because the conduct and behavior of the candidates showed that they were devoid of any tribal status, affinity of conditions, milieu, acceptance etc. to be deemed as a member of scheduled tribe community and also community has not accepted them as the member. Court also held that the caste of a person, thus, depends on birth. It is, thus, obvious that the Government cannot determine the caste of a particular person or a class of persons. If there is dispute, it depends upon the evidence as to in which caste one is born and is brought up, as to the practices and customs one may follow, the acceptance of the incumbent by the caste or group in a caste to which he/she claims to belong and several other related aspects. It is to be determined by a competent authority based on evidence, in case of doubt or dispute. Government cannot, thus, issue any general order determining the caste of any particular class of persons. So, G.O.11/ 77 cannot have any effect in determining the caste of one, as Government cannot determine caste of any one or a group.

---

[11] *Indra Sawhney and Ors. v. Union of India* (1992 Supp. (3) SCC 217).
[12] (2000 (2) KLT 913)

So, a particular community, caste, race or tribe or part or group thereof can be declared as Scheduled Caste or Scheduled Tribe initially by the President and a new group can be added to the lists only by a legislation by the Parliament. The State Government, cannot by an executive fiat, direct to treat any particular group of persons as Scheduled Caste or Scheduled Tribe.

34

Freedom of Speech & Right to Fly National Flag[1]

Question before the Court:

Important question that arises for consideration was whether the right to fly the National Flag by Indian citizen is a fundamental right within the meaning of Article 19(1)(a)[2] of the Constitution of India.

Facts in Nutshell:

Naveen Jindal, the respondent is a Joint Managing Director of a public limited company incorporated under the Companies Act. He being in charge of the factory of the said company situated at Raigarh in Madhya Pradesh was flying National Flag at the office premises of his factory. He was not allowed to do so by the government officials on the ground that the same is impermissible under the Flag Code of India. Questioning the said action, the respondent filed a writ petition before the High Court, inter alia, on the ground that no law could prohibit flying of National Flag by Indian citizens. Flying of National Flag with respect and dignity being a fundamental right, the Flag Code which contains only executive instructions On the government of India and, thus, being not a law, cannot be considered to have imposed reasonable restrictions in respect thereof within the meaning of Clause (2) of Article 19[3] of the Constitution of India.

---

[1] Appellants: **Union of India (UOI) Vs.** Respondent: **Naveen Jindal and Anr.**
AIR2004SC1559

Hon'ble Judges: V. N. Khare , C.J., Brijesh Kumar and S. B. Sinha , JJ.

[2] **Article 19(1)(a) in The Constitution Of India 1949**
(a) to freedom of speech and expression;

[3] **Article 19(2) in The Constitution Of India 1949**
(2) Nothing in sub clause (a) of clause (1) shall affect the operation of any existing law, or prevent the State from making any law, in so far as such law imposes reasonable restrictions

Appellant –Union of India Contentions before High Court:

1. That the Central government is authorised to impose restrictions on the use of National Flag at any public place or building and can regulate the same by the authority vested in it under Section 3 of the Emblems and Names (Prevention of Improper Use) Act. 1950[4];

2. That the restriction imposed by the Act and orders issued by the government are constitutionally valid being reasonable restrictions on the freedom of speech and expression under Article 19(2) of the Constitution

3. That the question of permitting free use of National Flag or to restrict its use is a matter of policy option available to the Parliament and to the government. Since it is a policy option constitutionally permissible, the courts ought not to interfere with the same.

Judgments Cited:

Will of People will prevail

In S.C. *Advocates-on-Record Assn. v. Union of India,*[5] it was held : "Constitution is the "will" of the people whereas the statutory laws are the creation of the legislators who are the elected representatives of the people. Where the will of the legislature-declared in the statutes-stands in opposition to that of the people-declared in the Constitution-the will of the people must prevail."

Constitution must be kept alive:

In *People's Union for Civil Liberties (PUCL) and Anr. etc. v. Union of India and Anr.*[6] Court held:

---

on the exercise of the right conferred by the said sub clause in the interests of the sovereignty and integrity of India, the security of the State, friendly relations with foreign States, public order, decency or morality or in relation to contempt of court, defamation or incitement to an offence

[4] 3. **Prohibition of improper use of certain emblems and names.** Notwithstanding anything contained in any law for the time being in force, no person shall, except in such cases and under such conditions as may be prescribed by the Central Government, use or continue to use, for the purpose of any trade, business, calling or profession, or in the title of any patent, or in any trade mark or design, any name or emblem specified in the Schedule or any colourable imitation thereof without the previous permission of the Central Government or of such officer of Government as may be authorized in this behalf by the Central Government.

[5] AIR1994SC268

[6] [2003]2SCR1136

"...It is established that fundamental rights themselves have no fixed content, most of them are empty vessels into which each generation must pour its content in the light of its experience. The attempt of the court should be to expand the reach and ambit of the fundamental rights by process of judicial interpretation. The Constitution is required to be kept young, energetic and alive".

Speech is God's Gift

In L.I.C. v. Professor Manubhai D. Shah,[7] it was observed :

" Speech is God's gift to mankind. Through speech a human being conveys his thoughts, sentiments and feelings to others. Freedom of speech and expression is thus a natural right which a human being acquires on birth. It is, therefore, a basis human right. Everyone has the right to freedom of opinion and expression: the right includes freedom to hold opinions without interference and to seek and receive and impart information and ideas through any media and regardless of frontiers.

In *Secretary, Ministry of Information and Broadcasting v. Cricket Association of Bengal and Ors.,* [8] it was observed :

"The freedom of speech and expression includes right to acquire information and to disseminate it. Freedom of speech and expression is necessary, for self-expression which is an important means of free conscience and self-fulfilment. It enables people to contribute to debates on social and moral issues. It is the best way to find a truest model of anything, since it is only through it that the widest possible range of ideas can circulate. It is the only vehicle of political discourse so essential to democracy. Equally important is the role if plays in facilitating artistic and scholarly endeavours of all sorts."

Observation by High Court:

The restrictions imposed by the Flag Code on flying the National Flag being not law within the meaning of Clause (2) of Article 19 of the Constitution of India, the same cannot be construed to be a penal provision. Referring to the debates held in the constituent assembly as also a passage from the

---

[7] [1992]3SCR595
[8] [1995]1SCR1036

book titled 'Our National Flag' by K.V. Singh, the High Court observed that the citizens were required to be educated by issue of Flag Code and the National Flag must be flown in a respectful manner and so long as a citizen of India does so, no restriction can be imposed on the basis of instructions contained in the Flag Code.

Decision by Supreme Court:

Court held that- (i) Right to fly the National Flag freely with respect and dignity is a fundamental right of a citizen within the meaning of Article 19(1)(a) of the Constitution of India being an expression and manifestation of his allegiance and feelings and sentiments of pride for the nation; (ii) The fundamental right to fly National Flag is not an absolute right but a qualified one being subject to reasonable restrictions under Clause 2 of Article 19 of the Constitution of India; (iii) The Emblems and Names (Prevention of Improper Use) Act, 1950 and the Prevention of Insults to National Honour Act, 1971 regulate the use of the National Flag ; (iv) Flag Cede although is not a law within the meaning of Article 13(3)(a) of the Constitution of India[9] for the purpose of Clause (2) of Article 19 thereof, it would not restrictively regulate the free exercise of the right of flying the National Flag. However, the Flag Code to the extent it provides for preserving respect and dignity of the National Flag, the same deserves to be followed. (v) For the purpose of interpretation of the constitutional scheme and for the purpose of maintaining a balance between the fundamental/legal rights of a citizen vis-a-vis, the regulatory measures/ restrictions, both Parts IV and IVA of the Constitution of India can be taken recourse to.

Leave granted in the S.L.P (Special Leave Petition).

---

[9] **Article 13(3) in The Constitution Of India 1949**

(3) In this article, unless the context otherwise requires law includes any Ordinance, order, bye law, rule, regulation, notification, custom or usages having in the territory of India the force of law; laws in force includes laws passed or made by Legislature or other competent authority in the territory of India before the commencement of this Constitution and not previously repealed, notwithstanding that any such law or any part thereof may not be then in operation either at all or in particular areas

35

Right to Sleep[1]

Facts in Nutshell:

In 2008, Baba Ramdev was the first person to raise the issue of black money publically. The black money outside the country was estimated at total of Rs. 400 lakh crore or nearly nine trillion US Dollar. On 27th February, 2011, an Anti-Corruption Rally was held at Ramlila Maidan, New Delhi where more than one lakh persons are said to have participated. The persons present at the rally included Baba Ramdev, Acharya Balakrishna, Ram Jethmalani, Anna Hazare and many others. On 20th April, 2011, the President of Bharat Swabhiman Trust, Delhi Pardesh submitted an application to the MCD proposing to take Ramlila Maidan on rent, subject to the general terms and conditions, for holding a yoga training camp for 4 to 5 thousand people between 1st June, 2011 to 20th June, 2011. He had also submitted an application to the Deputy Commissioner of Police (Central District) seeking permission for holding the Yoga Training Camp which permission was granted by the DCP (Central District) vide his letter dated 25th April, 2011. This permission was subject to the terms and conditions stated therein.

Continuing with his agitation for the return of black money to the country, Baba Ramdev wrote a letter to the Prime Minister on 4th May, 2011 stating his intention to go on a fast to protest against the Government's inaction in that regard. The Government made attempts to negotiate with Baba Ramdev and to tackle the problem on the terms, as may be commonly arrived at between the Government and Baba Ramdev. This process started with effect from 19th May, 2011 when the Prime Minister wrote a letter to

---

[1] Appellants: **Ramlila Maidan Incident Vs.** Respondent: **Home Secretary, Union of India (UOI) and Ors.**

2012(1)Crimes241(SC)

Hon'ble Judges: Swatanter Kumar and B.S. Chauhan, JJ.

Baba Ramdev asking him to renounce his fast. The Finance Minister also wrote a letter to Baba Ramdev informing him about the progress in the matter. On 23rd May, 2011, Baba Ramdev submitted an application for holding a dharna at Jantar Mantar, which permission was also granted to him .

On 27th May, 2011, the DCP (Central District), on receiving the media reports about Baba Ramdev's intention to organize a fast unto death at the Yoga Training Camp, made further enquiries from Acharya Virendra Vikram requiring him to clarify the actual purpose for such huge gathering. His response to this, vide letter dated 28th May, 2011, was that there would be no other programme at all, except residential yoga camp. However, the Special Branch, Delhi Police also issued a special report indicating that Baba Ramdev intended to hold indefinite hunger strike along with 30,000-35,000 supporters and that the organizers were further claiming that the gathering would exceed one lakh.

In the meanwhile, large number of followers of Baba Ramdev had gathered at Ramlila Maidan by the afternoon of 4th June, 2011. In the evening of that very day, one of the Ministers who had met Baba Ramdev at the Airport, Mr. Kapil Sibal, made public a letter from Baba Ramdev's camp calling off their agitation. This was not appreciated by Baba Ramdev, as, according to him, the Government had not stood by its commitments and, therefore, he hardened his position by declaring not to take back his satyagraha until a proper Government Ordinance was announced in place of forming a Committee. The ministers talked to Baba Ramdev in great detail but of no avail. It is stated that even the Prime Minister had gone the extra mile to urge Baba Ramdev not to go ahead with the hunger strike, promising him to find a "pragmatic and practical" solution to tackle the issue of corruption. Various attempts were made at different levels of the Government to resolve this issue amicably. Even a meeting of the ministers with Baba Ramdev was held at Hotel Claridges. It was reported by the Press/Media that many others supported the stand of Baba Ramdev.

As already noticed, Baba Ramdev had been granted permission to hold satyagraha at Jantar Mantar, of course, with a very limited number of persons. Despite the assurance given by Acharya Virendra Vikram, the event was converted into an Anshan and the crowd at the Ramlila Maidan swelled to more than fifty thousand. No yoga training was held for the entire day. At about 1.00 p.m., Baba Ramdev decided to march to Jantar Mantar for holding a dharna along with the entire gathering. Keeping in view the fact that Jantar Mantar could not accommodate such a large crowd, the permission dated 24/26th May, 2011 granted for holding the dharna was withdrawn by the authorities. Certain negotiations took place between Baba Ramdev and some of the ministers on telephone, but, Baba Ramdev revived his earlier condition of time-bound action, an ordinance to bring black money back and the items missing on his initial list of demands. At about 11.15 p.m., it is stated that Centre's emissary reached Baba Ramdev at Ramlila Maidan with the letter assuring a law to declare black money hoarded abroad as a national asset. The messenger kept his mobile on so the Government negotiators could listen to Baba Ramdev and his aides. The conversation with Baba Ramdev convinced the Government that Baba Ramdev will not wind up his protest. At about 11.30 p.m., a team of Police, led by the Joint Commissioner of Police, met Baba Ramdev and informed him that the permission to hold the camp had been withdrawn and that he would be detained. At about 12.30 a.m., a large number of CRPF, Delhi Police force and Rapid Action Force personnel, totaling approximately to 5000 (as stated in the notes of the Amicus. However, from the record it appears to be 1200), reached the Ramlila Maidan. At this time, the protestors were peacefully sleeping. Thereafter, at about 1.10 a.m., the Police reached the dais/platform to take Baba Ramdev out, which action was resisted by his supporters. At 1.25 a.m., Baba Ramdev jumped into the crowd from the stage and disappeared amongst his supporters. He, thereafter, climbed on the shoulders of one of his supporters, exhorting women to form a barricade around him. A scuffle between the security forces and the supporters of Baba Ramdev took place and eight rounds of teargas shells were fired. By 2.10 a.m., almost all the supporters had been driven out of the Ramlila Maidan. The Police sent them towards the New Delhi Railway Station. Baba Ramdev, who had disappeared from the dais earlier, was apprehended by the Police near Ranjit Singh Flyover at about 3.40 a.m. At that time, he was dressed in salwar-kameez with a dupatta over his beard. He was taken to the Airport guest-house. It was planned by the Government to fly Baba Ramdev in a chopper from Safdarjung Airport. However, at about 9.50 a.m. the Government shelved this plan and put him in an Indian Air Force helicopter and flew him out of the Indira Gandhi International Airport.

Submissions on behalf of Amicus Curiae[2]

Pointing out certain ambiguities and contradictions in various affidavits filed on behalf of various officers of the Government and the Police, learned amicus curiae pointed out certain factors by way of conclusions:

It may be concluded that

(i) the ground became a major protest area after the government abolished rallies at the Boat Club.

(ii) The police's capacity for Ramlila is 50,000 but it limited Baba Ramdev's meet to 5000.

(iii) The ground appears to be accommodative but with only one major exit and entrance.

(iv) There are aspects of the material that show considerable mobilization. But the figure of 5000 inside the tent is exaggerated.

(v) The numbers of people in the tent has varied but seems, according to the Police 20,000 or so at the time of the incident. But the Home Secretary suggests 60,000 which is an exaggeration.

(vi) The logs etc supplied seem a little haphazard, but some logs reflect contemporary evidence which shows things to the courts notice especially.

The crowd entered the Ramlila Ground from one entrance without any hassle and co- operatively (see CD marked CD003163" of 23 minutes @ 17 minutes) Police was screening each and every individual entering the premises. On 04th June 2011 many TV new (sic) channel live coverage shows about two kilometer long queue to enter the Maidan not even a single was armed, lathi or baseball bats etc. (pg.8 Vol.2)

It was also submitted by amicus Curie

(i) The crowd does not appear to be armed in anway - not even with 'baseball' bats.

(ii) The Police (sic - personnel) were throwing bricks.

---

[2] **Amicus curiae** - an adviser to the court on some matter of law who is not a party to the case; usually someone who wants to influence the outcome of a lawsuit involving matters of wide public interest

(iii) Baba Ramdev was abruptly woken up.

(iv) The crowd was asleep.

(v) The Police used lathis.

(vi) The crowd also threw bricks.

(vii) The Police used tear gas around that time.

viii) Water cannon was also used by the Police.

Submission of learned amicus curiae that passing of the order under Section 144 Cr.PC[3] and the force and brutality with which the persons present at the Ramlila Maidan were dispersed is nothing but a show of power of the State as opposed to a citizen's right. Citizens have a fundamental right

---

[3] The Code of Criminal Procedure, 1973 (CrPc) 144.

Power to issue order in urgent cases of nuisance or apprehended danger.

(1) In cases where, in the opinion of' a District Magistrate, a Sub-divisional Magistrate or any other Executive Magistrate specially empowered by the State Government in this behalf, there is sufficient ground for proceeding under this section and immediate prevention or speedy remedy is desirable, such Magistrate may, by a written order stating the material fact of the case and served in the manner provided by section 134, direct any person to abstain from a certain act or to take certain order with respect to certain property in his possession or under his management, if such Magistrate considers that such direction is likely to prevent, or tends to prevent, obstruction, annoyance or injury to any person lawfully employed, or danger to human life, health or safety, or a disturbance of the public tranquility, or a riot, or an affray.

(2) An order under this section may, in cases of' emergency or in cases where the circumstances do not admit of the serving in due time of a notice upon the person against whom the order is directed, be passed ex-parte.

(3) An order under this section may be directed to a particular individual, or to persons residing in a particular place or area, or to the public generally when frequenting or visiting a particular place or area.

(4) No order under this section shall remain in force for more than two months from the making thereof:

Provided that, if the State Government considers it necessary so to do for preventing danger to human life, health or safety or for preventing a riot or any, affray, it may by notification, direct that an order made by a Magistrate under this section shall remain in force for such further period not exceeding six months from the date on which the order made by the Magistrate would have, but for such order, expired, as it may specify in the faid notification.

(5) Any Magistrate may, either on his own motion or on the application of any person aggrieved, rescind or alter any order made under this section, by himself or any Magistrate Subordinate to him or by his predecessor-in-office.

(6) The State Government may either on its own motion or on the application of any person aggrieved, rescind or alter an order made by it under the proviso to sub-section (4).

(7) Where an application under subsection (5), or sub-section (6) is received, the Magistrate, or the State Government, as the case may be shall afford to the applicant an early opportunity of appearing before him or it, either in person or by pleader and showing cause against the order, and if the Magistrate or the State Government, as the case may be, rejects the application wholly or in part he or it shall record in writing the reasons-for so doing.

to assembly and peaceful protest which cannot be taken away by an arbitrary executive or legislative action. The law prescribes no requirements for taking of permission to go on a fast.

It was contended that Police itself was an unlawful assembly. It had attacked the sleeping persons, after midnight, by trespassing into the property, which had been leased to the Respondent-Trust. The use of teargas, lathi charge, brick-batting and chasing the people out of the Ramlila Maidan were unjustifiable and brutal acts on the part of the Police. It was completely disproportionate not only to the exercise of the rights to freedom of speech and expression and peaceful gathering, but also to the requirement for the execution of a lawful order. The restriction imposed, being unreasonable, its disproportionate execution renders the action of the Police unlawful. This brutality of the State resulted in injuries to a large number of persons and even in death of one of the victims. There has also been loss and damage to the property.

Question Raised before Court:

The question raised before Court included the loss and damage to the person and property that resulted from such unreasonable restriction imposed, its execution and invasion of fundamental right to speech and expression and the right to assembly, as protected under Articles $19(1)(a)^4$ and $19(1)(b)^5$. It was contended that the order was unreasonable, restriction imposed was contrary to law and the entire exercise by the Police and the authorities was an indirect infringement of the rights and protections available to the persons present there, including Article 21 of the Constitution[6].

Order 152 Police Rules:

Standing Order 152 deals particularly with the use of tear smoke in dispersal

---

[4] **Article 19(1) in The Constitution Of India 1949**

(1) All citizens shall have the right

(a) to freedom of speech and expression;

[5] **Article 19(1) in The Constitution Of India 1949**

(1) All citizens shall have the right

(b) to assemble peaceably and without arms;

[6] **Article 21 in The Constitution Of India**

Protection of life and personal liberty No person shall be deprived of his life or personal liberty except according to procedure established by law

of unlawful assemblies and processions. This Standing Order concerns with various aspects prior as well as steps which are required to be taken at the time of use of tear smoke. It requires that before tear smoke action is commenced, a suitable position should be selected for the squad, if circumstances permit, forty yards away from the crowd. A regular warning by the officer should be issued while firing the tear smoke shells, the speed of wind, area occupied by the crowd and the temper of the crowd, amongst others, should be taken into consideration. It states that apparently the object of use of force should be to prevent disturbance of peace or to disperse an unlawful assembly which threatens such disturbance.

When Section 144 Cr.PC[7] can be imposed:

On the bare reading of the language of Section 144 Code of Criminal Procedure, it is clear that the entire basis of an action under this Section is the 'urgency of the situation' and the power therein is intended to be availed for preventing 'disorder, obstruction and annoyance', with a view to secure the public weal by maintaining public peace and tranquility. In the case of *Gulam Abbas v. State of Uttar Pradesh[8]*, the Court clearly stated that preservation of public peace and tranquility is the primary function of the Government and the aforesaid power is conferred on the executive. In a given situation, a private right must give in to public interest.

Article 355 of the Constitution[9] provides that the Government of every State would act in accordance with the provisions of the Constitution. The

---

[7] **The Code of Criminal Procedure, 1973 (CrPc)**

Section 144. Power to issue order in urgent cases of nuisance or apprehended danger.

In cases where, in the opinion of' a District Magistrate, a Sub-divisional Magistrate or any other Executive Magistrate specially empowered by the State Government in this behalf, there is sufficient ground for proceeding under this section and immediate prevention or speedy remedy is desirable, such Magistrate may, by a written order stating the material fact of the case and served in the manner provided by section 134, direct any person to abstain from a certain act or to take certain order with respect to certain property in his possession or under his management, if such Magistrate considers that such direction is likely to prevent, or tends to prevent, obstruction, annoyance or injury to any person lawfully employed, or danger to human life, health or safety, or a disturbance of the public tranquility, or a riot, or an affray.

[8] AIR 1981 SC 2198

[9] **Article 355 in The Constitution Of India 1949**

355. Duty of the Union to protect States against external aggression and internal disturbance
It shall be the duty of the Union to protect every State against external aggression and internal disturbance and to ensure that the government of every State is carried on in accordance with the provisions of this Constitution.

primary task of the State is to provide security to all citizens without violating human dignity. Powers conferred upon the statutory authorities have to be, perforce, admitted. In *H.H. Maharajadhiraja Madhav Rao Jivaji Rao Scindia Bahadur and Ors.* v. *Union of India* [10], Court held that even in civil commotion or even in war or peace, the State cannot act catastrophically outside the ordinary law and there is legal remedy for its wrongful acts against its own subjects or even a friendly alien within the State.

The citizens/persons have a right to leisure; to sleep; not to hear and to remain silent. The knock at the door, whether by day or by night, as a prelude to a search without authority of law amounts to be police incursion into privacy and violation of fundamental right of a citizen.[11]

Decision of Court:

Court held that in the facts of the present case, the State and the Police could have avoided the tragic incident by exercising greater restraint, patience and resilience. The orders were passed by the authorities in undue haste and were executed with force and overzealousness, as if an emergent situation existed. The decision to forcibly evict the innocent public sleeping at the Ramlila grounds in the midnight of 4th/5th June, 2011, whether taken by the police independently or in consultation with the Ministry of Home Affairs is amiss and suffers from the element of arbitrariness and abuse of power to some extent. The restriction imposed on the right to freedom of speech and expression was unsupported by cogent reasons and material facts. It was an invasion of the liberties and exercise of fundamental freedoms. The members of the assembly had legal protections available to them even under the provisions of the Code of Criminal Procedure. Thus, the restriction was unreasonable and unwarrantedly executed. The action demonstrated the might of the State and was an assault on the very basic democratic values enshrined in our Constitution. Except in cases of emergency or the situation unexceptionably demanding so, reasonable notice/ time for execution of the order or compliance with the directions issued in the order itself or in furtherance thereto is the pre-requisite. It was primarily an error of performance of duty both by the police and Respondent No. 4 (Baba Ramdev) but the ultimate sufferer was the public at large.

[10] AIR 1971 SC 530

[11] (See: *Wolf* v. *Colorado* (1948) 338 US 25).

It is believed that a person who is sleeping, is half dead. His mental faculties are in an inactive state. Sleep is an unconscious state or condition regularly and naturally assumed by man and other living beings during which the activity of the nervous system is almost or entirely suspended. It is the state of slumber and repose. It is a necessity and not a luxury. It is essential for optimal health and happiness as it directly affects the quality of the life of an individual when awake inducing his mental sharpness, emotional balance, creativity and vitality. Sleep is, therefore, a biological and essential ingredient of the basic necessities of life. If this sleep is disturbed, the mind gets disoriented and it disrupts the health cycle. If this disruption is brought about in odd hours preventing an individual from getting normal sleep, it also causes energy disbalance, indigestion and also affects cardiovascular health. These symptoms, therefore, make sleep so essential that its deprivation would result in mental and physical torture both. It has a wide range of negative effects. It also impairs the normal functioning and performance of an individual which is compulsory in day-to-day life of a human being. Sleep, therefore, is a self rejuvenating element of our life cycle and is, therefore, part and partial of human life. The disruption of sleep is to deprive a person of a basic priority, resulting in adverse metabolic effects. It is a medicine for weariness which if impeded would lead to disastrous results.

An individual is entitled to sleep as comfortably and as freely as he breathes. Sleep is essential for a human being to maintain the delicate balance of health necessary for its very existence and survival. Sleep is, therefore, a fundamental and basic requirement without which the existence of life itself would be in peril. To disturb sleep, therefore, would amount to torture which is now accepted as a violation of human right. It would be similar to a third degree method which at times is sought to be justified as a necessary police action to extract the truth out of an accused involved in heinous and cold- blooded crimes. It is also a device adopted during warfare where prisoners of war and those involved in espionage are subjected to treatments depriving them of normal sleep.

Court directed the State Government and the Commissioner of Police to register and investigate cases of criminal acts and offences, destruction of private and public property against the police officers/personnel along with those members of the assembly, who threw bricks at the police force causing injuries to the members of the force as well as damage to the property, issued the following directions:

a. Take disciplinary action against all the erring police officers/ personnel who have indulged in brick-batting, have resorted to lathi charge and excessive use of tear gas shells upon the crowd, have exceeded their authority or have acted in a manner not permissible under the prescribed procedures, rules or the standing orders and their actions have an element of criminality. This action shall be taken against the officer/personnel irrespective of what ranks they hold in the hierarchy of police.

b. The police personnel who were present in the pandal and still did not help the evacuation of the large gathering and in transportation of sick and injured people to the hospitals have, in my opinion, also rendered themselves liable for appropriate disciplinary action.

c. The police shall also register criminal cases against the police personnel and members of the gathering at the Ramlila ground (whether they were followers of Baba Ramdev or otherwise) who indulged in damage to the property, brick-batting etc. All these cases have already been reported to the Police Station Kamla Market. The police shall complete the investigation and file a report under section 173 of the Code of Criminal Procedure[12] within three months.

---

[12] **The Code of Criminal Procedure, 1973 (CrPc)**

Section 173 Report of police officer on completion of investigation.

(1) Every investigation under this Chapter shall be completed without unnecessary delay.

(2) (i) as soon as it is completed, the officer in charge of the police station shall forward to a Magistrate empowered to take cognizance of the offence on a police report, a report in the form prescribed by the State Government, stating-

(a) the names of the parties;

(b) the nature of the information;

(c) The names of the persons who appear to be acquainted with the circumstances of the case;

(d) whether any offence appears to have been committed and, if so, by whom;

(e) whether the accused has been arrested;

(f) whether he has been released on his bond and, if so, whether with or without sureties;

(g) whether he has been forwarded in custody under section 170.

Smt. Rajbala, who got spinal injury in the incident and subsequently died, would be entitled to the ad-hoc compensation of Rs. 5 lacs while persons who suffered grievous injuries and were admitted to the hospital would be entitled to compensation of Rs. 50,000/- each and persons who suffered simple injuries and were taken to the hospital but discharged after a short while would be entitled to a compensation of Rs. 25,000/- each. Court also directed that 25% of the awarded compensation shall be paid by the Trust owned by Baba Ramdev (Respondent No-4) because of Contributory Negligence.

(ii) The officer shall also communicate, in such manner as may be prescribed by the State Government, the action taken by him, to the person, if any by whom the information relating to the commission of the offence was first given.

(3) Where a superior officer of police has been appointed under section 158, the report, shall, in any case in which the State Government by general or special order so directs, be submitted through that officer, and he may, pending the orders of the Magistrate, direct the officer in charge of the police station to make further investigation.

(4) Whenever it appears from a report forwarded under this section that the accused has been released on his bond, the Magistrate shall make such order for the discharge of such bond or otherwise as he thinks fit.

36

No use of fire crackers in silence zone[1]

Facts in Nutshell:

Shri Anil K. Mittal, an engineer by profession moving the Court *pro bono publico*[2]. The immediate provocation for filing the petition was that a 13 year old girl was a victim of rape (as reported in newspapers of January 3, 1998). Her cries for help sunk and went unheard due to blaring noise of music over loudspeaker in the neighbourhood. The victim girl, later in the evening, set herself ablaze and died of 100% burn injuries. The petition complains of noise created by the use of the loudspeakers being used in religious performances or singing *bhajans* and the like in busy commercial localities on the days of weekly offs. Best quality hi-fi audio systems are used. Open space, meant for use by the schools in the locality, is let out for use in marriage functions and parties wherein merry making goes on with hi-fi amplifiers and loudspeakers without any regard to timings. Modern residents of the locality organize terrace parties for socializing and use high capacity stereo systems in abundance. These are a few instances of noise pollution generated much to the chagrin of students taking examinations who find it utterly difficult to concentrate on studies before and during examinations. The noise polluters have no regard for the inconvenience and discomfort of the people in the vicinity. Noise pollution has had its victims in the past and continues to have victims today as well. The petitioner invoked

---

[1] Appellants: **Forum, Prevention of Envn. and Sound Pollution Vs.**Respondent: **Union of India (UOI) and Anr.**
AIR2005SC3136

Hon'ble Judges: R. C. Lahoti, C.J. and Ashok Bhan, J.

[2] Pro bono adj. short for pro bono publico, Latin "for the public good," legal work performed by lawyers without pay to help people with legal problems and limited or no funds, or provide legal assistance to organizations involved in social causes such as the environmental, consumers, minorities, youth, battered women and education organizations and charities.

the writ jurisdiction of Court so that there may not be victims of noise pollution in future. The principal prayer is that the existing laws for restricting the use of loudspeakers and other high volume noise producing audio-video systems, be directed to be rigorously enforced.

The Government of India framed and published Noise Pollution Control and Regulation Rules, 1999- On 11.10.2002 the Government of India brought in an amendment in the Rules. The amendment empowered the State Government to permit the use of loudspeaker or public address system during night hours (between 10 pm and 12 pm) on or during the cultural or religious occasions for a limited period not exceeding 15 days.

Some of the interveners have sought for:-

(i) noise created by horns of engines, pressure horns in automobiles, loudspeakers, denting painting of cars, particularly, in residential areas and from unauthorized premises being prohibited;

(ii) use of loudspeakers in religious places such as temples, mosque, churches, gurudwaras and other places being discontinued or at least regulated;

(iii) firecrackers burst during Diwali festival and on other occasions for fun or merry making being prohibited completely, if the noise created exceeds certain decibels and being so regulated as to prevent bursting during night hours.

Article 21 of the Indian Constitution

Article 21 of the Constitution guarantees life and personal liberty to all persons. It is well settled by repeated pronouncements of Court as also the High Courts that right to life enshrined in Article 21 is not of mere survival or existence. It guarantees a right of person to life with human dignity. Therein are included, all the aspects of life which go to make a person's life meaningful, complete and worth living. The human life has its charm and there is no reason why the life should not be enjoyed along with all permissible pleasures. Anyone who wishes to live in peace, comfort and quiet within his house has a right to prevent the noise as pollutant reaching him. No one can claim a right to create noise even in his own premises which would travel beyond his precincts and cause nuisance to neighbours or others. Any noise which has the effect of materially interfering with the ordinary comforts of life judged by the standard of a reasonable man is nuisance. How and when a nuisance created by noise becomes actionable has to be answered by reference to its degree and the surrounding circumstances including the place and the time.

Noise - what it is?

The word noise is derived from the Latin term "nausea". It has been defined as "unwanted sound, a potential hazard to health and communication dumped into the environment with regard to the adverse effect it may have on unwilling ears"

Noise is defined as unwanted sound. Sound which pleases the listeners is music and that which causes pain and annoyance is noise. At times, what is music for some can be noise for others.

According to Encyclopaedia Britannica : "In acoustics 'noise' is defined as 'any undesired sound'."

According to Chambers 20th Century Dictionary, 'noise' means- sound especially of loud, harsh or confused kind; a sound of any kind; an over loud or disturbing sound; frequent or public talk.

In Chambers 21st Century Dictionary, the definition of noise has undergone a change. Noise pollution stands carved out as a phrase separately from noise. The two are defined as under :

"**Noise** - a sound; a harsh disagreeable sound, or such sound; a din. **pollution** - an excessive or annoying degree of noise in a particular area, e.g. from traffic or aeroplane engines."

"Pollution" is a noun derived from the verb "pollute". Section 2 of the Environment (Protection) Act, 1986 defines "environmental pollution" to mean the presence in the environment of any environmental pollutant. Section 2 of the said Act defines "environmental pollutant" to mean any solid, liquid or gaseous substance present in such concentration as may be, or tends to be injurious to environment.

Thus, the disturbance produced in our environment by the undesirable sound of various kinds is called "noise pollution".

Noise as nuisance and health hazard

In the modern days noise has become one of the major pollutants and it has serious effects on human health. Effects of noise depend upon sound's pitch, its frequency and time pattern and length of exposure. Noise has both auditory and non-auditory effects depending upon the intensity and the duration of the noise level. It affects sleep, hearing, communication, mental and physical health. It may even lead to the madness of people.

Disturbance of sleep.

Noise intrusion can cause difficulty in falling asleep and can awaken people who are asleep.

Hearing Loss

"Deafness, like poverty, stunts and deadens its victims."- says Helen Keller. Hearing loss can be either temporary or permanent. *Noise-induced temporary threshold shift* (NIPTS) is a temporary loss of hearing acuity experienced after a relatively short exposure to excessive noise. Pre-exposure hearing is recovered fairly rapidly after cessation of the noise. *Noise induced permanent threshold shift* (NIPTS) is an irreversible loss of hearing that is caused by prolonged noise exposure. Both kinds of loss together with presbyacusis, the permanent hearing impairment that is attributable to the natural aging process, can be experienced simultaneously.

NIPTS occurs typically at high frequencies, usually with a maximum loss at around 4,000 Hz. It is now accepted that the risk of hearing loss is negligible at noise exposure levels of less than 75 dB(A) Leq (8-hr). Based on national judgments concerning acceptable risk, many countries have adopted industrial noise exposure limits of 85 dB(A) +5 dB(A) in their regulations and recommended practices. [N.B.- Hz. is abbreviation of Hertz which is the unit of frequency, equal to one cycle per second. Hertz (Hz) is the name, by international agreement, for the number of repetitions of similar pressure variations per second of time; this unit of frequency was previously called "cycles per second" (cps or c/s)].

Effect on performance

Noise can change the state of alertness of an individual and may increase or decrease efficiency. Performance of tasks involving motor or monotonous activities is not always degraded by noise. At the other extreme, mental activities involving vigilance, information gathering and analytical processes appear to be particularly sensitive to noise.

Noise pollution in the special context of Fireworks

Fireworks are used all over the world to celebrate special occasions. In India, fireworks are burst on festivals like Dussehra, Diwali and on special occasions like social gatherings, marriages, Independence day, Republic day, New year day, etc. In other countries of the world, fireworks are generally burst either on the New Year day or on the birthday of their respective countries. However, bursting of firecrackers is a health hazard since it is responsible for both air pollution and noise pollution.

The use of Fireworks has led to air pollution in the form of noise and smoke. Their excessive use has started to be a public hazard and violation of their fundamental rights as enshrined in the Constitution of India.

It has been held in the case of *Om Birangana Religious Society v. State*[3], that the "Freedom of speech and expression guaranteed under Article 19 of the Constitution of India includes, by necessary implication, freedom not to listen and/or to remain silent. A citizen has a right to leisure, right to sleep, right not to hear and right to remain silent. He also has the right to read and speak with others". Because of the tremendous sound and noise, the citizens cannot exercise all these fundamental rights.

Statutory Laws in India

Indian Penal Code

Noise pollution can be dealt under Sections 268[4], 290[5] and 291[6] of the Indian

---

[3] MANU/WB/0105/1996

[4] **Section 268 in The Indian Penal Code, 1860**

268. Public nuisance.— A person is guilty of a public nuisance who does any act or is guilty of an illegal omission which causes any common injury, danger or annoyance to the public or to the people in general who dwell or occupy property in the vicinity, or which must necessarily cause injury, obstruction, danger or annoyance to persons who may have occasion to use any public right. A common nuisance is not excused on the ground that it causes some convenience or advantage.

[5] **Section 290 in The Indian Penal Code, 1860 290.** Punishment for public nuisance in cases not otherwise provided for.- Whoever commits a public nuisance in any case not otherwise punishable by this **Code**, shall be punished with fine which may extend to two hundred rupees.

Penal Code, as a public nuisance. Under Section 268 of this Code, it is mentioned that 'A person is guilty of a public nuisance who does any act or is guilty of an illegal omission which causes any common injury, danger or annoyance to the public or the people in general who dwell or occupy property in the vicinity, or which must necessarily cause injury, obstruction, danger or annoyance to persons who may have occasion to use any public right.

A common nuisance is not excused on the ground that it causes some convenience or advantage.' Sections 290 and 291 of the Indian Penal Code deal with the punishment for public nuisance.

Criminal Procedure Code

Under Section 133 of the Code of Criminal Procedure, 1973[7] the magistrate has the power to make conditional order requiring the person causing nuisance to remove such nuisance.

---

[6] **Indian Penal Code (IPC) Section 291.**

Continuance of nuisance after injunction to discontinue

Whoever repeats or continues a public nuisance, having been enjoined by any public servant who has lawful authority to issue such injunction not to repeat or continue such nuisance, shall be punished with simple imprisonment for a term which may extend to six months, or with fine, or with both.

CLASSIFICATION OF OFFENCE

Punishment—Simple imprisonment for 6 months, or fine, or both—Cognizable-Bailable—Triable by any Magistrate—Non-compoundable.

[7] **The Code of Criminal Procedure, 1973 (CrPc)**

133 Conditional order for removal of nuisance.

(1) Whenever a District Magistrate or a Sub-Divisional Magistrate or any other Executive Magistrate specially empowered in this behalf by the State Government on receiving the report of a police officer or other information and on taking such evidence (if any) as he thinks fit, considers —

(a) that any unlawful obstruction or nuisance should be removed from any public place or from any way, river or channel, which is or may be lawfully used by the public; or

(b) that the conduct of any trade or occupation or the keeping of any goods or merchandise; is injurious to the health or physical comfort of the community, and that in consequence such trade or occupation should be prohibited or regulated or such, goods or merchandise should be removed or the keeping thereof regulated; or

(c) that the construction of any building, or the disposal of any substance, as is likely to occasion conflagration or explosion, should be prevented or stopped; or

(d) that any building, tent or structure, or any tree is in such a condition that it is likely to fall and thereby cause injury to persons living or carrying on business in the neighborhood or passing by, and that in consequence the removal, repair or support of such building, tent or structure, or the removal or support of such tree, is necessary; or

(e) that any tank, well or excavation adjacent to any such way or public place should be fenced in such manner as to prevent danger arising to the public; or

Motor Vehicles Act, 1988, and Rules framed thereunder

Rules 119 and 120 of the Central Motor Vehicles Rules, 1989, deal with reduction of noise.

Judicial Opinion In India

In *Ivour Heyden v. State of Andhra Pradesh* [8], the High Court of Andhra Pradesh excused the act of playing radio loudly on the ground that it was a trivial act. Careful reading of Section95 of IPC[9] shows that only that harm is excused which is not expected to be complained by the person of ordinary temper and sense.

In *Free Legal Aid Cell Shri Sugan Chand Aggarwal alias Bhagatji v. : Govt. of NCT of Delhi and Ors.*,[10] it was said that "Pollution

---

(f) that any dangerous animal should be destroyed, confined or otherwise disposed of,

Such Magistrate may make a conditional order requiring the person causing such obstruction or nuisance, or carrying on such trade or occupation, or keeping any such goods or merchandise, or owning, possessing or controlling such building, tent, structure, substance, tank, well or excavation, or owning or possessing such animal or tree, within time to be fixed in the order-

(i) to remove such obstruction or nuisance; or

(ii) to desist from carrying on, or to remove or regulate in such manner as may be directed, such trade or occupation, or to remove such goods or merchandise, or to regulate the keeping thereof in such manner as may be directed; or

(iii) to prevent or stop the construction of such building, or to alter the disposal of such substance; or

(iv) to remove, repair or support such building, tent or structure, or to remove or support such trees; or

(v) to fence such tank, well or excavation; or

(vi) to destroy, confine or dispose of such dangerous animal in the manner provided in the said order;

or, if he objects so to do, to appear before himself or some other Executive Magistrate Subordinate to him at a time and place to be fixed by the order, and show cause, in the manner hereinafter provided, why the order should not be made absolute.

(2) No order duly made by a Magistrate under this section shall be called in question in any civil court.

Explanation. A "public place" includes also property belonging to the state, camping grounds and grounds left unoccupied for sanitary or recreative purposes.

[8] 1984 Cr LJ 16 (NOC)

[9] **Indian Penal Code (IPC)**

Section 95. Act causing slight harm

Nothing is an offence by reason that it causes, or that it is intended to cause, or that it is known to be likely to cause, any harm, if that harm is so slight that no person of ordinary sense and temper would complain of such harm.

[10] AIR2001Delhi455

being wrongful contamination of the environment which causes material injury to the right of an individual, noise can well be regarded as a pollutant because it contaminates environment, causes nuisance and affects the health of a person and would therefore, offend Article 21, if it exceeds a reasonable limit."

Noise standards for fire- crackers

1.(i) The manufacture, sale or use of firecrackers generating noise level exceeding 125 dB(AI) or 145 dB(C)pk at 4 meters distance from the point of bursting shall be prohibited.

(ii) For individual fire-cracker constituting the series (joined fire-crackers), the above mentioned limit be reduced by $5 \log 10(N)$ dB, where N = number of crackers joined together."

(2) The use of fireworks or fire-crackers shall not be permitted except between 6.00 a.m. and 10.00p.m. No firework or firecracker shall be allowed between 10.00 p.m. and 6.00 a.m.

(3) Firecrackers shall not be used at any time in silence zones, as defined in S.O. 1046(E) issued on 22.11.2000 by the Ministry of Environment and Forests. In the said Notification Silence Zone has been defined as: *"Silence Zone is an area comprising not less than 100 meters around hospitals, educational institutions, courts, religious places or any other area which is declared as such by the competent authority."*

(4) The State Education Resource Centers in all the States and the Union Territories as well as the management/principals of schools in all the States and Union Territories shall take appropriate steps to educate students about the ill effects of air and noise pollution and appraise them of directions (1) to (3) above."

Decision of Court

"The use of fireworks or firecrackers shall not be permitted except between 6.00 a.m. and 10.p.m. No fireworks or firecrackers shall be used between 10.00 p.m. and 6.00 a.m. The Government of India, has also expressed its opinion that there should be no relaxation in the time limit for bursting firecrackers. Relaxation of restrictions on bursting of crackers from 10.00 p.m. to 6.00 a.m. shall not be given as it is night time. During the night time, people sleep and the high level of noise has deleterious effects on the health and well being of the people." The total restriction on bursting firecrackers between 10 pm and 6 am must continue without any relaxation in favour of anyone.

Whether such restriction is violative of Article 25 of the Constitution[11] ?

The Court by restricting the time of bursting the firecrackers has not in any way violated the religious rights of any person as enshrined under Article 25 of the Constitution. The festival of Diwali is mainly associated with pooja performed on the auspicious day and not with firecrackers. In no religious text book it is written that Diwali has to be celebrated by bursting crackers. Diwali is considered as a festival of lights, not of noises. Shelter in the name of religion cannot be sought for, for bursting firecrackers and that too at odd hours.

Directions/Guidelines of Court:

I. Firecrackers

1. The Department of Explosives may divide the firecrackers into two categories- (i) Sound emitting firecrackers, and (ii) Colour/light emitting firecrackers.

2. There shall be a complete ban on bursting sound emitting firecrackers between 10 pm and 6 am. It is not necessary to impose restrictions as to time on bursting of colour/light emitting firecrackers.

---

[11] **Article 25 in The Constitution Of India 1949**

25. Freedom of conscience and free profession, practice and propagation of religion

(1) Subject to public order, morality and health and to the other provisions of this Part, all persons are equally entitled to freedom of conscience and the right freely to profess, practise and propagate religion

(2) Nothing in this article shall affect the operation of any existing law or prevent the State from making any law

(a) regulating or restricting any economic, financial, political or other secular activity which may be associated with religious practice;

(b) providing for social welfare and reform or the throwing open of Hindu religious institutions of a public character to all classes and sections of Hindus Explanation I The wearing and carrying of kirpans shall be deemed to be included in the profession of the Sikh religion Explanation II In sub clause (b) of clause reference to Hindus shall be construed as including a reference to persons professing the Sikh, Jaina or Buddhist religion, and the reference to Hindu religious institutions shall be construed accordingly

3. Every manufacturer shall on the box of each firecracker mention details of its chemical contents and that it satisfies the requirement as laid down by DOE. In case of a failure on the part of the manufacturer to mention the details or in cases where the contents of the box do not match the chemical formulae as stated on the box, the manufacturer may be held liable.

4. Firecrackers for the purpose of export may be manufactured bearing higher noise levels subject to the following conditions: (i) The manufacturer should be permitted to do so only when he has an export order with him and not otherwise;(ii) The noise levels for these firecrackers should conform to the noise standards prescribed in the country to which they are intended to be exported as per the export order; (iii) These firecrackers should have a different colour packing, from those intended to be sold in India; (iv) They must carry a declaration printed thereon something like 'not for sale in India' or 'only for export to country AB' and so on.

II. Loudspeakers

1. The noise level at the boundary of the public place, where loudspeaker or public address system or any other noise source is being used shall not exceed 10 dB(A) above the ambient noise standards for the area or 75 dB(A) whichever is lower.

2. No one shall beat a drum or tom-tom or blow a trumpet or beat or sound any instrument or use any sound amplifier at night (between 10. 00 p.m. and 6.a.m.) except in public emergencies. 3. The peripheral noise level of privately owned sound system shall not exceed by more than 5 dB(A) than the ambient air quality standard specified for the area in which it is used, at the boundary of the private place.

III. Vehicular Noise

No horn should be allowed to be used at night (between 10 p.m. and 6 a.m.) in residential areas except in exceptional circumstances.

IV. Awareness

1. There is a need for creating general awareness towards the hazardous effects of noise pollution. Suitable chapters may be added in the text-books which teach civic sense to the children and youth at the initial/early level of education. Special talks and lectures be organised in the schools to highlight the menace of noise pollution and the role of the children and younger generation in preventing it. Police and civic administration should be trained to understand the various methods to curb the problem and also the laws on the subject.

2. The State must play an active role in this process. Residents Welfare Associations, Service Clubs and Societies engaged in preventing noise pollution as a part of their projects need to be encouraged and actively involved by the local administration.

3. Special public awareness campaigns in anticipation of festivals, events and ceremonial occasions whereat firecrackers are likely to be used, need to be carried out.

Generally

The States shall make provision for seizure and confiscation of loudspeakers, amplifiers and such other equipments as are found to be creating noise beyond the permissible limits.

37

Public Trust Doctrine[1]

Facts in Nutshell:

Court took notice of the News item appearing in the "Indian Express" dated February 25, 1996 under the caption – "Kamal Nath dares the mighty Beas to keep his dreams afloat". The relevant part or the news item is as under:

Kamal Nath's family has direct links with a private company, Span Motels Private Limited, which owns a resort - Span Resorts - for tourists in the Kullu-Manali valley. The problem is with another ambitious venture floated by the same company - Span Club.

The club represents Kamal Nath's dream of having a house on the bank of the Beas in the shadow of the snow-capped Zanskar ranges. The club was built after encroaching upon 27.12 bighas of land, including substantial forest land, in 1990. The land was later regularised and leased out to the company on April 11, 1994. The regularisation was done when Mr. Kamal Nath was Minister of Environment and Forests. ...The swollen Beas changed its course and engulfed the Span Club and the adjoining lawns, washing it away.

The motel has constructed 190m wire crates on the bank of the river (upstream). The dredged material is piled up on the banks of the river. The dredging and channelising of the left bank has been done on a large scale with a view to keep high intensity of flow away from the motel. The dredging of the main channel of river was done by blasting the big boulders and removing the debris. The mouth of the natural relief/spill channel has been

---

[1] Appellants: **M.C. Mehta Vs.** Respondent: **Kamal Nath and Ors.**
(1997)1SCC388
Hon'ble Judges: Kuldip Singh and S. Saghir Ahmad, JJ.

blocked by wire crates and dumping of boulders. The construction work was not done under expert advice. The construction work undertaken by the motel for channelising the main course has divided the main stream into two, one of which goes very near to the left bank because of which, according to the report, fresh land slip in future cannot be ruled out.

The forest lands which have been given on lease to the Motel by the State Governments are situated at the bank of the river Beas. Beas is a young and dynamic river. It runs through Kullu valley between the mountain ranges of the Dhauladhar in the right bank and the Chandrakheni in the left. The river is fast - flowing, carrying large boulders, at the time of flood. When water velocity is not sufficient to carry the boulders, those are deposited in the channel often blocking the flow of water. Under such circumstances the river stream changes its course, remaining within the valley but swinging from one bank to the other. The right bank of the river Beas where motel is located mostly comes under forest, the left bank consists of plateaus, having steep - bank facing the river, where fruit orchards and cereal cultivation are predominant. The area being ecologically fragile and full of scenic-beauty should not have been permitted to be ' converted into private ownership and for commercial gains.

Doctrine of Public Trust:

The ancient Roman Empire developed a legal theory known as the "Doctrine of the Public Trust". It was founded on the ideas that certain common properties such as rivers, sea-shore, forests and the air were held by Government in trusteeship for the free and unimpeded use of the general public. Under the Roman Law these resources were either owned by no one (Res Nullious) or by every one in common (Res Communious). Under the English common law, however, the Sovereign could own these resources but the ownership was limited in nature, the Crown could not grant these properties to private owners if the effect was to interfere with the public interests in navigation of fishing. Resources that were suitable for these uses were deemed to be held in trust by the Crown for the benefit of the public, Joseph L. Sax, Professor of Law, University of Michigan proponent of the Modern Public Trust Doctrine in an erudite article "Public Trust Doctrine in natural resource law; effective judicial intervention"[2] has given the historical background of the Public Trust Doctrine as under:

---

[2] Michigan Law Review Vol. 68 Part-I page 473

The source of modern public trust law is found in a concept that received much attention in Roman and English law - the nature of property rights in rivers, the sea, and the seashore. That history has been given considerable attention in the legal literature, need not be repeated in detail here. But two points should be emphasized. First, certain interests, such as navigation and fishing, were sought to be preserved for the benefit of the public, accordingly, property used for the those purposes was distinguished from general public property which the sovereign could routinely grant to private owners. Second, while it was understood that in certain common properties - such as the seashore, highways, and running water - "perpetual use was dedicated to the public," it has never been clear whether the public had an enforceable right to prevent infringement of those interests. Although the state apparently did protect public uses, no evidence is available that public rights could be legally asserted against a recalcitrant government.

The Public Trust Doctrine primarily rests on the principle that certain resources like air, sea, waters and the forests have such a great importance to the people as a whole that it would be wholly unjustified to make them a subject of private ownership. The said resources being a gift of nature. They should be made freely available to everyone irrespective of the status in life. The doctrine enjoins upon the Government to protect the resources for the enjoyment of the general public rather than to permit then- use for private ownership or commercial purposes. According to Professor Sax the Public Trust Doctrine imposes the following restrictions on governmental authority:

Three types of restrictions on governmental authority are often thought to be imposed by the public trust: first, the property subject to the trust must not only be used for a public purpose, but it must be held available for use by the general public; second, the property may not be sold, even for a fair cash equivalent; and third, the property must be maintained for particular types of uses.

Our Indian legal system-based on English Common Law - includes the public trust doctrine as part of its jurisprudence. The State is the trustee of all natural resources which are by nature meant for public use and enjoyment. Public at large is beneficiary of the sea-shore, running waters, airs, forests and ecologically fragile lands. The State as a trustee is under a legal duty to protect the natural resources. These resources meant for public use cannot be converted into private ownership.

Observation of Court (para 28):

Court observed that the issues presented in the present case illustrate the classic struggle between those members of the public who would preserve our rivers, forests, parks and open lands in their pristine purity and those charged with administrative responsibilities who, under the pressures of the changing needs of an increasing complex society, find it necessary to encroach to some extent open lands heretofore considered in-violate to change. The resolution of this conflict in any given case is for the legislature and not the courts. If there is a law made by Parliament or the State Legislature the courts can serve as an instrument of determining legislative intent in the exercise of its powers of judicial review under the Constitution. But in the absence of any legislation, the executive acting under the doctrine of public trust cannot abdicate the natural resources and convert them into private ownership or for commercial use. The esthetic use and the pres time glory of the natural resources, the environment and the eco-systems of our country cannot be permitted to be eroded for private, commercial or any other use unless the courts find it necessary in good faith, for the public good and in public interest to encroach upon the said resources.

Decision of the Court:

Court held that the Himachal Pradesh Government committed patent breach of public trust by leasing the ecologically fragile land to the Motel management. Both the lease - transactions are in patent breach of the trust held by the State Government.

Court has also referred *Vellore Citizens Welfare Forum v. Union of India and Ors.*[3], explained the "Precautionary Principle" and "Polluters Pays principle" as under:

Some of the salient principles of "Sustainable Development", as culled out from Brundtland Report and other international documents, are inter-Generational Equity, Use and Conservation of Natural Resources, Environmental Protection, the Precautionary Principle, Polluter pays principle,

---

[3]   AIR1996SC2715

Obligation to assist and cooperate, Eradication of Poverty and Financial Assistance to the developing countries. But courts are, however, of the view that "the Precautionary Principle" and "the Polluter Pays" principle are essential features of "Sustainable Development". The "precautionary Principle" - in the context of the municipal law - means:

(i)   Environment measures - by the State Government and the statutory authorities - must anticipate, prevent and attack the causes of environmental degradation.

(ii) Where there are threats of serious and irreversible damage, lack of scientific certainty should not be used as a reason for postponing measures to prevent environmental degradation.

(iii) The "Onus of proof" is on the actor or the developer/industrialist to show that his action is environmentally benign.

The Polluter Pays principle has been held to be a sound principle by Court in *Indian Council for Environ-Legal Action v. Union of India*[4]. The Court observed, "We are of the opinion that any principle evolved in this behalf should be simple, practical and suited to the conditions obtaining in this country". The Court ruled that "Once the activity carried on is hazardous or inherently dangerous, the persons carrying on such activity is liable to make good the loss caused to any other person by his activity irrespective of the fact whether he took reasonable care while carrying on his activity. The rule is premised upon the very nature of the activity carried on". Consequently the polluting industries are "absolutely liable to compensate for the harm caused by them to villagers in the affected area, to the soil and to the underground water and hence, they are bound to take all necessary measures to remove sludge and other pollutants lying in the affected areas". The "Polluter Pays" principle as interpreted by Court means that the absolute liability for harm to the environment extends not only the compensate the victims of pollution but a.lso the cost of restoring the environmental degradation. Remediation of the damaged environment is part of the process of "Sustainable Development" and as such polluter is liable to pay the cost to the individual sufferers as well as the cost of reversing the damaged ecology.

---

[4]   [1996]2SCR503

The precautionary principle and the polluter pays principle have been accepted as part of the law of the land. It is thus settled by Court that one who pollutes the environment must pay to reverse the damage caused by his acts.

Directions of the Court:

1. The public trust doctrine, is a part of the law of the land.

2. The prior approval granted by the Government of India, Ministry of Environment and Forest by the letter dated November 24, 1993 and the lease-deed dated April 11, 1994 in favour of the Motel were quashed. The lease granted to the Motel by the said lease-deed in respect of 27 bighas and 12 biswas of area, is cancelled and set aside. The Himachal Pradesh Government shall take over the area and restore it to its original-natural conditions.

3. The Motel shall pay compensation by way of cost for the restitution of the environment and ecology of the area. The pollution caused by various constitutions made by the Motel in the river bed and the banks on the river Beas has to be removed and reversed.

4. The Motel through its management shall show cause why pollution fine in addition be not imposed on the Motel.

5. The Motel shall construct a boundary wall at a distance of not more than four meters from the cluster of rooms (main building of the Motel) towards the river basin. The boundary wall shall be on the area of the Motel which is covered by the lease dated September 29, 1981. The Motel shall not encroach/cover/utilise any part of the river basin. The boundary wall shall separate the Motel building from the river basin. The river bank and the river basin shall be left open for the public use.

6. The Motel shall not discharge untreated effluent into the river.

7. The Himachal Pradesh Pollution Control Board shall not permit the discharge of untreated effluent into river Beas. The Board shall inspect all the hotels/institutions/factories in Kullu- Manali area and in case any of them are discharging untreated effluent/waste into the river, the Board shall take action in accordance with law.

Court Ordered Span Motels Pvt. Ltd. to pay Rs Ten Lakh as exemplary damages.

38

Fundamental Right to Education[1]

Facts in Nutshell:

The writ petitions filed by private educational institutions engaged in or proposing to engage in imparting medical and engineering education - the correctness of the decision rendered by a Division Bench comprising Kuldip Singh and R.M. Sahai, JJ. in Miss *Mohini Jain v. State of Karnataka and Ors*[2]. is called in question. The petitioners, running medical/engineering colleges in the States of Andhra Pradesh, Karnataka, Maharashtra and Tamil Nadu, say that if Mohini Jain is correct and is followed and implemented by the respective State Governments as indeed they are bound to they will have to close down; no other option is left to them.

Question before the Court:

1. Whether a citizen has a Fundamental Right to education for a medical, engineering or other professional degree.

2. Whether the Constitution of India guarantees a fundamental right to education to its citizens?

3. Whether there is a fundamental right to establish an educational institution under Article 19(1)(g)[3]?

---

[1] Appellants: **Unni Krishnan, J.P. and others etc. etc. Vs.** Respondent: **State of Andhra Pradesh and others etc. etc.**

AIR1993SC2178

Hon'ble Judges: L. M. Sharma, C.J., S. Ratnavel Pandian, S. Mohan, B.P. Jeevan Reddy and S. P. Bharucha,

[2] 1992 AIR 1858

[3] **Article 19(1)(g) in The Constitution Of India 1949**

(g) to practise any profession, or to carry on any occupation, trade or business

Right to Life

The Court Interpreted in *Bandhua Mukti Morcha v. Union of India* [4]: It is the fundamental right of everyone in this country, assured under the interpretation given Article 21[5] by the Court in Francis Mullin's case, to live with human dignity, free from citation. This right to live with human dignity enshrined in Article 21 derives its life breath the Directive Principles of State Policy and particularly Clauses (e) and (f) of Article 39[6] Articles 41[7] and 42[8] and at the least, therefore, it must include protection of the health and strength of workers, men and women, and of the tender age of children against abuse, unities and facilities for children to develop in a healthy manner and in conditions of freedom and dignity, educational facilities, just and humane conditions of work and maternity relief. These are the minimum requirements which must exist in order to enable a person to (with human dignity and no State - neither the Central Government nor any State eminent has the right to take any action which will deprive a person of the enjoyment basic essentials. Since the Directive Principles of State Policy contained in Clauses (e) and (f) of Article 39, Articles 41 and 42 are not enforceable in a court of law, it may not be possible to compel the State through the judicial process to make provision by statutory enactment or executive fiat for ensuring these basic essentials which go to make up a life of dignity but where legislation is already enacted by the State providing these basic requirements to the workmen and thus investing their right to

---

[4] (3) SCC 161

[5] **Article 21 in The Constitution Of India 1949**

21. Protection of life and personal liberty No person shall be deprived of his life or personal liberty except according to procedure established by law

[6] **Article 39 Certain principles of policy to be followed by the State.**

(e) That the health and strength of workers, men and women, and the tender age of children are not abused and that citizens are not forced by economic necessity to enter avocations unsuited to their age or strength

[(f) That children are given opportunities and facilities to develop in a healthy manner and in conditions of freedom and dignity and that childhood and youth are protected against exploitation and against moral and material abandonment.]

[7] **Article 41 - Right to work, to education and to public assistance in certain cases.**

The State shall, within the limits of its economic capacity and development, make effective provision for securing the right to work, to education and to public assistance in cases of unemployment, old age, sickness and disablement, and in other cases of undeserved want.

[8] **Article 42 – provision for just and humane conditions of work and maternity relief**

The State shall make provision for securing just and humane conditions of work and for maternity relief

live with basic human dignity, concrete reality and content, the State can certainly be obligated to ensure observance of legislation for inaction on the part of the State in securing implementation of such Nation would amount to denial of the right to live with human dignity enshrined in Article 21, more so in the context of Article 256 which provides that the executive power of every State so exercised as to ensure compliance with the laws made by Parliament and any 's which apply in that State.

In Bandhua Mukti Morcha Court held that the right to life guaranteed by Article 21 does take in "educational facilities".

Right to Education and Right to Life[9]

Right to life is the compendious expression for all those rights which the courts must enforce because they are basic to the dignified enjoyment of life. It extends to the full range of conduct which the individual is free to pursue. The right to education flows directly from right to life. The right to life under Article 21 and the dignity of an individual cannot be assured unless it is accompanied by the right to education. The State Government is under an obligation to make endeavor to provide educational facilities at all levels to its citizens.

Right to education after the child/citizen completes the age of 14 years.

The right to free education is available only to children until they complete the age of 14 years. Thereafter, the obligation of the State to provide education is subject to the limits of its economic capacity and development[10].

The expression 'professional colleges' in the scheme includes:

(i) medical colleges, dental colleges and other institutions and colleges imparting Nursing, Pharmacy and other courses allied to Medicine, established and/or run by private education institutions,

(ii) colleges of engineering and colleges and institutions imparting technical education including electronics, computer sciences, established and/or run by private education institutions, and

---

[9] *Mohini Jain Vs State of Karnataka and ors.*1992 AIR 1858
[10] *Francis C. Mullin Administrator vs Union Territory of* Delhi 1981CriLJ306

(iii) such other colleges to which this scheme is made applicable by the Government, recognising and/or affiliating authority.

Whether there is a fundamental right to establish an educational institution. Article 19(1)(g). That reads as follows: To practice any profession, or to carry on any occupation, trade or business,

The question before the court was: what is the meaning to be attributed to the words "profession", "occupation", "trade" or "business".

In P. Ramanatha Aiyar's Law Lexicon Reprint Edition 1987 at page 897 "Occupation" means:

The principal business of one's life, vocation, calling, trade, the business which a man follows to procure a living or obtain wealth: that which occupies or engages one's time or attention, vocation, employment, calling, trade; the business in which a man is usually engaged, to the knowledge of his neighbour.

According to Black's Law Dictionary Fifth Edition at page 973 "Occupation" means:

Possession; control; tenure; use. The act or process by which real property is possessed and enjoyed. Where a person exercises physical control over land.

That which principally takes up one's time thought, and energies, especially, one's regular business or employment; also, whatever one follows as the means of making a livelihood. Particular business, profession, trade, or calling which engages individual's time and efforts; employment in which one regularly engages or vocation of his life.

In *P. V.G. Raju v. Commissioner of Expenditure*[11] it is observed thus:

The activity termed as "Occupation", if of wider import than vocation or profession. It is also distinct from a hobby which can be resorted to only in leisure hours for the purpose of killing time. Occupation, therefore, is that with which a person occupies himself either temporarily or permanently or for a considerable period with continuity of activity. It is analogous to a business, calling or pursuit. A person may have more than one occupation in

---

[11] 36 ITR . 267

a previous year. The Occupations may be seasonal or for the whole year.

The meaning of "business' can be gathered from Law Lexicon Edition 1987 by Ramnath Iyer:

Business is that which engages the time, talent and interest of a man" and is what a man proposes to himself. There may be a "Business" without pecuniary profit being at all contemplated.

In *State of Andhra Pradesh -vs- Abdul Bakshi*[12]

The expression "business" though extensively used as a word of indefinite import, in taxing statutes it is used in the sense of an occupation, or profession which occupies the time, attention and labour of a person, normally with the object of making profit. To regard an activity as business there must be a course of dealings, either actually continued or contemplated to be continued with a profit motive, and no for sport of pleasure.

The expression "Business" includes every Trade, occupation, or profession. Section 2(b) of the Indian Partnership Act, 1932[13] also defines "Business" thus: Business includes every trade, occupation and profession.

In **Ahmedabad St. Xaviers College Society** v. **State of Gujarat** [14] it was observed:

The right to establish and administer educational institutions of their choice has been conferred on religious and linguistic minorities so that the majority who can always have their right by having proper legislation do not pass a legislation prohibiting minorities to establish and administer educational institutions of their choice. If the scope of Article 30(1)[15] is made an extension of the right under Article 29(1)[16] as the right to establish and administer educational institutions for giving religious instruction or for imparting education in their religious teachings or tenets

---

[12] [1964]7SCR664

[13] **Section 2(b) in The Indian Partnership Act, 1932**

(b) " business" includes every trade, occupation and profession;

[14] [1975]1SCR173

[15] **Article 30- Right of minorities to establish and administer educational institutions.**

Article 30(1) All minorities, whether based on religion or language, shall have the right to establish and administer educational institutions of their choice.

the fundamental right of minorities to establish and administer educational institution of their choice will be taken away.

In *R.M.D.C. v. State till Bombay* [17], it was held that imparting education cannot be treated as trade or business. Education cannot be allowed to be converted into commerce nor can the petitioners seek to obtain the said result by relying upon the wider meaning of "occupation". The content of the ' expression "occupation" has to be ascertained keeping in mind the fact that Clause (g) employs all the four expressions viz., profession, occupation, trade and business.

It is significant to notice the words "to practice any profession". [18] Establishing educational institutions can by no stretch of imagination be treated as "practicing any profession". Teaching may be as profession but establishing an institution, employing teaching and non-teaching staff, procuring the necessary intrastate for running a school or college is not 'practising profession'. It may be anything but not practising a profession.

Case Referred— *Mohini Jain vs State of Karnataka and Ors* [19]

Miss Mohini Jain, a non-Karnataka student (she was from Meerut in Uttar Pradesh) applied for admission in M.B.B.S. course in one of the private medical colleges in Karnataka. She was informed by the college that if she pays Rs. 60,000/- towards the first year's tuition fee and furnishes a Bank guarantee for the fees payable for the remaining years of the M.B.B.S. course, she will be admitted. Her parents were not in a position to pay the same and hence she could not be admitted. Her further case, which was denied by the Management of the college, was that she was asked to pay a capitation fee of Rs. 4,50,000/- as a condition of admission. She approached

---

[16] **Article 29- Protection of Interests of Minorities**

(1) Any section of the citizens residing in the territory of India or any part thereof having a distinct language, script or culture of its own shall have the right to conserve the same.

(2) No citizen shall be denied admission into any educational institution maintained by the State or receiving aid out of State funds on grounds only of religion, race, caste, language or any of them.

[17] [1957]1SCR874

[18] *Employees v. Industrial Tribunal* A.I.R. 1962 S.C. 1085.

[19] 1992 AIR 1858

the Court under Article 32[20] challenging the aforesaid notification of the Karnataka Government and asking for a direction to be admitted on payment of the same fee as was payable by the Karnataka students admitted against the "Government Seats".

Questions before the Court in Mohini Jain Case:

(i) Is there a 'right to education' guaranteed to the people of India under the Constitution? If so, does the concept of 'capitation fee' infarct the same?

(ii) Whether the charging of capitation fee in consideration of admission to educational institutions is arbitrary, unfair, unjust and as such violates the equality clause contained in Article 14 of the Constitution[21]?

(iii) Whether the impugned notification permits the Private Medical Colleges to charge capitation fee in the guise of regulating fees under the Act? And

(iv) Whether the notification is violative of the provisions of the Act which in specific terms prohibits the charging of capitation fee by any educational institution in the State of Karnataka?

Decision of Court in Mohini Jain Case

On the first question, the Bench held, on a consideration of Articles 21[22], 38[23], 39(a)[24] and (f)[25], 41[26] and 45[27] of the constitution:

    (a) the framers of the Constitution made it obligatory for the State to provide education for citizens";

---

[20] **Article 32- Remedies for enforcement of rights conferred by this part**

(1) The right to move the Supreme Court by appropriate proceedings for the enforcement of the rights conferred by this Part is guaranteed.

(2) The Supreme Court shall have power to issue directions or orders or writs, including writs in the nature of habeas corpus, mandamus, prohibition, quo warranto and certiorari, whichever may be appropriate, for the enforcement of any of

(3) Without prejudice to the powers conferred on the Supreme Court by clauses (1) and (2), Parliament may by law empower any other court to exercise within the local limits of its jurisdiction all or any of the powers exercisable by the Supreme Court under clause (2).

(4) The right guaranteed by this article shall not be suspended except as otherwise provided for by this Constitution.

[21] **Article 14- Equality before Law**

The State shall not deny to any person equality before the law or the equal protection of the laws within the territory of India.

[22] **Article 21- Protection of Life and Personal Liberty**

No person shall be deprived of his life or personal liberty except according to procedure established by law.

(b) the objectives set forth in the preamble to the Constitution cannot be achieved unless education is provided to the citizens of this country;

(c) the preamble also assures dignity of the individual. Without education, dignity of the individual cannot be assured;

(d) Parts III and IV of the Constitution are supplementary to each other. Unless the 'right to education' mentioned in Article 41 is made a reality, the fundamental rights in part III will remain beyond the reach of the illiterate majority;

(e) Article 21 has been interpreted by this Court to include the right to live with human dignity and all that goes along with it. The "right to education' flows directly from right to life." In other words, 'right to education' is concomitant to the fundamental rights enshrined in part II the Constitution. The State is under a constitutional mandate to provide educational Institutions at all levels for the benefit of citizens." The benefit of education cannot be confined to richer classes.

---

[23] **Article 38- State to secure a social order for the promotion of welfare of the people**

[(1)] The State shall strive to promote the welfare of the people by securing and protecting as effectively as it may a social order in which justice, social, economic and political, shall inform all the institutions of the national life.

[(2) The State shall, in particular, strive to minimise the inequalities in income, and endeavour to eliminate inequalities in status, facilities and opportunities, not only amongst individuals but also amongst groups of people residing in different areas or engaged in different vocations.]

[24] **Article 39 –Certain principles of policy to be followed by state**

39 (a) That the citizens, men and women equally, have the right to an adequate means of livelihood;

[25] **Article 39- Certain principles of policy to be followed by state**

39 (f) That children are given opportunities and facilities to develop in a healthy manner and in conditions of freedom and dignity and that childhood and youth are protected against exploitation and against moral and material abandonment

[26] **Article 41- Right to work, to education and to public assistance in certain cases.**

The State shall, within the limits of its economic capacity and development, make effective provision for securing the right to work, to education and to public assistance in cases of unemployment, old age, sickness and disablement, and in other cases of undeserved want.

[27] **Article-45 Provision for early childhood care and education to children below the age of six years**

Provision for early childhood care and education to children below the age of six years.

The State shall endeavours to provide early childhood care and education for all children until they complete the age of six years.

(f) Capitation fee is nothing but a consideration for admission. The concept of "teaching hops" is alien to our Constitutional scheme. Education in India has never been a commodity for sale.

(g) "Court held that every citizen has a "right to education' under the Constitution.

The State is under an obligation to establish educational institutions to enable the citizens to enjoy the said right. The State may discharge its obligation through state-owned for state-recognized educational institutions. When the State Government grants recognition to the private educational institutions it creates an agency to fulfill its obligation under the Constitution. The students are given admission to the educational institutions - whether state-owned or state-recognised - in recognition of their "right to education' under the Constitution. Charging capitation fee in consideration of admission to educational institutions, is a patent denial of citizen's right to education under the Constitution.

On the second question, the bench held that "the State action in permitting capitation fee be charged by state-recognised educational institutions is wholly arbitrary and as such violative of Article 14 of the Constitution of India.... The Capitation fee brings to the fore a clear class bias." Admission of no meritorious students by charging capitation fees - in any form whatsoever strikes at the very root of the constitutional scheme and our educational system. D.P. Joshi does not come to the rescue of the private institutions.

On the third question, the Bench held that having regard to the scheme of the Act, charging of Rs. 60,000/- for admission is "nothing but a capitation fee". The private medical colleges have further been given a free hand in the matter of admission of non-Karnataka students irrespective merit. It held further: "if the State Government fixes Rs. 2000 per annum as the tuition fee in government colleges and for "Government Seats" in private medical colleges then it is the state responsibility to see that any private college which has been set up with Government permission being run with Government recognition is prohibited from charging more than Rs. 2000 from any student who may be resident of any part of India. When the State Government permits private medical college to be set up and recognises its curriculum and degrees then the said college is performing a function which under the Constitution has been assigned to the State Government. Court held that Rs. 60,000 per annum permitted to be charged from Indian students from outside Karnataka in Para 1 (d) of the notification is not tuition fee but in fact a capitation fee and as such cannot be sustained and is liable to be struck down."

Decision of the Court with regard to Fundamental Right to Education:

1. The citizens of this country have a fundamental right to education. The said right flows from Article 21. This right is, however, not an absolute right. Its content and para meters have to be determined in the light of Articles 45 and 41. In other words every child/citizen of this country has a right to free education until he completes the age of fourteen years. Thereafter his right to education is subject to the limits of economic capacity and development of the State

2. The obligations created by Articles 41, 45 and 46 of the Constitution can be discharged by the State either by establishing institutions of its own or by aiding, recognising and/or granting affiliation to private educational institutions. Where aid is not granted to private educational institutions and merely recognition or affiliation is granted it may not be insisted that the private education institution shall charge only that fee as is charged for similar courses in governmental institutions. The private educational institutions have to and are entitled to charge a higher fee, not exceeding the ceiling fixed in that behalf. The admission of students and the charging of fee in these private educational institutions shall be governed by the scheme evolved herein - set out in Part-Ill of this Judgment.

3. A citizen of this country may have a right to establish an educational institution but no citizen, person or institution has a right much less a fundamental right, to affiliation or recognition or to grant-in-aid from the State. The recognition and/or affiliation shall be given by the State subject only to the conditions set out in, and only accordance with the scheme continued in Part-Ill of this Judgment. No Government/University or authority shall be competent to grant

recognition or affiliation except in accordance with the said scheme. The said scheme shall constitute a condition of such recognition or affiliation, as the case may be, in addition to such other conditions and terms which such Government, University or other authority may choose to impose. Those receiving aid shall, however, be subject to all such terms and conditions, as the aid giving authority may impose in the interest of general public.

39

Eleven Guidelines to be followed in all cases of Arrest and Detention[1]

Ratio Decidendi[2]: *"Where right is one guaranteed by State, it is against the State that the remedy must be sought if there has been a failure to discharge the constitutional obligation imposed."*

Facts in Nutshell:

The Executive Chairman, Legal Aid Services, West Bengal, a non-political organisation registered under the Societies Registration Act, on 26th August, 1986 addressed a letter to the Chief Justice of India drawing his attention to certain news items published in the Telegraph dated 20, 21 and 22 of July, 1986 and in the Statesman and Indian Express dated 17th August, 1986 regarding deaths in police lock-ups and custody. The Executive Chairman after reproducing the news items submitted that it was imperative to examine the issue in depth and to develop "custody jurisprudence" and formulate modalities for awarding compensation to the victim and/or family members of the victim for atrocities and death caused in police custody and to provide for accountability of the officers concerned. It was also stated in the letter that efforts are often made to hush up the matter of lock-up deaths and thus the crime goes unpunished and "flourishes". It was requested that the letter along with the news items be treated as a writ petition under "public interest litigation" category.

---

[1] Appellants: **D.K.Basu Vs.** Respondent: **State of West Bengal**
AIR1997SC610

Hon'bleJudges: Kuldip Singh and Dr. A. S. Anand, JJ.

[2] **Meaning of Ratio Decidendi**

Ratio decidendi is a Latin phrase meaning "the reason" or "the rationale for the decision." The *ratio decidendi* is "[t]he point in a case which determines the judgment" or "the principle which the case establishes."

Considering the importance of the issue raised in the letter and being concerned by frequent complaints regarding custodial violence and deaths in police lock up, the letter was treated as a writ petition and notice was issued to the respondents.

Reply of Respondents:

In response to the notice, the State of West Bengal filed a counter. It was maintained that the police was not hushing up any matter of lock-up death and that wherever police personnel were found to the responsible for such death, action was being initiated against them. The respondents characterised the writ petition as misconceived, misleading and untenable in law.

Suggestion by Law Commission:

The Law Commission of India in response to the notice issued by Court forwarded a copy of the 113th Report regarding "Injuries in police custody and suggested incorporation of Section 114-B in the Indian Evidence Act[3]."

The Universal Declaration of Human Rights in 1948, which marked the emergence of a worldwide trend of protection and guarantee of certain basic human rights, stipulates in Article 5 that "No one shall be subjected to torture[4] or to cruel, inhuman or degrading treatment or punishment."

Fundamental rights occupy a place of pride in the Indian Constitution

Article 21 provides "no person shall be deprived of his life or personal liberty except according to procedure established by law". Personal liberty, thus, is a sacred and cherished right under the Constitution. The expression "life or personal liberty" has been held to include the right to live with human

---

[3] **Section 114 in The Indian Evidence Act, 1872**

Court may presume existence of certain facts. The Court may presume the existence of any fact which it thinks likely to have happened, regard being had to the common course of natural events, human conduct and public and private business, in their relation to the facts of the particular case. Illustrations The Court may presume—

(b) that an accomplice is unworthy of credit, unless he is corroborated in material particulars;

[4] "Torture" has not been defined in the Constitution or in other penal laws. 'Torture' of a human being by another human being is essentially an instrument to impose the will of the 'strong' over the 'weak' by suffering. The word torture today has become synonymous with the darker side of the human civilisation.

Torture is a wound in the soul so painful that sometimes you can almost touch it, but it is also such intangible that there is no way to heal it. Torture is anguish squeezing in your chest, cold as ice and heavy as a stone paralyzing as sleep and dark as the abyss. Torture is despair and fear and rage and hate. It is a desire to kill and destroy including yourself. —Adriana P. Bartow

dignity and thus it would also include within itself a guarantee against torture and assault by the State or its functionaries. Article 22 guarantees protection against arrest and detention in certain cases and declares that no person who is arrested shall be detained in custody without being informed of the grounds of such arrest and he shall not be denied the right to consult and defend himself by a legal practitioner of his choice. Clause (2) of Article 22 directs that the person arrested and detained in custody shall be produced before the nearest Magistrate within a period of 24 hours of such arrest, excluding the time necessary for the journey from the place of arrest to the court of the Magistrate. Article 20(3) of the Constitution lays down that a person accused of an offence shall not be compelled to be a witness against himself. These are some of the constitutional safeguards provided to a person with a view to protect his personal liberty against any unjustified assault by the State. In tune with the constitutional guarantee a number of statutory provisions also seek to protect personal liberty, dignity and basic human rights of the citizens. Chapter V of Criminal Procedure Code, 1973 deals with the powers of arrest of a person and the safeguards which are required to be followed by the police to protect the interest of the arrested person. Section 41, Cr. P.C.[5] confers powers on any police officer to arrest a person under the circumstances specified therein without any order or a

---

[5] **The Code of Criminal Procedure, 1973 (CrPc)**

When police may arrest without warrant.

(1) Any police officer may without an order from a Magistrate and without a warrant, arrest any person :-

(a) who has been concerned in any cognizable offence, or against whom a reasonable complaint has been made, or credible information has been received, or a reasonable suspicion exists, of his having been so concerned; or

(b) who has in his possession without lawful excuse, the burden of proving which excuse shall lie on such person, any implement of house-breaking; or

(c) who has been proclaimed as an offender either under this Code or by order of the State Government; or

(d) in whose possession anything is found which may reasonably be suspected to be stolen property and who may reasonably be suspected of having committed an offence with reference to such thing; or

(e) who obstructs a police officer while in the execution of his duty, or who has escaped, or attempts to escape, from lawful custody; or

(f) who is reasonable suspected of being a deserter from any of the Armed Forces of the Union; or

(g) who has been concerned in, or against whom a reasonable complaint has been made, or credible information has been received, or a reasonable suspicion exists, of his having been concerned in, any act committed at any place out of India which, if committed in India, would have been punishable as an offence, and for which he is, under any law relating to extradition, or otherwise, liable to be apprehended or detained in custody in India; or

warrant of arrest from a Magistrate. Section 46[6] provides the method and manner of arrest. Under this Section no formality is necessary while arresting a person. Under Section 49,[7] the police is not permitted to use more restraint than is necessary to prevent the escape of the person. Section 50[8] enjoins every police officer arresting any person without warrant to communicate to him the full particulars of the offence for which he is arrested and the grounds for such arrest. The police officer is further enjoined to inform the person arrested that he is entitled to be released on bail and he may arrange for sureties in the event of his arrest for a non-bailable offence. Section 56[9] contains a mandatory provision requiring this police officer making an arrest without warrant to produce the arrested person before a Magistrate without unnecessary delay and Section 57[10] echoes Clause (2) of Article 22 of the Constitution of India. There are some other provisions also

---

[6] **The Code of Criminal Procedure, 1973 (CrPc)**
Arrest how Made
(1) In making an arrest the police officer or other person making the same shall actually touch or confine the body of the person to be arrested, unless there be a submission to the custody by word or action.
(2) If such person forcibly resists the endeavour to arrest him, or attempts to evade the arrest, such police officer or other person may use all means necessary to effect the arrest.
(3) Nothing in this section gives a right to cause the death of a person who is not accused of an offence punishable with death or with imprisonment for life.

[7] **The Code of Criminal Procedure, 1973 (CrPc)**
No unnecessary restraint.
The person arrested shall not be subjected to more restraint than is necessary to prevent his escape.

[8] **The Code of Criminal Procedure, 1973 (CrPc)**
Person arrested to be informed of grounds of arrest and of right to bail.
(1) Every police officer or other person arresting any person without warrant shall forthwith communicate to him full particulars of the offence for which he is arrested or other grounds for such arrest.
(2) Where a police officer arrests without warrant any person other than a person accused of a non-bailable offence, he shall inform the person arrested that he is entitled to be released on bail and that he may arrange for sureties on his behalf.

[9] **The Code of Criminal Procedure, 1973 (CrPc)**
Person arrested to be taken before Magistrate or officer in charge of police station.
A police officer making an arrest without warrant shall, without unnecessary delay and subject to the provisions herein contained as to bail, take or send the person arrested before a Magistrate having jurisdiction in the case, or before the officer in charge of a police station.

[10] **The Code of Criminal Procedure, 1973 (CrPc)**
Person arrested not to be detained more than twenty-four hours.
No police officer shall detain in custody a person arrested without warrant for a longer period than under all the circumstances of the case is reasonable, and such period shall not, in the absence of a special order of a Magistrate under section 167, exceed twenty four hours exclusive of the time necessary for the journey from the place of arrest to the Magistrate's court.

like Sections 53[11] 54[12] and 167[13] which are aimed at affording procedural safeguards to a person arrested by the police. Whenever a person dies in custody of the police, Section 176[14] requires the Magistrate to hold an enquiry into the cause of death.

Recommendations by National Police Commission

The Third Report of the National Police Commission in India expressed its deep concern with custodial violence and lock-up deaths. It appreciated the demoralising effect which custodial torture was creating on the society as a whole. It made some very useful suggestions. It suggested:

---

[11] The Code of Criminal Procedure, 1973 (CrPc).

Examination of accused by medical practitioner at the request of police officer.

(1) When a person is arrested on a charge of committing an offence of such a nature and alleged to have been committed under such circumstances that there are reasonable grounds for believing that an examination of his person will afford evidence as to the commission of an offence, it shall be lawful for a registered medical practitioner, acting, at the request of a police officer not below the rank of sub-inspector, and for- any person acting in good faith in his aid and -under his direction, to make such all examination of the person arrested as is reasonably necessary in order to ascertain the facts which may afford such evidence, and to use such force as is reasonably necessary for that purpose.

(2) Whenever the person of a female is to be examined under this section, the examination shall be made only by, or under the supervision of, a female registered medical practitioner.

[12] The Code of Criminal Procedure, 1973 (CrPc)

Examination of arrested person by medical practitioner at the request of the arrested person.

When a person who is arrested, whether on a charge or otherwise, alleges, at the time when he is produced before a Magistrate or at any time during the period of his detention in custody that the examination of his body will afford evidence which will disprove the commission by him of any offence or which will establish the commission by any other person of any offence against his body, the Magistrate shall, if requested by the arrested person so to do direct the examination of the body of such person by a registered medical practitioner unless the Magistrate considers that the request is made for the purpose of vexation or delay or for defeating the ends of justice.

[13] The Code of Criminal Procedure, 1973 (CrPc)

Procedure when investigation cannot be completed in twenty-four hours.

(1) Whenever any person is arrested and detained in custody, and it appears that the investigation cannot be completed within the period of twenty-four hours fixed by section 57, and there are grounds for believing that the accusation or information is well-founded, the officer in charge of the police station or the police officer making the investigation, if he is not below the rank of sub-inspector, shall forthwith transmit to the nearest Judicial Magistrate a copy of the entries in the diary hereinafter prescribed relating to the case, and shall at the same time forward the accused to such Magistrate.

(2) The Magistrate to whom an accused person is forwarded under this section may, whether he has or not jurisdiction to try the case, from time to time, authorise the detention of the accused in such custody as such Magistrate thinks fit, a term not exceeding fifteen days in the whole; and if he has no jurisdiction to try the case or commit it for trial, and considers further detention unnecessary, he may order the accused to be forwarded to a Magistrate having such

...An arrest during the investigation of a cognizable[15] case may be considered justified in one or other of the following circumstances:

(i)   The case involves a grave offence like murder, dacoity, robbery, rape etc., and it is necessary to arrest the accused and bring his movements under restraint to infuse confidence among the terror stricken victims.

(ii) The accused is likely to abscond and evade and the processes of law.

(iii) The accused is given to violent behavior and is likely to commit further offences unless his movements are brought under restraint.

(iv) The accused is a habitual offender and unless kept in custody he is likely to commit similar offences again. It would be desirable to insist through departmental instructions that a police officer making an arrest should also record in the case diary the reasons for making the arrest, thereby clarifying his conformity to the specified guidelines....

---

[14] **The Code of Criminal Procedure, 1973 (CrPc)**
Inquiry by Magistrate into cause of death
When the case is of the nature referred to in clause (i) or clause (ii) of sub-section (3) of section 174], the nearest Magistrate empowered to hold inquests shall, and in any other case mentioned in sub-section (1) of section 174, any Magistrate so empowered may hold an inquiry into the cause of death either instead of, or in addition to, the investigation held by the police officer; and if he does so, he shall have all the powers in conducting it which he would have in holding an inquiry into an offence.

[(1A) Where,-

(I) any person dies or disappears, on

(II) rape is alleged to have been committed on any woman,

while such person or woman is in the custody of the police or in any other custody authorised by the Magistrate or the Court, under this Code in addition to the enquiry or investigation held by the police, an inquiry shall be held by the Judicial Magistrate or the Metropolitan Magistrate, as the case may be, within whose local jurisdiction the offence has been committed.]

(2) The Magistrate holding such inquiry shall record the evidence taken by him in connection therewith in any manner hereinafter prescribed according to the circumstances of the case.

(3) Whenever such Magistrate considers it expedient to make an examination of the dead body of any person who has been already interred, in order to discover the causes of his death, the Magistrate may cause the body to be disinterred and examined.

(4) Where an inquiry is to be held under this section, the Magistrate shall, wherever practicable, inform the relatives of the deceased whose names and addresses are known, and shall allow them to remain present at the inquiry.

[15] "cognizable offence" means an offence for which, and "cognizable case" means a case in which, a police officer may, in accordance with the First Schedule or under and other law for the time being in force, arrest without warrant.

Cases Referred:

In *Joginder Kumar v. State*[16], considered the dynamics of misuse of police power of arrest and opined:

No arrest can be made because it is lawful for the police officer to do so. The existence of the power of arrest is one thing. The justification for the exercise of it is quite another.... No arrest should be made without a reasonable satisfaction reached after some investigation about the genuineness and bonafides of a complaint and a reasonable belief both as to the person's complicity and even so as to the need to effect arrest. Denying a person his liberty is a serious matter.

Decision of Court —ordered requirements to be followed in all cases of Arrest and Detention:

(1) The police personnel carrying out the arrest and handling the interrogation of the arrestee should bear accurate, visible and clear identification and name tags with their designations. The particulars of all such police personnel who handle interrogation of the arrestee must be recorded in a register.

(2) That the police officer carrying out the arrest of the arrestee shall prepare a memo of arrest at the time of arrest and such memo shall be attested by atleast one witness, who may be either a member of the family of the arrestee or a respectable person of the locality from where the arrest is made. It shall also be counter signed by the arrestee and shall contain the time and date of arrest.

(3) A person who has been arrested or detained and is being held in custody in a police station or interrogation center or other lock-up, shall be entitled to have one friend or relative or other person known to him or having interest in his welfare being informed, as soon as practicable, that he has been arrested and is being detained at the particular place, unless the attesting witness of the memo of arrest is himself such a friend or a relative of the arrestee.

(4) The time, place of arrest and venue of custody of an arrestee must be notified by the police where the next friend or relative of the arrestee lives outside the district or town through the Legal Aid Organisation in the District

---

[16] 1994CriLJ1981

and the police station of the area concerned telegraphically within a period of 8 to 12 hours after the arrest.

(5) The person arrested must be made aware of this right to have someone informed of his arrest or detention as soon as he is put under arrest or is detained.

(6) An entry must be made in the diary at the place of detention regarding the arrest of the person which shall also disclose the name of the next friend of the person who has been informed of the arrest and the names and particulars of the police officials in whose custody the arrestee is.

(7) The arrestee should, where he so requests, be also examined at the time of his arrest and major and minor injuries, if any present on his/her body, must be recorded at that time. The "Inspection Memo" must be signed both by the arrestee and the police officer effecting the arrest and its copy provided to the arrestee.

(8) The arrestee should be subjected to medical examination by a trained doctor every 48 hours during his detention in custody by a doctor on the panel of approved doctors appointed by Director, Health Services of the concerned State or Union Territory. Director, Health Services should prepare such a penal for all Tehsils and Districts as well.

(9) Copies of all the documents including the memo of arrest, referred to above, should be sent to the illaqa Magistrate for his record.

(10) The arrestee may be permitted to meet his lawyer during interrogation, though not throughout the interrogation.

(11) A police control room should be provided at all district and state headquarters, where information regarding the arrest and the place of custody of the arrestee shall be communicated by the officer causing the arrest, within 12 hours of effecting the arrest and at the police control room it should be displayed on a conspicuous notice board.

The requirements mentioned above were forwarded to the Director General of Police and the Home Secretary of every State/Union Territory and it shall be their obligation to circulate the same to every police station under their charge and get the same notified at every police station at a conspicuous place.

40

Any member of public acting bona fide can file writ petition[1]

Facts in Nutshell:

The petitioner[2] is an organization dedicated to the cause of release of bonded labourers in the country. The petitioner made a survey of some of the stone quarries in Faridabad district near the city of Delhi and found that there were a large number of labourers from Maharashtra, Madhya Pradesh, Uttar Pradesh and Rajasthan who were working in these stone quarries under "inhuman and intolerable conditions" and many of whom were bonded labourers. The petitioner therefore addressed a letter to Judges pointing out that in the mines a large number of labourers were languishing under abject conditions of bondage for last about ten years.

The letter dated 25th February 1982 addressed by the petitioner was treated as a writ petition under article 32 of the Constitution[3] and by an order Court issued notice on the writ petition and appointed two advocates, as commissioners to visit the stone quarries and to interview each of the persons.

---

[1] Appellants: **Bandhua Mukti Morcha Vs.** Respondent: **Union of India (UOI) and Ors.** AIR1984SC802

   Hon'ble Judges: A. N. Sen, P. N. Bhagwati and R.S. Pathak, JJ.

[2] Someone who gives a court an official document in which they ask it to take legal action

[3] Article 32 in so far it is material is in the following terms :

   Article 32(1) : The right to move the Supreme Court by appropriate proceedings for the enforcement of the rights conferred by this Part is guaranteed.

   (2) : The Supreme Court shall have power to issue directions or orders or writs, including writ in the nature of habeas corpus, mandamus, prohibition, quo warranto and certiorari, whichever may be appropriate, for the enforcement of any of the rights conferred by this Part.

System of Bonded Labour

The system of bonded labour has been prevalent in various parts of the country since long prior to the attainment of political freedom and it constitutes an ugly and shameful feature of our national life. This system under which one person can be bonded to provide labour to another for years and years until an alleged debt is supposed to be wiped out which never seems to happen during the life time of the bonded labourer, is totally incompatible with the new egalitarian socio-economic order which we have promised to build and it is not only an affront to basic human dignity but also constitutes gross and revolting violation of constitutional values. Article 23 of the Constitution[4] which prohibits "traffic in human beings and begar and other similar forms of forced labour" practised by any one. The system of bonded labour therefore stood prohibited by Article 23 and there could have been no more solemn and effective prohibition than the one enacted in the Constitution in Article 23. But, it appears that though the Constitution was enacted as far back as 26th January, 1950 and many years passed since then, no serious effort was made to give effect to Article 23 and to stamp out the shocking practice of to bonded labour. It was only in 1976 that Parliament enacted the Banded Labour System (Abolition) Act, 1976 providing for the abolition of bonded labour system with a view to preventing the economic and physical exploitation of the weaker sections of the people. There are still a number of bonded labourers in various parts of the country and significantly, as pointed out in the Report of the National Seminar on "Identification and Rehabilitation of Bonded Labour" a large number of them belong to Scheduled Castes and Scheduled Tribes account for the next largest number while the few who are not from Scheduled Castes or Scheduled Tribes are generally landless agricultural labourers.

---

[4] **Article 23 in The Constitution Of India 1949**

23. Prohibition of traffic in human beings and forced labour

(1) Traffic in human beings and begar and other similar forms of forced labour are prohibited and any contravention of this provision shall be an offence punishable in accordance with law

(2) Nothing in this article shall prevent the State from imposing compulsory service for public purpose, and in imposing such service the State shall not make any discrimination on grounds only of religion, race, caste or class or any of them

Bonded Labour System (Abolition) Act 1976.

The expression 'bonded labourer' is defined in Clause (f) to mean "a labourer who incurs, or has or is presumed to have incurred a bonded debt". Clause (g) defines "bonded labour system" to mean : The system of forced, or partly forced, labour under which a debtor enters, or has, or is presumed to have, entered, into an agreement with the creditor to the effect that,-

(i) in consideration of an advance obtained by him or by any of his lineal ascendants or descendants (whether or not such advance is evidenced by any document) and in consideration of the interest, if any, due on such advance, or

(ii) in pursuance of any customary or social obligation, or

(iii) for any economic consideration received by him or by any of his lineal ascendants or descendants, or he would-

(1) render, by himself or through any member of his family, or any person dependent on him, labour or service to the creditor, or for the benefit of the creditor, for a specified period or for an unspecified period, either without wages or for nominal wages, or

(2) forfeit the freedom of employment or other means of livelihood for a specified period or for an un-specified period, or

(3) forfeit the right to move freely throughout the territory of India, or

(4) forfeit the right to appropriate or sell at market value any of his property of his product of his labour or the labour of a member of his family or any person dependent on him.

Article 32 of the Constitution

Article 32(1) : The right to move the Supreme Court by appropriate proceedings for the enforcement of the rights conferred by this Part is guaranteed.

(2) : The Supreme Court shall have power to issue directions or orders or writs, including writ in the nature of habeas corpus, mandamus, prohibition, quo warranto and certiorari, whichever may be appropriate, for the enforcement of any of the rights conferred by this Part.

Clause (1) of Article 32confers the right to move the Supreme Court for enforcement of any of the fundamental rights[5], but it does not say as to who shall have this right to move the Supreme Court nor does it say by what proceedings the Supreme Court may be so moved. There is no limitation in the words of Clause (1) of Article 32 that the fundamental right which is sought to be enforced by moving the Supreme Court should be one belonging to the person who moves the Supreme Court nor does it say that the Supreme Court should be moved only by a particular kind of proceeding. *It is clear on the plain language of Clause (1) of Article 32that whenever there is a violation of a fundamental right, any one can move the Supreme Court for enforcement of such fundamental right.*

Then again Clause (1) of Article 32 says that the Supreme Court can be moved for enforcement of a fundamental right by any 'appropriate' proceeding. There is no limitation in regard to the kind of proceeding envisaged in Clause (1) of Article 32 except that the proceeding must be "appropriate" and this requirement of appropriateness must be judged in the light of the purpose for which the proceeding is to be taken, namely,

---

[5] The six fundamental rights recognized by the constitution are:

1) Right to equality, including equality before law, prohibition of discrimination on grounds of religion, race, caste, sex or place of birth, and equality of opportunity in matters of employment, abolition of untouchability and abolition of titles.

2) Right to freedom which includes speech and expression, assembly, association or union or cooperatives, movement, residence, and right to practice any profession or occupation (some of these rights are subject to security of the State, friendly relations with foreign countries, public order, decency or morality), right to life and liberty, right to education, protection in respect to conviction in offences and protection against arrest and detention in certain cases.

3) Right against exploitation, prohibiting all forms of forced labour, child labour and traffic in human beings;

4) Right to freedom of religion, including freedom of conscience and free profession, practice, and propagation of religion, freedom to manage religious affairs, freedom from certain taxes and freedom from religious instructions in certain educational institutes.

5) Cultural and Educational rights preserving Right of any section of citizens to conserve their culture, language or script, and right of minorities to establish and administer educational institutions of their choice.

6) Right to constitutional remedies for enforcement of Fundamental Rights. Fundamental rights for Indians have also been aimed at overturning the inequalities of pre-independence social practices. Specifically, they have also been used to abolish untouchability and hence prohibit discrimination on the grounds of religion, race, caste, sex, or place of birth. They also forbid trafficking of human beings and forced labour. They also protect cultural and educational rights of ethnic and religious minorities by allowing them to preserve their languages and also establish and administer their own education institutions.

Right to property was originally a fundamental right, but is now a legal right.

enforcement of a fundamental right. The Constitution makers deliberately did not lay down any particular form of proceeding for enforcement of a fundamental right nor did they stipulate that such proceeding should conform to any rigid pattern or straight jacket formula as, for example, in England, because they knew that in a country like India where there is so much of poverty, ignorance, illiteracy, deprivation and exploitation, any insistence on a rigid formula of proceeding for enforcement of a fundamental right would become self-defeating because it would place enforcement of fundamental rights beyond the reach of the common man and the entire remedy for enforcement of fundamental rights which the Constitution makers regarded as so precious and invaluable that they elevated it to the status of a fundamental right, would become a more rope of sand so far as the large masses of the people in this country are concerned. The Constitution makers therefore advisedly provided in Clause (1) of Article 32that the Supreme Court may be moved by any 'appropriate' proceeding, 'appropriate' not in terms of any particular form but 'appropriate' with reference to the purpose of the proceeding.

Cases Referred

In *S.P. Gupta v. Union of India (* Judges Appointment and Transfer Case)[6] Court for the first time took the view that where a person or class of persons to whom legal injury is caused by reason of violation of a fundamental right is unable to approach the court for judicial redress on account of poverty or disability or socially or economically disadvantaged position, any member of the public acting bona fide can move the court for relief under Article 32 and a fortiorari, also under Article 226[7], so that the fundamental rights may become

---

[6] [1982]2SCR365

[7] **Article 226 of the Indian Constitution, 1950**: Power of High Courts to issue certain writs.

(1) Notwithstanding anything in Article 32 every High Court shall have powers, throughout the territories in relation to which it exercise jurisdiction, to issue to any person or authority, including in appropriate cases, any Government, within those territories directions, orders or writs, including writs in the nature of habeas corpus, mandamus, prohibitions, quo warranto and certiorari, or any of them, for the enforcement of any of the rights conferred by Part III and for any other purpose.

(2) The power conferred by clause (1) to issue directions, orders or writs to any Government, authority or person may also be exercised by any High Court exercising jurisdiction in relation to the territories within which the cause of action , wholly or in part, arises for the exercise of such power, notwithstanding that the seat of such Government or authority or the residence of such person is not within those territories.

meaningful not only for the rich and the well-to-do who have the means to approach the court but also for the large masses of people who are living a life of want and destitution and who are by reason of lack of awareness, assertiveness and resources unable to seek judicial redress. Where a member of the public acting bona fide moves the Court for enforcement of a fundamental right on behalf of a person or class of persons who on account of poverty or disability or socially or economical disadvantaged position cannot approach the court for relief, such member of the public may move the court even by just writing a letter, because it would not be right or fair to expect a person acting pro bono publico to incur expenses out of his own pocket for going to a lawyer and preparing a regular writ petition for being filed in court for enforcement of the fundamental right of the poor and deprived sections of the community and in such a case, a letter addressed by him can legitimately be regarded as an "appropriate' proceeding.

In *Asiad Construction Worker*[8] case that the State is under a constitutional obligation to see that there is no violation of the fundamental right of any person, particularly when he belongs to the weaker sections of the community and is unable to wage a legal battle against a strong and powerful opponent who is exploiting him. The Central Government is therefore bound to ensure observance of various social welfare and labour laws enacted by Parliament for the purpose of securing to the workmen a life of basic human dignity in compliance with the Directive Principles of State Policy.

---

(3) Where any party against whom an interim order, whether by way of injunction or stay or in any other manner, is made on, or in any proceedings relating to, a petition under clause (1), without-

(a) furnishing to such party copies of such petition and all documents in support of the plea for such interim order; and

(b) giving such party an opportunity of being heard, makes an application to the High Court for the vacation of such order and furnishes a copy of such application to the party in whose favor such order has been made or the counsel of such party, the High Court shall dispose of the application within a period of two weeks from the date on which it is received or from the date on which the copy of such application is so furnished, whichever is later, or where the High Court is closed on the last day of that period, before the expiry of the next day afterwards on which the High Court is open; and if the application is not so disposed of, the interim order shall, on the expiry of that period, or , as the case may be, the expiry of the aid next day, stand vacated.

(4) The power conferred on a High Court by this article shall not be in derogation of the power conferred on the Supreme court by clause (2) of Article 32.

[8] (1982)IILLJ454SC

Directions of the Court:

(1) The State Government as also the Vigilance Committees and the district magistrates will take the assistance of nonpolitical social action groups and voluntary agencies for the purpose of ensuring implementation of the provisions of the Bonded Labour System (Abolition) Act, 1976.

(2) The Central Board of Workers Education will organise periodic camps near the sites of stone quarries and stone crushers in Faridabad district for the purpose of educating the workmen in the rights and benefits conferred upon them by social welfare and labour laws and the progress made shall be reported to this Court by the Central Board of Workers Education at least once in three months.

(3) The Central Government and the State Government will ensure that conservancy facilities in the shape of latrines and urinals in accordance with the provisions contained in Section 20 of the Mines Act, 1950[9].

(4) The Central Government and the State Government will take steps to immediately ensure that appropriate and adequate medical and first aid facilities as required by Section 21 of the Mines Act 1952[10] are provided to

---

[9] **Section 20 of Mines Act, 1950**

(1) Conservancy. There shall be provided, separately for males and females in every mine, a sufficient number of latrines and urinals of prescribed types so situated as to be convenient and accessible to persons employed in the mine at all times.

(2) All latrines and urinals provided under sub- section (1) shall be adequately lighted, ventilated and at all times maintained in a clean and sanitary condition.

(3) The Central Government may specify the number of latrines and urinals to be provided in any mine, in proportion to the number of males and females employed in the mine and provide for such other matters in respect of sanitation in mines (including the obligations in this regard of persons employed in the mine) as it may consider necessary in the interests of the health of the persons so employed.

[10] **Section 21 in The Mines Act, 1952**

(1) Medical appliances. In every mine there shall be provided and maintained so as to be readily accessible during all working hours such number of first- aid boxes or cupboards equipped with such contents as may be prescribed.

(2) Nothing except the prescribed contents shall be kept in a first- aid box or cupboard or room.

(3) Every first- aid box or cupboard shall be kept in the charge of a responsible person who is trained in such first- aid treatment as may be prescribed and who shall always be readily available during the working hours of the mine.

(4) In every mine there shall be made so as to be readily available such arrangements as may be prescribed for the conveyance to hospitals or dispensaries of persons who, while employed in the mine, suffer bodily injury or become ill.

(5) In every mine wherein more than one hundred and fifty persons are employed, there shall be provided and maintained a first- aid room of such size with such equipment and in the charge of such medical and nursing staff as may be prescribed.

the workmen.

(5) The Central Government and the State Government will immediately take steps to ensure that proper and adequate medical treatment is provided by the mine lessees and owners of stone crushers to the workmen employed by them as also to the members of their families free of cost and such medical assistance shall be made available to them without any cost of transportation or otherwise and the doctor's fees as also the cost of medicines prescribed by the doctors including hospitalisation charges, if any, shall also be reimbursed to them.

(6) The Central Government and the State Government will ensure that the provisions of the Maternity Benefit Act 1961, the Maternity Benefit (Mines and Circus) Rules 1963 and the Mines Creche Rules 1966 where applicable in any particular stone quarry or stone crusher are given effect to by the mine lessees and stone crusher owners.

41

Banning Slaughter of Cows[1]

Facts in Nutshell:

The 12 petitions under Art. 32 of Constitution[2] raise the question of the constitutional validity of three several legislative enactments banning the slaughter of certain animals passed by the States of Bihar, Uttar Pradesh and Madhya Pradesh respectively. The controversy concerning the slaughter of cows has been raging in this country for a number of years and in the past it generated considerable ill will amongst the two major communities resulting even in riots and civil commotion in some places. The Bill, which was eventually passed as the Bihar Act, was published in the Bihar Gazette on April 20, 1953. The scheme of the Bill, as originally drafted, was, it is said, to put a total ban only on the slaughter of cows and calves of cows below three years of age. Petition No. 103 of 1956 has been filed by two petitioners, who are both Muslims residing in Uttar Pradesh and carrying on business in that State, the first one as a hide merchant and the second as a butcher. Petitioners in Petition No. 129 are eight in number all of whom are

---

[1] Appellants: **Mohd. Hanif Quareshi and Ors. Vs.** Respondent: **The State of Bihar** AIR1958SC731

Hon'ble Judges: Sudhi Ranjan Das, C.J., P. B. Gajendragadkar, S. K. Das, T. L. Venkatarama Aiyar and Vivian Bose, JJ.

[2] **Article 32. Remedies for enforcement of rights conferred by this Part**

(1) The right to move the Supreme Court by appropriate proceedings for the enforcement of the rights conferred by this Part is guaranteed

(2) The Supreme Court shall have power to issue directions or orders or writs, including writs in the nature of habeas corpus, mandamus, prohibition, quo warranto and certiorari, whichever may be appropriate, for the enforcement of any of the rights conferred by this Part

(3) Without prejudice to the powers conferred on the Supreme Court by clause (1) and (2), Parliament may by law empower any other court to exercise within the local limits of its jurisdiction all or any of the powers exercisable by the Supreme Court under clause (2)

(4) The right guaranteed by this article shall not be suspended except as otherwise provided for by this Constitution

Muslims residing and carrying on business in Uttar Pradesh either as gut merchants or cattle dealers, or Kasais or beef vendors or bone dealers or hide merchants or cultivators. All the petitioners in these two applications are citizens of India. By these two petitions the petitioners challenge the validity of the Uttar Pradesh Prevention of Cow Slaughter Act, 1955 (U.P. I of 1956), hereinafter referred to as the U.P. Act and pray for a writ in the nature of mandamus[3] directing the respondent State of Uttar Pradesh not to take any steps in pursuance of the U.P. Act or to interfere with the fundamental rights of the petitioners.

Petitions Nos. 117 of 1956, 126 of 1956, 127 of 1956, 128 of 1956, 248 of 1956, 144 of 1956 and 145 of 1956 have been filed by 6, 95, 541, 58, 37, 976 and 395 petitioners respectively, all of whom are Muslims belonging to the Quraishi Community and are mainly engaged in the butchers' trade and its subsidiary undertaking such as the supply of hides, tannery, glue making, gut-making and blood-dehydrating. By these petitions the petitioners all of whom are citizens of India, challenge the validity of the C.P. and Berar Animal Preservation Act, 1949 (C.P. and Berar LII of 1949), as subsequently amended.

Arguments on behalf of Counsel for Petitioners:

The principal purpose of Article 48[4], according to learned counsel for the petitioners, is to direct the State to endeavour to organise agriculture and animal husbandry on modern and scientific lines. They contend that the States are required to take steps for preserving and improving the breeds and for prohibiting the slaughter of the animals specified therein only with a view to implement that principal purpose, that is to say, only as parts of the general scheme for organising our agriculture and animal husbandry on modern and scientific lines. They also rely on entry 15 in List II of the

---

[3] **A writ of mandamus** (which means "we command" in latin), or sometimes mandates, is the name of one of the prerogative writs in the common law, and is "issued by a superior court to compel a lower court or a government officer to perform mandatory or purely ministerial duties correctly"

[4] **Article 48 in The Constitution Of India 1949**

48. Organisation of agriculture and animal husbandry The State shall endeavour to organise agriculture and animal husbandry on modern and scientific lines and shall, in particular, take steps for preserving and improving the breeds, and prohibiting the slaughter, of cows and calves and other milch and draught cattle

Seventh Schedule to the Constitution[5]. There is no separate legislative head for prohibition of slaughter of animals and that fact, they claim, lends support to their conclusion that the prohibition of the slaughter of animals specified in the last part of Art. 48 is only ancillary to the principal directions for preservation, protection and improvement of stock, which is what is meant by organising agriculture and animal husbandry. Learned counsel appearing for the petitioners challenge the constitutional validity of the Acts respectively applicable to them on three grounds, namely, that they offend the fundamental rights guaranteed to them by Arts. 14[6], 19(1)(g)[7] and 25[8].

Learned counsel also argues that Article 13(2) expressly says that the State shall not make any law which takes away or abridges the rights conferred by Chapter III of our Constitution which enshrines the fundamental rights.

"That the petitioners further submitted that the said section also violates the fundamental rights of the petitioners guaranteed under Article 25 of the Constitution in-as-much as on the occasion of their Bakr Id Day, it is the religious practice of the petitioners' community to sacrifice a cow on the said occasion. The poor members of the community usually sacrifice one cow for every 7 members whereas it would require one sheep or one goat for each member which would entail considerably more expense[9]. As a result of the total ban imposed by the impugned section the petitioners

---

[5] That entry reads : "Preservation, protection and improvement of stock and prevention of animal diseases; veterinary training and practice."

[6] **Article 14 in The Constitution Of India 1949**

14. Equality before law The State shall not deny to any person equality before the law or the equal protection of the laws within the territory of India Prohibition of discrimination on grounds of religion, race, caste, sex or place of birth

[7] **Article 19(1)(g) in The Constitution Of India 1949**

(g) to practise any profession, or to carry on any occupation, trade or business

[8] Art. 25(1). That article runs as follows :

"Subject to public order, morality and health and to the other provisions of this Part, all persons are equally entitled to freedom of conscience and the right freely to profess, practise and propagate religion."

[9] Hamilton's translation of Hedaya Book XLIII at p. 592 that it is the duty of every free Mussulman, arrived at the age of maturity, to offer a sacrifice on the Yd Kirban, or festival of the sacrifice, provided he be then possessed of Nisab and be not a traveller. The sacrifice established for one person is a goat and that for seven a cow or a camel. It is therefore, optional for a Muslim to sacrifice a goat for one person or a cow or a camel for seven persons. It does not appear to be obligatory that a person must sacrifice a cow.

would not even be allowed to make the said sacrifice which is a practice and custom in their religion, enjoined upon them by the Holy Quran, and practised by all Muslims from time immemorial and recognised as such in India."

Ban on Slaughter of Cows from Ages (Para 20 of the Judgment):

It is part of the known history of India that the Moghul Emperor Babar saw the wisdom of prohibiting the slaughter of cows as and by way of religious sacrifice and directed his son Humayun to follow this example. Similarly Emperors Akbar, Jehangir, and Ahmad Shah, it is said, prohibited cow slaughter. Nawab Hyder Ali of Mysore made cow slaughter an offence punishable with the cutting of the hands of the offenders. Three of the members of the Gosamvardhan Enquiry Committee set up by the Uttar Pradesh Government in 1953 were Muslims and concurred in the unanimous recommendation for total ban on slaughter of cows.

The complaint of the petitioners under Art. 19(1)(g) is that the Acts, if enforced, will compel them at once to close down their business and will, in effect, amount to a complete denial of their right to carry on their occupation, trade or business in spite of the mandatory provisions of Art. 19(1)(g).

What do the Acts actually provide?

In Uttar Pradesh the petitioners can freely slaughter buffaloes (male or female adults or calves) and sell their meat for food. It is also open to them to slaughter goats and sheep and sell the meat. Therefore, so far as the butchers of Uttar Pradesh are concerned, there is obviously no total prohibition of their occupation but only some restrictions have been imposed on them in respect of one part of their occupation, namely, the slaughter of cows, bulls, bullocks, and calves of cows. In Madhya Pradesh the Act, it is true, totally forbids and slaughter of cows including bulls, bullocks and cows but permits the slaughter of buffaloes (male or female adults or calves) under certain conditions. Therefore, in Madhya Pradesh also there is no law totally prohibiting the carrying on of the business of a butcher. In Bihar there is, no doubt, a total ban against the slaughter of all animals belonging to the species of bovine cattle which includes buffaloes (male or female adults or calves) but it is still possible for the butchers of Bihar to slaughter goats and sheep and sell goats' meat and mutton for food.

Observation of the Court (Para 54 of the Judgement):

The country is in short supply of milch cattle, breeding bulls and working bullocks. If the nation is to maintain itself in health and nourishment and get adequate food, our cattle must be improved. In order to achieve this objective our cattle population fit for breeding and work must be properly fed and whatever cattle food is now at our disposal and whatever more we can produce must be made available to the useful cattle which are in presenti or will in future be capable of yielding milk or doing work. The maintenance of useless cattle involves a wasteful drain on the nation's cattle feed. To maintain them is to deprive the useful cattle of the much needed nourishment. The presence of so many useless animals tends to deteriorate the breed. Total ban on the slaughter of cattle, useful or otherwise, is calculated to bring about a serious dislocation, though not a complete stoppage, of the business of a considerable section of the people who are by occupation butchers (Kasais), hide merchants and so on. Such a ban will also deprive a large section of the people of what may be their staple food. At any rate, they will have to forego the little protein food which may be within their means to take once or twice in the weed. Preservation of useless cattle by establishment of Gosadans is not, for reasons already indicated, a practical proposition. Preservation of these useless animals by sending them to concentration camps to fend for themselves is to leave them to a process of slow death and does no good to them. On the contrary, it hurts the best interests of the nation in that the useless cattle deprive the useful ones of a good part of the cattle food, deteriorate the breed and eventually affect the production of milk and breeding bulls and working bullocks, besides involving an enormous expense which could be better utilised for more national needs.

Decision of the Court:

Court held: (i) that a total ban on the slaughter of cows of all ages and calves of cows and calves of she-buffaloes, male and female, is quite reasonable and valid and is in consonance with the directive principles laid down in Art. 48, (ii) that a total ban on the slaughter of she-buffaloes or breeding bulls or working bullocks (cattle as well as buffaloes) as long as they are as milch or draught cattle is also reasonable and valid and (iii) that a total ban on the slaughter of she-buffaloes, bulls and bullocks (cattle or buffalo) after they cease to be capable of yielding milk or of breeding or working as draught animals cannot be supported as reasonable in the interest of the general public.

The Bihar Act, in so far as it prohibits the slaughter of cows of all ages and calves of cows and calves of buffaloes, male and female, is valid. The Bihar Act makes no distinction between she-buffaloes, bulls and bullocks (cattle and buffaloes) which are useful as milch or breeding or draught animals and those which are not and indiscriminately prohibits slaughter of she-buffaloes, bulls and bullocks (cattle and buffalo) irrespective of their age or usefulness. In Court view the ban on slaughter of she-buffaloes, breeding bulls and working bullocks (cattle and buffalo) which are useful is reasonable but of those which are not useful is not valid. The result is that Court uphold and declare that the Bihar Act in so far as it prohibits the slaughter of cows of all ages and calves of cows and calves of buffaloes, male and female, is constitutionally valid and hold that, in so far as it totally prohibits the slaughter of she-buffaloes, breeding bulls and working bullocks (cattle and buffalo), without prescribing any test or requirement as to their age or usefulness, it infringes the rights of the petitioners under Art. 19(1)(g) and is to that extent void.

As regards the U.P. Act Court held that it is constitutionally valid in so far as it prohibits the slaughter of cows of all ages and calves of cows, male and female, but we hold that in so far as it purports to totally prohibit the slaughter or breeding bulls and working bullocks without prescribing and test or requirement as to their age or usefulness, it offends against Art. 19(1)(g) and is to that extent void.

As regards the Madhya Pradesh Act likewise declare that it is constitutionally valid in so far as it prohibits the slaughter of cows of all ages and calves of cows, male and female, but that it is void in so far as it totally prohibits the slaughter of breeding bulls and working bullocks without prescribing any test or requirement as to their age or usefulness. Court also hold that the act is valid in so far as it regulates the slaughter of other animals under certificates granted by the authorities mentioned therein. Court also directed respondent States not to enforce the respective Acts in so far as they have been declared void by Court.

42

Sexual Harassment of Women at Workplace[1]

Facts in Nutshell:

This writ petition[2] have been filed for the enforcement of the fundamental rights[3] of working women under Articles 14^4 19^5 and 21^6 of the Constitution of India. With the increasing awareness and emphasis on gender justice,

---

[1] Appellants:**Vishaka and others Vs.** Respondent: **State of Rajasthan and Others** AIR1997SC3011

Hon'ble Judges: J. S. Verma, C.J.I., Sujata V. Manohar and B. N. Kirpal, JJ.

[2] A writ petition is a right endowed by the law for a person to seek speedy trial before an appellate court after a trial court's judgment on his case. The petitioner seeks to rush his case to prevent irreparable harm.

[3] The six fundamental rights recognized by the constitution are:

1) Right to equality, including equality before law, prohibition of discrimination on grounds of religion, race, caste, sex or place of birth, and equality of opportunity in matters of employment, abolition of untouchability and abolition of titles.

2) Right to freedom which includes speech and expression, assembly, association or union or cooperatives, movement, residence, and right to practice any profession or occupation (some of these rights are subject to security of the State, friendly relations with foreign countries, public order, decency or morality), right to life and liberty, right to education, protection in respect to conviction in offences and protection against arrest and detention in certain cases.

3) Right against exploitation, prohibiting all forms of forced labour, child labour and traffic in human beings;

4) Right to freedom of religion, including freedom of conscience and free profession, practice, and propagation of religion, freedom to manage religious affairs, freedom from certain taxes and freedom from religious instructions in certain educational institutes.

5) Cultural and Educational rights preserving Right of any section of citizens to conserve their culture, language or script, and right of minorities to establish and administer educational institutions of their choice.

6) Right to constitutional remedies for enforcement of Fundamental Rights. Fundamental rights for Indians have also been aimed at overturning the inequalities of pre-independence social practices. Specifically, they have also been used to abolish untouchability and hence prohibit discrimination on the grounds of religion, race, caste, sex, or place of birth. They also forbid trafficking of human beings and forced labour. They also protect cultural and educational rights of ethnic and religious minorities by allowing them to preserve their languages and also establish and administer their own education institutions.

Right to property was originally a fundamental right, but is now a legal right.

there is increase in the effort to guard against such violations; and the resentment towards incidents of sexual harassment is also increasing. The petition has been brought as a class action by certain social activists and NGOs with the aim of focussing attention towards societal aberration, and assisting in finding suitable methods for realisation of the true concept of 'gender equality'; and to prevent sexual harassment of working women in all work places through judicial process, to fill the vacuum in existing legislation.

The cause for the filing of the writ petition was an incident of alleged brutal gang rape of a social worker in a village of Rajasthan. The incident reveals the hazards to which a working woman may be exposed and the depravity to which sexual harassment can degenerate; and the urgency for safeguards by an alternative mechanism in the absence of legislative measures. The fundamental right to carry on any occupation, trade or profession[7] depends on the availability of a "safe" working environment. Right to life means life with dignity.

---

[4] **Article 14 in The Constitution Of India 1949**

14. Equality before law The State shall not deny to any person equality before the law or the equal protection of the laws within the territory of India Prohibition of discrimination on grounds of religion, race, caste, sex or place of birth

[5] **Article 19 in Constitution of India**

Protection of certain rights regarding freedom of speech etc

(1) All citizens shall have the right

(a) to freedom of speech and expression;

(b) to assemble peaceably and without arms;

(c) to form associations or unions;

(d) to move freely throughout the territory of India;

(e) to reside and settle in any part of the territory of India; and

(f) omitted

(g) to practise any profession, or to carry on any occupation, trade or business

[6] **Article 21 in The Constitution Of India**

Protection of life and personal liberty No person shall be deprived of his life or personal liberty except according to procedure established by law

[7] Article 19(1) (g) of the Constitution of India

Article 19(1)(g) —To practise any profession, or to carry on any occupation, trade or business

Beijing Statement of Principles of the Independence of the Judiciary in the LAWASIA region

The obligation of Court under Article 32 of the Constitution[8] for the enforcement of the fundamental rights in the absence of legislation must be viewed along with the role of judiciary envisaged in the Beijing Statement of Principles of the Independence of the Judiciary in the LAWASIA region. These principles were accepted by the Chief Justices of the Asia and the Pacific at Beijing in 1995 as those representing the minimum standards necessary to be observed in order to maintain the independence and effective functioning of the judiciary. The objectives of the judiciary mentioned in the Beijing Statement are:

Objectives of the Judiciary:

The objectives and functions of the judiciary include the following:

(a) to ensure that all persons are able to live securely under the Rule of Law;

(b) to promote, within the proper limits of the judicial function, the observance and the attainment of human rights; and

(c) to administer the law impartially among persons and between persons and the State.

Sexual harassment

Sexual harassment includes such unwelcome sexually determined behavior as physical contacts and advances, sexually coloured remarks, showing pornography and sexual demands, whether by words or actions. Such conduct can be humiliating and may constitute a health and safety problem; it is

---

[8] **Article 32. Remedies for enforcement of rights conferred by this Part**

(1) The right to move the Supreme Court by appropriate proceedings for the enforcement of the rights conferred by this Part is guaranteed

(2) The Supreme Court shall have power to issue directions or orders or writs, including writs in the nature of habeas corpus, mandamus, prohibition, quo warranto and certiorari, whichever may be appropriate, for the enforcement of any of the rights conferred by this Part

(3) Without prejudice to the powers conferred on the Supreme Court by clause (1) and (2), Parliament may by law empower any other court to exercise within the local limits of its jurisdiction all or any of the powers exercisable by the Supreme Court under clause (2)

(4) The right guaranteed by this article shall not be suspended except as otherwise provided for by this Constitution

discriminatory when the woman has reasonable grounds to believe that her objection would disadvantage her in connection with her employment, including recruiting or promotion, or when it creates a hostile working environment. Effective complaints procedures and remedies, including compensation, should be provided.

Guidelines/Directions of the Court

It is necessary and expedient for employers in work places as well as other responsible persons or institutions to observe certain guidelines to ensure the prevention of sexual harassment of women:

1. Duty of the Employer or other responsible persons in work places and other institutions:

It shall be the duty of the employer or other responsible persons in work places or other institutions to prevent or deter the commission of acts of sexual harassment and to provide the procedures for the resolution, settlement or prosecution of acts of sexual harassment by taking all steps required.

2. Definition:

For this purpose, sexual harassment includes such unwelcome sexually determined behavior (whether directly or by implication) as:

a) physical contact and advances;

b) a demand or request for sexual favours;

c) sexually coloured remarks;

d) showing pornography;

e) any other unwelcome physical, verbal or non-verbal conduct of sexual nature.

Where any of these acts is committed in circumstances whereunder the victim of such conduct has a reasonable apprehension that in relation to the victim's employment or work whether she is drawing salary, or honorarium or voluntary, whether in Government, public or private enterprise such conduct can be humiliating and may constitute a health and safety problem. It is discriminatory for instance when the woman has reasonable grounds to believe that her objection would disadvantage her in connection with her employment or work including recruiting or promotion or when it creates a hostile work environment. Adverse consequences might be visited if the victim does not consent to the conduct in question or raises any objection thereto.

3. Preventive Steps:

All employers or persons in charge of work place whether in the public or private sector should take appropriate steps to prevent sexual harassment. Without prejudice to the generality of this obligation they should take the following steps:

(a) Express prohibition of sexual harassment as defined above at the work place should be notified, published and circulated in appropriate ways.

(b) The Rules/Regulations of Government and Public Sector bodies relating to conduct and discipline should include rules/regulations prohibiting sexual harassment and provide for appropriate penalties in such rules against the offender.

(c) As regards private employers steps should be taken to include the aforesaid prohibitions in the. standing orders under the Industrial Employment (Standing Orders) Act, 1946.

(d) Appropriate work conditions should be provided in respect of work, leisure, health and hygiene to further ensure that there is no hostile environment towards women at work places and no employee woman should have reasonable grounds to believe that she is disadvantaged in connection with her employment.

4. Criminal Proceedings:

Where such conduct amounts to a specific offence under the Indian Penal Code or under any other law, the employer shall initiate appropriate action in accordance with law by making a complaint with the appropriate authority.

In particular, it should ensure that victims, or witnesses are not victimized or discriminated against while dealing with complaints of sexual harassment.

The victims of sexual harassment should have the option to seek transfer of the perpetrator or their own transfer.

5. Disciplinary Action:

Where such conduct amounts to misconduct in employment as defined by the relevant service rules, appropriate disciplinary action should be initiated by the employer in accordance with those rules.

6. Complaint Mechanism:

Whether or not such conduct constitutes an offence under law or a breach of the service rules, an appropriate complaint mechanism should be created in the employer's organization for redress of the complaint made by the victim. Such complaint mechanism should ensure time bound treatment of complaints.

7. Complaints Committee:

The complaint mechanism, referred to in (6) above, should be adequate to provide, where necessary, a Complaints Committee, a special counselor or other support service, including the maintenance of confidentiality.

The Complaints Committee should be headed by a woman and not less than half of its member should be women. Further, to prevent the possibility of any undue pressure or influence from senior levels, such Complaints Committee should involve a third party, either NGO or other body who is familiar with the issue of sexual harassment.

The Complaints Committee must make an annual report to the Government department concerned of the complaints and action taken by them.

The employers and person in charge will also report on the compliance with the aforesaid guidelines including on the reports of the Complaints Committee to the Government department.

8. Workers' Initiative:

Employees should be allowed to raise issues of sexual harassment at workers' meeting and in other appropriate forum and it should be affirmatively discussed in Employer-Employee Meetings.

9. Awareness:

Awareness of the rights of female employees in this regard should be created in particular by prominently notifying the guidelines (and appropriate legislation when enacted on the subject) in a suitable manner.

10. Third Party Harassment:

Where sexual harassment occurs as a result of an act or omission by any third party or outsider, the employer and person in charge will take all steps necessary and reasonable to assist the affected person in terms of support and preventive action.

Court also held that the guidelines shall be observed by Private employers as well. The directions would be binding and enforceable in law until suitable legislation is enacted to occupy the field.

43

What Cricket Means to India [1]

Question before the Court:

Whether the Board of Control for Cricket in India (Board) which is a cricket controlling authority in terms of the ICC Rules answers the description of "Other Authorities" within the meaning of Article 12 of the Constitution of India[2].

ARTICLE 12:

Article 12 of the Constitution of India which reads as under:

"12. In this part, unless the context otherwise requires, "the State" includes the Government and Parliament of India and the Government and the Legislature of each of the States and all local or other authorities within the territory of India or under the control of the Government of India."

In this Article, the 'State' has not been defined. It is merely an inclusive definition. It includes all other authorities within the territory of India or under the control of the Government of India. It does not say that such other authorities must be under the control of the Government of India. The word 'or' is disjunctive and not conjunctive. The expression "Authority" has a definite connotation. It has different dimensions and, thus, must receive a liberal interpretation. To arrive at a conclusion, as to which "other

---

[1] Appellants: **Zee Telefilms Ltd. and Anr. Vs.** Respondent: **Union of India (UOI) and Ors.** AIR2005SC2677

Hon'ble Judges: N. Santosh Hedge, B. P. Singh, H. K. Sema, S. B. Sinha and S. N. Variava , JJ.

[2] "**Article 12 of Indian Constitution**: In this part, unless the context otherwise requires, "the State" includes the Government and Parliament of India and the Government and the Legislature of each of the States and all local or other authorities within the territory of India or under the control of the Government of India."

authorities" could come within the purview of Article 12, we may notice the meaning of the word 'authority". The word "Other Authorities" contained in Article 12 is not to be treated as ejusdam generis.

In Concise Oxford English Dictionary, 10th Edition, the word 'authority' has been defined as under :

"1. the power or right to give orders and enforce obedience. 2. a person or organization exerting control in a particular political or administrative sphere. 3. the power to influence others based on recognized knowledge or expertise."

Broadly, there are three different concepts which exist for determining the question which fall within the expression "other authorities".

(i) The Corporations and the Societies' created by the State for carrying on its trading activities in terms of Article 298 of the Constitution[3] where for the capital, infrastructure, initial investment and financial aid etc. are provided by the State and it also exercises regulation and control there over.

(ii) Bodies created for research and other developmental works which is otherwise a governmental function but may or may not be a part of the sovereign function.

(iii) A private body is allowed to discharge public duty or positive obligation of public nature and furthermore is allowed to perform regulatory and controlling functions and activities which were otherwise the job of the government.

BOARD A STATE?

The Board is a society registered under the Tamil Nadu Societies Act. It is not created under a Statute but it is an acknowledged fact that in terms of

---

[3] **Article 298 in The Constitution Of India 1949**

298. Power to carry on trade, etc The executive power of the Union and of each State shall extend to the carrying on of any trade or business and to the acquisition, holding and disposal of property and the making of contracts for any purpose: Provided that (a) the said executive power of the Union shall, in so far as such trade or business or such purpose is not one with respect to which Parliament may make laws, be subject in each State to legislation by the State; and

(b) the said executive power of each State shall, in so far as such trade or business or such purpose is not one with respect to which the State Legislature may make laws, be subject to legislation by Parliament

its Memorandum of Association and rules framed by it, it has not only the monopoly status as regard the regulation of the game of cricket but also can lay down the criteria for its membership and furthermore make the law of sport of cricket. The Board for all intent and purport is a recognized national federation recognized by the Union of India. By reason of said, recognition only, an enormous power is exercised by the second Respondent which from selection and preparation of players at the grass root level to organize Daleep Trophy, Ranji Trophy etc. select teams and umpires for international events. The players selected by the BCCI represent India as their citizen. They use the national colour in their attire. The team is known as Indian team. It is recognized as such by the ICC. For all intent and purport it exercises the monopoly.

MEMORANDUM OF ASSOCIATION OF BOARD (Para 206 of Judgment):

206. The Board is a society under the Tamil Nadu Societies Registration Act, 1975. In terms of its Memorandum of Association, its objects, inter alia, are to control the game of Cricket in India and to resolve the disputes and to give its decision on matters referred to it by any State, Regional or other Association, to promote the game, to frame the laws of cricket in India, to select the teams to represent India in Test Matches and various others and to appoint India's representative or representatives on the International Cricket Conference and other Conferences, Seminars, connected with the game of cricket;

Pleas of the parties :

The writ petitioners[4] allegedly demonstrate that the Board is an authority that would be subject to the constitutional discipline of Part III of the Constitution of India[5], as under:

"a. It undertakes all activities in relation to Cricket including entering into the contracts for awarding telecast and broadcasting rights, for advertisement revenues in the Stadium etc.

---

[4] A writ petition is a right endowed by the law for a person to seek speedy trial before an appellate court after a trial court's judgment on his case. The petitioner seeks to rush his case to prevent irreparable harm.

[5] http://en.wikisource.org/wiki/Constitution_of_India/Part_III

261

b The team fielded by the BCCI plays as "Indian Team" while playing One Day Internationals or Test Matches — it cannot be gainsaid that the team purports to represent India as a nation, and its wins are matters of national prestige. They wear uniform that carries the national flag, and are treated as sports ambassadors of India.

c. The sportsmen of today are professionals who devote their life to playing the game. They are paid a handsome remuneration by the BCCI for their participation in the team. Thus, they are not amateurs who participate on an honorary basis. Consequently they have a right under Article 19(1)(g)[6] to be considered for participation in the game. The BCCI claims the power to debar players from playing cricket in exercise of its disciplinary powers. Obviously, a body that purports to exercise powers that impinge on the fundamental rights of citizens would constitute at least an "authority" within the meaning of Article 12of the Constitution - it can hardly contend that it has the power to arbitrarily deny players all tights to even be considered for participation in a tournament which they are included as a team from "India".

d. It is also submitted that even domestically, all representative cricket can only be under its aegis. No representative tournament can be organized without the permission of BCCI or its affiliates at any level or cricket.

Reply of Union of India:

Union of India responded that the Board is a State. In support of the said plea a large number of documents have been filed to show that the Board had all along been acting as a recognized body and as regard international matches has always been seeking its prior permission. The Board had also been under the administrative control of the Government of India.

Reply of (BCCI):

In support of its plea that it is not a 'State', the BCCI in its Counter Affidavit asserted :

---

[6] **Article 19 in The Constitution Of India 1949**

19. Protection of certain rights regarding freedom of speech etc

(1) All citizens shall have the right

(g) to practise any profession, or to carry on any occupation, trade or business

"(a) Board of Control of Cricket in India, the Respondent No. 2 is an autonomous non-profit making Association limited and restricted to its Members only and registered under the Tamil Nadu Societies Registration Act. It is a private organization whose objects are to promote the game of Cricket. Its functions are regulated and governed by its own Rules and Regulations independent of any statute and are only related to its members. The Rules and Regulations of the Respondent No. 2 have neither any statutory force nor it has any statutory powers to make rules or regulations having statutory force.

(b) The Working Committee elected from amongst its members in accordance with its own Rules controls the entire affairs and management of the Respondent No. 2. There is no representation of the Government or any Statutory Body of whatsoever nature by whatever form in the Respondent No. 2. There exists no control of the Government over the function, finance, administration, management and affairs of the Respondent No. 2.

(c) ...The Respondent No. 2 does not discharge or perform any public or statutory duly.

(d) The Respondent No. 2 receives no grant of assistance in any form or manner from the Government in this context.

(e) The Respondent No. 2 organizes cricket matches and/or tournaments between the Teams of its Members and with the Teams of the members of International Cricket Council (ICC) which is also an autonomous Body dehors any Government control....Matches that are organized are played at places either belonging to Members in India or at the places of either belonging to its Members of ICC only. Only when for the purpose of organizing any match or tournament with foreign participants, the Respondent No. 2 requires normal and scheduled permissions from the Ministry of Sports for travel of foreign teams, it obtains the same like any other private organization, particularly in the subject matter of foreign exchange. The Respondent No. 2 is the only autonomous sporting body which not only does not obtain any financial grants but on the contrary earns foreign exchange.

(f) Organizing Cricket Matches and/or Tournaments between the Teams of the Members of the Respondent No. 2 and/or with the co-members of International Cricket Council cannot be said to be a facet of public function or government in character. No monopoly status has been conferred upon the Respondent No. 2 either by Statute or by the Government Any other body could organize any matches on its own and neither the Respondent No. 2 nor the Government could oppose the same. As a matter of fact, number of cricket matches including International matches are played in the Country which have nothing to do with the Respondent No. 2. Respondent No. 2 has no monopoly over sending teams overseas for the game of cricket and to control the entire game of cricket in India. Matches which are sanctioned or recognized by the ICC are only known as Official Test matches or One day International Matches. Respondent No. 2 is entitled to invite teams of other members of ICC or send teams to participate in such matches by virtue of its membership of ICC."

Response of Learned Counsel that BCCI is a State

Learned Counsel submitted that the Board (BCCI) is a 'State' within the meaning of Article 12 of the Constitution of India as:

(i) it regulates cricket;

(ii) It has a virtual monopoly;

(iii) it seeks to put restrictions on the fundamental rights of the players and umpires to earn their livelihood as envisaged under Article 19(1)(g) of the Constitution of India[7]

(iv) The cricket events managed by the third Respondent (President BCCI) have a definite concept, connotation and significance which have a bearing on the performance of individual players as also the team as a national team representing the country in the entire field of cricket.

What Cricket Means to India (Para 205 of Judgment):

205. Cricket in India is the most popular game. When India plays in international fora, it attracts the attention of millions of people. The win or loss of the game brings 'joy' or 'sorrow' to them. To, some lovers of the

---

[7] **Article 19 in The Constitution Of India 1949**

19. Protection of certain rights regarding freedom of speech etc

(1) All citizens shall have the right

(g) to practise any profession, or to carry on any occupation, trade or business

game, it is a passion, to a lot more it is an obsession, nay a craze. For a large number of viewers, it is not enthusiasm alone but involvement.

Decision of the Court:

Court held that BCCI is a state under article 12 of the constitution. One of the important factors which has been taken note of in rendering the decision is the fact that the game of cricket has a special place in India. No other game attracts so much attention or favour. Further, no other sport, in India, affords an opportunity to make a livelihood out of it. Court also held that only because it is a State within the meaning of Article 12, the same by itself would not mean that it is bound by rule of reservation as contained in Clause 4 of Article 15[8] and Clause 4 of the Article 16 of the Constitution of India[9].

---

[8] **Article 15(4) in The Constitution Of India 1949**

(4) Nothing in this article or in clause (2) of Article 29 shall prevent the State from making any special provision for the advancement of any socially and educationally backward classes of citizens or for the Scheduled Castes and the Scheduled Tribes

[9] **Article 16(4) in The Constitution Of India 1949**

(4) Nothing in this article shall prevent the State from making any provision for the reservation of appointments or posts in favor of any backward class of citizens which, in the opinion of the State, is not adequately represented in the services under the State

44

Handcuffing should not be forced on Prisioners[1]

Facts in Nutshell:

Mr. Kuldip Nayar, an eminent journalist in his capacity as President of "Citizens for Democracy" wrote a letter dated December 22, 1994 to Court wherein he stated as under: "A few days ago when he was in Guwahati he went to see a patient at the Govt. Hospital. To his horror, he found 7 TADA detenus put in one room, handcuffed to their bed. This was despite the fact that the room in which they were locked had bars and was locked. Outside a posse of policemen stood with guns on their shoulders. After talking to the detenus he found that they had to pay for the medicine from their own pocket. The undisputed facts are that while lodged inside the ward of the Guwahati Medical College Hospital the seven detenus were handcuffed and on top of that tied with a long rope to contain their movement. He fail to understand how the Assam Government could do all this in spite of various Court orders. He drew the attention of the State Chief Minister through a letter but got no reply. Therefore, he approached court.

Court treated the letter as a petition under Article 32 of the Constitution[2] of

---

[1] Appellants:**Citizen for Democracy through its President Vs.** Respondent: **State of Assam and others**

AIR1996SC2193

Hon'ble Judges: Kuldip Singh and N. Venkatachala, JJ.

[2] **Article 32. Remedies for enforcement of rights conferred by this Part**

(1) The right to move the Supreme Court by appropriate proceedings for the enforcement of the rights conferred by this Part is guaranteed

(2) The Supreme Court shall have power to issue directions or orders or writs, including writs in the nature of habeas corpus, mandamus, prohibition, quo warranto and certiorari, whichever may be appropriate, for the enforcement of any of the rights conferred by this Part

(3) Without prejudice to the powers conferred on the Supreme Court by clause (1) and (2), Parliament may by law empower any other court to exercise within the local limits of its jurisdiction all or any of the powers exercisable by the Supreme Court under clause (2)

(4) The right guaranteed by this article shall not be suspended except as otherwise provided for by this Constitution

India and issued notice to the State of Assam, through its Chief Secretary, Home Secretary and Secretary, Health.

Reply of Govt. of Assam through Affidavit :

The seven detenus in question mentioned in Shri Kuldip Nayar's letter were lodged in Guwahati Medical College Hospital. As the Guwahati Medical College Hospital is not a part of any jail, a part of the ward of the said hospital was set apart with a collapsible gate for their lodgment in the Hospital under Police guard. When inside the ward they were bound by long ropes tied to one of their hands with a handcuff, which allowed them to move freely within the ward; but prevented their escape, which was a very real apprehension having regard to the number of TADA detenus escaping from Police, Judicial and Hospital custody as mentioned above... Also seven detenus are hardcore activists of ULFA, which is notorious for insurgent and secessionist activities. The seven detenus are all accused of terrorist and disruptive activities, murder, extortion, hoarding and smuggling of arms and ammunition and other allied offences...

Handcuffing is prima facie inhuman

The Court in *Prem Shankar Shukla v. Delhi Administration*[3] categorically held that handcuffing is prima facie inhuman, unreasonable, arbitrary and as such repugnant to Article 21 of the Constitution[4] of India. To prevent the escape of an under-trial is, no doubt, in public interest, but "to bind a man hand-and-foot, fetter his limbs with hoops of steel, shuffle him along in the streets and stand him for hours in the Courts is to torture him, defile his dignity, vulgarise society and foul the soul of our constitutional culture."

Court has, clearly and firmly, laid down that the police and the jail authorities are under a public duty to prevent the escape of prisoners and provide them with safe custody but at the same time the rights of the prisoners guaranteed

---

[3] 1980CriLJ930

[4] **Article 21 in The Constitution Of India**

Protection of life and personal liberty No person shall be deprived of his life or personal liberty except according to procedure established by law

to them under Articles 14[5] 19[6] and 21[7] of the Constitution of India cannot be infracted. The authorities are justified in taking suitable measures, legally permissible, to safeguard the custody of the prisoners, but the use of fetters purely at the whims or subjective discretion of the authorities is not permissible.

Decision of the Court:

The handcuffing and in addition tying with ropes of the patient-prisoners who are lodged in the hospital is inhuman and in utter violation of the human rights guaranteed to an individual under the International Law and the law of the land. Court directed and lay down as a rule that handcuffs or other fetters shall not be forced on a prisoner convicted or under-trial while lodged in a jail anywhere in the country or while transporting or in transit from one jail to another or from jail to Court and back. The police and the jail authorities, on their own, shall have no authority to direct the handcuffing of any inmate of a jail in the country or during transport from one jail to another or from jail to Court and back. Court also directed that when the police arrests a person in execution of a warrant of arrest obtained from a Magistrate, the person arrested shall not be handcuffed unless the police has also obtained orders from the Magistrate for the handcuffing of the person to be so arrested. In all the cases where a person arrested by police, is produced before the Magistrate and remand judicial or non-judicial is given by the Magistrate the

---

[5] **Article 14 in The Constitution Of India 1949**

14. Equality before law The State shall not deny to any person equality before the law or the equal protection of the laws within the territory of India Prohibition of discrimination on grounds of religion, race, caste, sex or place of birth

[6] 19. Protection of certain rights regarding freedom of speech etc

(1) All citizens shall have the right

(a) to freedom of speech and expression;

(b) to assemble peaceably and without arms;

(c) to form associations or unions;

(d) to move freely throughout the territory of India;

(e) to reside and settle in any part of the territory of India; and

(f) omitted

(g) to practise any profession, or to carry on any occupation, trade or business

[7] **Article 21 in The Constitution Of India**

Protection of life and personal liberty No person shall be deprived of his life or personal liberty except according to procedure established by law

person concerned shall not be hand-cuffed unless special orders in that respect are obtained from the Magistrate at the time of the grant of the remand[8].

---

[8] **Meaning of Remand:** The term 'remand' basically implies the act of sending the accused back to custody either to provide security or to provide surety for bail.

45

Capitation Fees[1]

Facts in Nutshell:

Miss Mohini Jain a resident of Meerut was informed by the Management of Sri Siddhartha Medical College, in the State of Karnataka that she could be admitted to the MBBS course in the session. According to the management she was asked to deposit Rs. 60,000/- as the tuition fee for the first year and furnish a bank guarantee in respect of the fee for the remaining years of the MBBS course. The petitioner's father informed the management that it was beyond there means to pay the exorbitant annual fee of Rs. 60,000/- and as a consequence she was denied admission to the medical college. Mohini Jain had alleged that the management demanded a further capitation fee[2] of rupees four and a half lakhs.

Therefore Mohini Jain filed a petition under Article 32 of the Constitution[3] of India challenging the notification of the Karnataka Government permitting the Private Medical Colleges in the State of Karnataka to charge exorbitant tuition fees from the students other than those admitted to the "Government seats".

---

[1] Appellants: **Miss. Mohini Jain Vs.**Respondent: **State of Karnataka and others** AIR1992SC1858

Hon'ble Judges: Kuldip Singh and R.M. Sahai, JJ.

[2] Capitation fee" means any amount, by whatever name called, paid or collected directly or indirectly in excess of the fee prescribed

[3] **Article 32. Remedies for enforcement of rights conferred by this Part**

(1) The right to move the Supreme Court by appropriate proceedings for the enforcement of the rights conferred by this Part is guaranteed

(2) The Supreme Court shall have power to issue directions or orders or writs, including writs in the nature of habeas corpus, mandamus, prohibition, quo warranto and certiorari, whichever may be appropriate, for the enforcement of any of the rights conferred by this Part

(3) Without prejudice to the powers conferred on the Supreme Court by clause (1) and (2), Parliament may by law empower any other court to exercise within the local limits of its jurisdiction all or any of the powers exercisable by the Supreme Court under clause (2)

(4) The right guaranteed by this article shall not be suspended except as otherwise provided for by this Constitution

Arguments on behalf of the Counsel:

Counsel appearing for the medical college contended that the students from whom higher tuition fee is charged belong to a different class. According to him those who are admitted to the "Government seats" are meritorious and the remaining non-meritorious. He states that classification of candidates into those who possess merit and these who do not possess merits a valid classification and as such the college- management is within its right to charge more fee from those who do not possess merit. He also stated that the object sought to be achieved by the said classification is to collect money to meet the expenses incurred by the college in providing medical education to the students.

Points of Consideration before the Court:

(1) Is there a 'right to education' guaranteed to the people of India under the Constitution? If so, does the concept of 'capitation fee' infracts the same?

(2) Whether the charging of capitation fee in consideration of admissions to educational institutions is arbitrary, unfair, unjust and as such violates the equality clause contained in Article 14 of the Constitution[4]?

Right to Education

It is correct that "right to education" as such has not been guaranteed as fundamental right under Part III of the Constitution[5] but reading Constitution provisions[6] cumulatively it becomes clear that the framers of the Constitution made it obligatory for the State to provide education for its citizens.

---

[4] **Article 14 in The Constitution Of India 1949**

14. Equality before law The State shall not deny to any person equality before the law or the equal protection of the laws within the territory of India Prohibition of discrimination on grounds of religion, race, caste, sex or place of birth

[5] http://en.wikisource.org/wiki/Constitution_of_India/Part_III

[6] **Article 41 Right to work, to education and to public assistance in certain cases. -** The State shall, within the limits of its economic capacity and development, make effective provision for securing the right to work, to education and to public assistance in cases of unemployment, old age, sickness and disablement, and in other cases of undeserved want.

Article 45. Provision for free and compulsory education for children. - The State shall endeavour to provide, within a period of ten years from the commencement of this Constitution, for free and compulsory education for ah children until they complete the age of fourteen years.

The "right to education", therefore, is concomitant to the fundamental rights enshrined under Part III of the Constitution. The State is under a constitutional-mandate to provide educational institutions at all levels for the benefit of the citizens. The educational institutions must function to the best advantage of the citizens. Opportunity to acquire education cannot be confined to the richer section of the society. Increasing demand for medical education has led to the opening of large number of medical colleges by private persons, groups and trusts with the permission and recognition of State Governments.

This Court in *E.P. Royappa v. State of Tamil Nadu and Anr.* [7] gave new dimension to Article 14 of the Constitution in the following words:

The capitation fee brings to the fore a clear class bias, It enables the rich to take admission whereas the poor has to withdraw due to financial inability. A poor student with better merit cannot get admission because he has no money whereas the rich can purchase the admission. Such a treatment is patently unreasonable, unfair and unjust. There is, threfore, no escape from the conclusion that charging of capitation fee in consideration of admissions to educational institutions is wholly arbitrary and as such infracts Article 14 of the Constitution.

Decision of the Court:

Court held that every citizen has a 'right to education' under the Constitution. The State is under an obligation to establish educational institutions to enable the citizens to enjoy the said right. The State may discharge its obligation through State-owned or State-recognised educational institutions. When the State Government grants recognition to the private educational institutions it creates an agency to fulfill its obligation under the Constitution. The students are given admission to the educational institutions - whether State-owned or State recognised in recognition of their 'right to education' under the Constitution. *Charging capitation fee in consideration of admission to educational institutions, is a patent denial of a citizen's right to education under the Constitution.*

---

[7] (1974)ILLJ172SC

Capitation fee makes the availability of education beyond the reach of the poor. The State action in permitting capitation fee to be charged by State-recognised educational institutions is wholly arbitrary and as such violative of Article 14 of the Constitution of India. Court also held that charging of capitation fee by the private educational institutions as a consideration for admission is wholly illegal and cannot be permitted.

46

Prohibition of Smoking in Public Areas[1]

Ratio Decidendi[2]:

"In the interest of citizen, smoking in public places will be prohibited."

Facts in Nutshell:

Petition under Article 32 of the Constitution[3] was filed to ban smoking in Public Areas. Fundamental right guaranteed under Article 21 of Constitution[4] of India, *inter alia,* provides that none shall be deprived of his life without due process of law. Then-why a non-smoker should be afflicted by various diseases including lung cancer or of heart, only because he is required to go to public places? Is it not indirectly depriving of his life without any process of law? Undisputedly smoking is injurious to health and may affect the

---

[1]   Appellants: **Murli S. Deora** vs. Respondent: **Union of India and ors**
      AIR2002SC40

      Hon'ble Judges: M. B. Shah and R. P. Sethi, JJ.

[2]   **Meaning of Ratio Decidendi**

      Ratio decidendi is a Latin phrase meaning "the reason" or "the rationale for the decision." The ratio decidendi is "[t]he point in a case which determines the judgment" or "the principle which the case establishes."

[3]   **Article 32. Remedies for enforcement of rights conferred by this Part**

      (1) The right to move the Supreme Court by appropriate proceedings for the enforcement of the rights conferred by this Part is guaranteed

      (2) The Supreme Court shall have power to issue directions or orders or writs, including writs in the nature of habeas corpus, mandamus, prohibition, quo warranto and certiorari, whichever may be appropriate, for the enforcement of any of the rights conferred by this Part

      (3) Without prejudice to the powers conferred on the Supreme Court by clause (1) and (2), Parliament may by law empower any other court to exercise within the local limits of its jurisdiction all or any of the powers exercisable by the Supreme Court under clause (2)

      (4) The right guaranteed by this article shall not be suspended except as otherwise provided for by this Constitution

[4]   **Article 21 of the Constitution of India, 1950**: Protection of Life and Personal Liberty

      No person shall be deprived of his life or personal liberty except according to procedure established by law.

health of smokers but there is no reason that health of passive smokers[5] should also be injuriously affected. In any case there is no reason to compel non-smokers to be helpless victims of air pollution.

(The) Cigarettes (Regulation of Production. Supply and Distribution) Act. 1975

The statement of objects and reason of (The) Cigarettes (Regulation of Production. Supply and Distribution) Act. 1975, *inter alia,* provides, Smoking of cigarettes is a harmful habit and, in course of time, can lead to grave health hazards.

Similarly, the statement of objects and reasons of the Cigarettes and Other Tobacco Products (Prohibition of Advertisement and Regulation of Trade and Commerce, Production, Supply and Distribution) Bill, 2001, provides, Tobacco is universally regarded as one of the major public health hazards and is responsible directly or indirectly for an estimated eight lakh deaths annually in the country.

Tobacco smoking contains harmful contents including nicotine, tar, potential carcinogens, carbon monoxide irritants, asphyxiates and smoke particles which are the cause of many diseases including the cancer.

Submissions on Behalf of Attorney General of India:

Learned Attorney General submitted that considering harmful effect of smoking, smoking in public places is required to be prohibited. The persons not indulging in smoking cannot be compelled to or subject to passive smoking on a account of acts of the smokers.

Supreme Court Directions:

Supreme Court of India issued directions to the Union of India, State Governments as well as the Union Territories to take effective steps to ensure prohibiting smoking in public places, namely:

---

[5] **Passive smoking** is the inhalation of smoke, called **second-hand smoke (SHS)**, or **environmental tobacco smoke (ETS)**, by persons other than the intended 'active' smoker. It occurs when tobacco smoke permeates any environment, causing its inhalation by people within that environment.

1. Auditoriums

2. Hospital Buildings

3. Health Institutions

4. Educational Institutions

5. Libraries

6. Court Buildings

7. Public Office

8. Public Conveyances, including Railways.

47

Who can File a PIL[1]

Ratio Decidendi[2]:

Jurisdiction of the court cannot be invoked in a matter where the controversy itself is no longer res integra[3].

Facts in Nutshell:

The appointment of L. P. Nathani was challenged before the High Court in a Public Interest Litigation[4] on the ground that he could not hold the august Office of the Advocate General of Uttarakhand in view of Article 165[5] read

---

[1] **Appellants:** State of Uttaranchal **Vs. Respondent:** Balwant Singh Chaufal and Ors. AIR2010SC2550

Hon'ble Judges: Dalveer Bhandari and Mukundakam Sharma , JJ.

[2] **Meaning of Ratio Decidendi**

Ratio decidendi is a Latin phrase meaning "the reason" or "the rationale for the decision. " The *ratio decidendi* is "[t]he point in a case which determines the judgment" or "the principle which the case establishes."

[3] **Res Integra.** An entire thing; an entirely new or untouched matter. This term is applied to those points of law which have not been decided, which are is applied to those points of law which have not been decided, which are "untouched by dictum or decision

[4] **Public Interest Litigation has been defined in the Black's Law Dictionary (6th Edition) as under:**

Public Interest - Something in which the public, the community at large, has some pecuniary interest, or some interest by which their legal rights or liabilities are affected. It does not mean anything so narrow as mere curiosity, or as the interests of the particular localities, which may be affected by the matters in question. Interest shared by citizens generally in affairs of local, state or national government....

Advanced Law Lexicon has defined 'Public Interest Litigation' as under:

The expression 'PIL' means a legal action initiated in a Court of law for the enforcement of public interest or general interest in which the public or a class of the community has pecuniary interest or some interest by which their legal rights or liabilities are affected.

[5] **Article 165 of the Constitution:** The Advocate-General for the State.- (1) The Governor of each State shall appoint a person who is qualified to be appointed a Judge of a High Court to be Advocate-General for the State.

(2) It shall be the duty of the Advocate-General to give advice to the Government of the State upon such legal matters, and to perform such other duties of a legal character, as may from time to time be referred or assigned to him by the Governor, and to discharge the functions conferred on him by or under this Constitution or any other law for the time being in force.

with Article 217 of the Constitution[6]. According to the respondent[7], Mr. Nathani was ineligible to be appointed as the Advocate General because he had attained the age of 62 years much before he was appointed as the Advocate General. The High Court entertained the petition. The State of Uttaranchal filed special leave petition[8] before Supreme Court.

Cases Referred:

In *Ghanshyam Chandra Mathur v. The State of Rajasthan and Ors.*[9] the appointment of the Advocate General was challenged. The court held that "...no age of superannuation has been mentioned in Article 165 of the Constitution of India. This clearly means that the age of superannuation which applies to a High Court Judge, does not apply to the office of the Advocate General".

---

(3) The Advocate-General shall hold office during the pleasure of the Governor, and shall receive such remuneration as the Governor may determine.

[6] **Article 217 which deals with the appointment and the conditions of the office of a Judge of a High Court is set out as under:**

217 - Appointment and conditions of the office of a Judge of a High Court .- (1) Every Judge of a High Court shall be appointed by the President by warrant under his hand and seal after consultation with the Chief Justice of India, the Governor of the State, and, in the case of appointment of a Judge other than the Chief Justice, the Chief Justice of the High court, and shall hold office, in the case of an additional or acting Judge, as provided in Article 224, and in any other case, until he attains the age of sixty-two years:

Provided that—

(a) a Judge may, by writing under his hand addressed to the President, resign his office;

(b) a Judge may be removed from his office by the President in the manner provided in Clause (4) of Art

(c) the office of a Judge shall be vacated by his being appointed by the President to be a Judge of the Supreme Court or by his being transferred by the President to any other High Court within the territory of India.

(2) A person shall not be qualified for appointment as a Judge of a High Court unless he is a citizen of India and—

(a) has for at least ten years held a judicial office in the territory of India; or

(b) has for at least ten years been an advocate of a High Court or of two or more such courts in succession;

[7] A person against whom a petition or complaint is filed in a court.

[8] **Article 136 Constitution of India**

Special Leave to appeal by the Supreme Court

(1) Notwithstanding anything in this Chapter, the Supreme Court may, in its discretion, grant special leave to appeal from any judgment, decree, determination, sentence or order in any cause or matter passed or made by any court or tribunal in the territory of India.

(2) Nothing in clause (1) shall apply to any judgment, determination, sentence or order passed or made by any court or tribunal constituted by or under any law relating to the Armed Forces.

[9] 1979 WLN 773

In *Dr. Chandra Bhan Singh v. State of Rajasthan and Ors.*[10] the question regarding the validity of the appointment of the Advocate General was challenged. The Court had held that the age of superannuation of a High Court Judge did not apply to the post of the Advocate General. The court noted that all provisions in the Constitution for High Court Judges, such as remuneration and tenure of office do not apply to the post of the Advocate General.

Decision of the Supreme Court:

Court held that when the controversy is no longer res-integra[11] and the same controversy is raised repeatedly, then it not only wastes the precious time of the Court and prevent the Court from deciding other deserving cases, but also has the immense potentiality of demeaning a very important constitutional office and person who has been appointed to that office. In Courts considered view, it was a clear case of the abuse of process of court in the name of the Public Interest Litigation. The Court cautioned by observing that:

Public interest litigation is a weapon which has to be used with great care and circumspection and the judiciary has to be extremely careful to see that behind the beautiful veil of public interest an ugly private malice, vested interest and/or publicity seeking is not lurking. It is to be used as an effective weapon in the armory of law for delivering social justice to the citizens. The attractive brand name of public interest litigation should not be used for suspicious products of mischief. It should be aimed at redressal of genuine public wrong or public injury and not publicity oriented or founded on personal vendetta.

Court in order to preserve the purity and sanctity of the PIL has issued the following directions:

(1) The courts must encourage genuine and bona fide PIL and effectively discourage and curb the PIL filed for extraneous considerations.

(2) Instead of every individual judge devising his own procedure for dealing with the public interest litigation, it would be appropriate for each High Court to properly formulate rules for encouraging the genuine PIL and

---

[10] AIR 1983 Raj. 149

discouraging the PIL filed with oblique motives. Consequently, we request that the High Courts who have not yet framed the rules, should frame the rules within three months. The Registrar General of each High Court is directed to ensure that a copy of the Rules prepared by the High Court is sent to the Secretary General of this Court immediately thereafter.

(3) The courts should prima facie verify the credentials of the petitioner before entertaining a P.I.L.

(4) The court should be prima facie satisfied regarding the correctness of the contents of the petition before entertaining a PIL.

(5) The court should be fully satisfied that substantial public interest is involved before entertaining the petition.

(6) The court should ensure that the petition which involves larger public interest, gravity and urgency must be given priority over other petitions.

(7) The courts before entertaining the PIL should ensure that the PIL is aimed at redressal of genuine public harm or public injury. The court should also ensure that there is no personal gain, private motive or oblique motive behind filing the public interest litigation.

(8) The court should also ensure that the petitions filed by busybodies for extraneous and ulterior motives must be discouraged by imposing exemplary costs or by adopting similar novel methods to curb frivolous petitions and the petitions filed for extraneous considerations.

48

Working Hours of child not more than four to six hours a Day[1]

Facts in Nutshell:

In our country, Sivakasi was once taken as the worst offender in the matter of violating prohibition of employing child labour. As the situation there had became intolerable, the public spirited lawyer, Shri M.C. Mehta, thought it necessary to invoke the court's power under Article 32[2], as after all the fundamental right of the children guaranteed by Article 24[3] of the Constitution was being grossly violated. He, therefore, filed petition in Court.

Constitution call (Articles in Constitution of India related to Child)

Article 24. Prohibition of employment of children in factories, etc. - No child below the age of fourteen years shall be employed to work in any factory or mine or engaged in any other hazardous employment.

---

[1] Appellants: **M.C. Mehta** Vs. Respondent: **State of Tamil Nadu and others** AIR1997SC699

Hon'ble Judges: Kuldip Singh, B. L. Hansaria and S.B. Majmudar, JJ.

[2] **Article 32. Remedies for enforcement of rights conferred by this Part**

(1) The right to move the Supreme Court by appropriate proceedings for the enforcement of the rights conferred by this Part is guaranteed

(2) The Supreme Court shall have power to issue directions or orders or writs, including writs in the nature of habeas corpus, mandamus, prohibition, quo warranto and certiorari, whichever may be appropriate, for the enforcement of any of the rights conferred by this Part

(3) Without prejudice to the powers conferred on the Supreme Court by clause (1) and (2), Parliament may by law empower any other court to exercise within the local limits of its jurisdiction all or any of the powers exercisable by the Supreme Court under clause (2)

(4) The right guaranteed by this article shall not be suspended except as otherwise provided for by this Constitution

[3] **Article 24. Prohibition of employment of children in factories, etc**. - No child below the age of fourteen years shall be employed to work in any factory or mine or engaged in any other hazardous employment.

Article 39.(e). that the health and strength of workers, men and women, and the tender age of children are not abused and that citizens are not forced by economic necessity to enter avocations unsuited to their age or strength;

Article 39(f). that children are given opportunities and facilities to develop in a healthy manner and in conditions of freedom and dignity and that childhood and youth are protected against exploitation and against moral and material abandonment.

Article 41. Right to work, to education and to public assistance in certain cases. - The State shall, within the limits of its economic capacity and development, make effective provision for securing the right to work, to education and to public assistance in cases of unemployment, old age, sickness and disablement and in other cases of undeserved want.

Article 45. Provision for free and compulsory education for children. - The State shall endeavour to provide, within a period often years from the commencement of this Constitution, for free and compulsory education for all children until they complete the age of fourteen years.

Article 47. Duty of the State to raise the level of nutrition and the standard of living and to improve public health. - The State shall regard the raising of the level of nutrition and the standard of living of its people and the improvement of public health as among its primary duties and, in particular, the State shall endeavour to bring about prohibition of the consumption except for medical purposes of intoxicating drinks and of drugs which are injurious to health.

Recommendations on Prohibition of Child Labour:

Suo moto cognizance[4] was taken itself when news about an unfortunate accident, in one of the Sivakasi cracker factories was published. The Court gave certain directions regarding the payment of compensation and formed a committee. The Committee gave following recommendations:

---

[4] **Suo moto cognizance** means "take notice of the fact on its own ". The source of information may be Newspaper, television or any other source and the Commission acts of its own initiative and calls for a report from the concerned department or may order for investigation to be done by its own investigation team.

(a) State of Tamilnadu shall be directed to ensure that children are not employed in fire works factories.

(b) The children employed in the match factories for packing, purposes must work in a separate premises for packing.

(c) Employers should not be permitted to take work from the children for more than six hours a day.

(d) Proper transport facilities should be provided by the employers and State Govt. for travelling of the children from their homes to their work places and back.

(e) Facilities for recreation, socialisation and education should be provided either in the factory or close to the factory.

(f) Employers should make arrangements for providing basic diets for the children and in case they fail to do so, the Government may be directed to provide for basic diet - one meal a day programme of the State of Tamil Nadu for school children may be extended to the child worker.

(g) Piece-rate wages should be abolished and payment should be made on monthly basis. Wages should be commensurate to the work done by the children.

(h) All the workers working in the industry, whether in registered factories or in unregistered factories, whether in cottage industry or on contract basis, should be brought under the Insurance Scheme.

(i) Welfare Fund - For Sivakasi area, instead of present committee, a committee should be headed by a retired High Court Judge or a person of equal status with two social workers, who should be answerable either to this Hon'ble Court or to the High Court as may be directed by this Hon'ble Court. Employers should be directed to deposit Rs. 2 per month per worker towards welfare fund and the State should be directed to give the matching contribution. The employers of all the industries, whether it is registered or unregistered, whether it is cottage industry or on contract basis, to deposit Rs. 2 per month per worker.

(j) A National Commission for children's welfare should be set up to prepare a scheme for child labour abolition in a phased manner. Such a Commission should be answerable to Hon'ble Court directly and should report to Hon'ble Court at periodical intervals about the progress.

International Labour Organisation has been playing an important role in the process of gradual elimination of child labour and to protect child from industrial exploitation. It has focused five main issues:

1. Prohibition of children labour.

2. Protecting child labour at work.

3. Attacking the basic causes of child labour.

4. Helping children to adopt to future work.

5. Protecting the children of working parents.

Poverty is basic reason for Child Labour (Para 26 of the Judgment)

Poverty is basic reason which compels parents of a child, despite their unwillingness, to get it employed. Otherwise, no parents, specially no mother, would like that a tender aged child should toil in a factory in a difficult condition, instead of it enjoying its childhood at home under the paternal gaze.

Decision of the Court:

Court held that offending employer be asked to pay compensation for every child employed in contravention of the provisions of the Act (The Child Labour (Prohibition and Regulation) Act, 1986) A sum of Rs 20,000 . Court also fixed the Labour inspector duty that he shall have to see that working hours of child are not more than four to six hours a day and child receives education at least for two hours each day and the entire cost of education to be borne by employer.

49

Right of the employer to terminate the services of permanent employees[1]

Facts in Nutshell:

The (appellant) Delhi Transport Corporation, is a statutory body formed and established Under Section 3 of the Delhi Road Transport Act, 1950[2] read with Delhi Road Transport (Amendment) Act, 1971 (hereinafter called 'the Act'). The appellant carries out the objects of vital public utility, according to the appellant, i.e. transport of passengers in the Union Territory of Delhi and other areas. Respondent No. 2, Sri Ishwar Singh was appointed as conductor therein on probation for a period of 1 year in 1970. The probation period was extended thereafter for a further period of one year and thereafter he was regularised in service of the appellant. Similarly, respondent No. 3- Sri Ram Phal was appointed as Assistant Traffic Incharge and after the probation period he was regularised in service. Respondent No. 4- Sri Vir Bhan was appointed as driver and after completing the probation period he was also regularised in service. It is stated that respondents Nos. 2 to 4

---

[1] Appellants:**Delhi Transport Corporation Vs.** Respondent: **D.T.C. Mazdoor Congress and Ors.**

AIR1991SC101

Hon'ble Judges: Sabyasachi Mukherjee, C.J.,K. Ramaswamy,B. C. Ray,L. M. Sharma and P. B. Sawant, JJ.

[2] **Section 3 in The Road Transport Corporations Act, 1950**

3. Establishment of Road Transport Corporations in the States. The State Government, having regard to-

(a) the advantages offered to the public, trade and industry by the development of road transport;

(b) the desirability of coordinating any form of road transport with any other form of transport;

(c) the desirability of extending and improving the facilities for road transport in any area and of providing an efficient and economical system of road transport service therein; may, by notification in the Official Gazette, establish a Road Transport Corporation for the whole or any part of the State under such name as may be specified in the notification.

became, according to the appellant, inefficient in their work and started inciting other staff members not to perform their duties. They were served with termination notices under Regulation 9(b)[3] of the Delhi Road Transport Authority (Conditions of Appointment & Service) Regulations, 1952. On" 11th June, 1985 respondents Nos. 2 to 4 and their Union being respondent No. 1- DTC Mazdoor Congress, filed writ petition in Delhi High Court, challenging the constitutional validity of Regulation 9(b) of the Delhi Road Transport Act. High Court of Delhi struck down Regulation 9(b) of the said Regulations, and directed the appellant to pay back respondents' wages and benefits within 3 months. Than special leave petition[4] was filed in Supreme Court. The question, therefore, was whether the High Court justified in the view it took?

Question before the Court:

The only question involved in all these matters is whether the absolute power given to the Management of the public undertakings under their respective rules/regulations to terminate the services of an employee without assigning any reason, is constitutionally valid. The petitions[5] deal with the question of

---

[3] **Regulation 9 of the said regulations, reads as follows:**

9. Termination of service: (a) Except as otherwise specified in the appointment orders, the services of an employee of the authority may be terminated without any notice or pay in lieu of notice:

(i) During the period of probation and without assigning any reason thereof.

(ii) For misconduct,

(iii) On the completion of specific period of appointment.

(iv) In the case of employees engaged on contract for a specific period, on the expiration of such period in accordance with the terms of appointment.

(b) Where the termination is made due to reduction of establishment or in circumstances other than those mentioned at (a) above, one month notice or pay in lieu thereof will be given to all categories of employees.

(c) Where a regular/temporary employee wishes to resign from his post under the authority he shall give three/one month's notice in writing or pay in lieu thereof to the Authority provided that in special cases, the General Manager may relax, at his discretion, the conditions regarding the period of notice of resignation or pay in lieu thereof.

[4] **Article 136 in The Constitution Of India 1949**

136. Special leave to appeal by the Supreme Court

(1) Notwithstanding anything in this Chapter, the Supreme Court may, in its discretion, grant special leave to appeal from any judgment, decree, determination, sentence or order in any cause or matter passed or made by any court or tribunal in the territory of India

(2) Nothing in clause (1) shall apply to any judgment, determination, sentence or order passed or made by any court or tribunal constituted by or under any law relating to the Armed Forces

[5] A formal written application requesting a court for a specific judicial action

constitutional validity of the right of the employer to terminate the services of permanent employees without holding any inquiry in certain circumstances by reasonable notice or pay in lieu of notice.

High Court judgment

It was held by the court that the said provision gave absolute, unbridled and arbitrary powers to the Management to terminate the services of any permanent or temporary employee.

High Court of Delhi struck down Regulation 9(b) of the said Regulations, and directed the appellant to pay back respondents' wages and benefits within 3 months.

Arguments on behalf of the Counsel

When the service of a person employed for an indefinite period or till the age of retirement is terminated, then Article 14[6] is violated when there is no guidance for the exercise of power and reasons are not required to be recorded and principles of natural justice are abrogated. Similarly Article 19(1)(g)[7] is violated, according to Counsel, for the reasons that there is no guidance, no requirement of reasons to be recorded and there is violation of the principles of natural justice.

Decision of the Supreme Court:

Supreme Court struck down Regulation 9(b) of the said Regulations, and directed the appellant to pay back respondents' wages and benefits. Court also concluded that the regulation 9(b) of the Regulations are arbitrary, unjust, unfair and unreasonable offending Article 14, 16(1)[8], 19(1)(g) and 21[9] of the Constitution.

---

[6] **Article 14 in The Constitution Of India 1949**

14. Equality before law The State shall not deny to any person equality before the law or the equal protection of the laws within the territory of India Prohibition of discrimination on grounds of religion, race, caste, sex or place of birth

[7] **Article 19(1)(g) in The Constitution Of India 1949**

(g) to practise any profession, or to carry on any occupation, trade or business

[8] **Article 16(1) in The Constitution Of India 1949**

(1) There shall be equality of opportunity for all citizens in matters relating to employment or appointment to any office under the State

[9] **Article 21 in The Constitution Of India**

Protection of life and personal liberty No person shall be deprived of his life or personal liberty except according to procedure established by law

CIVIL LAW

Civil Law

Civil law is a unique type of law inspired by Roman law. Civil laws are based on the historic customs that are stuck in codified and writing not determined as in the case of common law.

"Civil laws are primary based on law system of Roman that usually provide a set of written and accessible collection of the laws which are applied to all citizens even to all legal professionals including lawyers, attorneys and judges must also follow the same. Legal code is the primary source of civil law which is arranged in a some pre specified order according to subject matters." Civil law is one of the oldest and prevalent surviving legal systems in the world.

Civil law deals with disputes between private parties, or negligent acts that cause harm to others . For example, if individuals or companies disagree over the terms of an agreement, or who owns land or buildings, or whether a person was wrongfully dismissed from their employment, they may file a lawsuit asking the courts to decide who is right. As well, the failure to exercise the degree of caution that an ordinarily prudent person would take in any situation may result in a negligence claim. Depending on the circumstances, a person may be held responsible for any damages or injury that occurs as a result of their negligence. Family law cases involving divorce, parental responsibility for children, spousal support, child support and division of property between spouses or common law couples represent a large portion of the civil law cases presented to the courts. Challenges to decisions of administrative tribunals, allegations of medical malpractice and applications for distribution of the estates of deceased persons are other examples of civil cases. The party who brings the legal action is known as the plaintiff or applicant, while the party being sued is the defendant or respondent. The courts may dismiss a case, or if it is found to have merit, the courts may order the losing party to take corrective action, although the usual outcome is an order to pay damages - a monetary award designed to make up for the harm inflicted. The state plays no role in civil cases, unless the government launches a lawsuit or is the party being sued. Parties retain a lawyer - or may choose to represent themselves - to gather evidence and present the case in court.

50

Hawking and Vending a Fundamental Right[1]

Ratio Decidendi[2]:

"Rights cannot be let to be gone merely because people belongs to poor sections."

Facts in Nutshell:

Hawking on the streets of Delhi, whose municipal limits have expanded over the years, has been the subject matter of several proceedings in Court. Initially in the early sixties, the problem surfaced when the Court, hearing an appeal from a decision dated 4th August, 1966 of the Punjab High Court, Circuit Bench at Delhi, dealt with this question in some detail in the case of *Pyare Lal v. New Delhi Municipal Committee and Anr*[3]. In **Pyare Lal case**, sale of cooked food on public streets which was creating the problems of unhygienic conditions came up before the Court in the context of a resolution of the New Delhi Municipal Committee stopping such sale. A three-Judge Bench of the Court held that no person carrying on the aforesaid business of selling cooked food has any *fundamental right* to carry on street vending particularly in a manner which creates unsanitary and unhygienic conditions in the neighbourhood.

Pursuant to the directions of the Hon'ble Court, a scheme was prepared by the NDMC (New Delhi Municipal Corporation) vide its Resolution No. 28 dated 10.11.1989 and the same was placed before the Lok Adalat.

---

[1] Appellants: **Gainda Ram and Ors. Vs.** Respondent: **M.C.D. and Ors.**
JT2010(11)SC228

Hon'ble Judges: G. S. Singhvi and Asok Kumar Ganguly, JJ.

[2] **Meaning of Ratio Decidendi**

Ratio decidendi is a Latin phrase meaning "the reason" or "the rationale for the decision." The *ratio decidendi* is "[t]he point in a case which determines the judgment" or "the principle which the case establishes."

[3] MANU/SC/0010/1967 : AIR 1968 SC 133.

Thereupon, a general order was passed by the Lok Adalat after going through the scheme submitted by NDMC on the guidelines laid down by the Court in **Sodan Singh case** (for creation of hawking jones) for implementation of the scheme. But several petitions were filed against the scheme of NDMC.

Judgments Referred:

The Court in *Sodan Singh and Ors. v. New Delhi Municipal Committee and Ors.*[4] come to the conclusion that the hawkers and squatters have a fundamental right to carry on business on the public street, but the same should be regulated. It was further held that the right of a hawker to transact business, while going from place to place, is recognized in India for a long period. Of course such right is subject to regulation since public streets demand its use by the public and the streets are not meant to facilitate some citizens to carry on any private business. However, such right of hawking for carrying on business on the street cannot be denied if they are properly regulated. The learned Judge made it very clear that the said right is subject to reasonable restrictions under Clause (6) of Article 19[5]. The Constitution Bench in **Sodan Singh** case clarified in paragraph 24 of the judgment that the demand of the petitioners that the hawkers must be permitted on every road in the city, could not be allowed, if the road was not wide enough to conveniently manage the traffic on it, no hawking may be permitted at all, or may be sanctioned only once a week, say on Sundays when the rush considerably thinned out. Hawking could also be justifiably prohibited near hospitals or where necessity of security measures so demanded. Court also held that it is, therefore, settled law that every citizen has a right to the use

---

[4] MANU/SC/0521/1989 : (1989) 4 SCC 155

[5] **Article 19 in The Constitution Of India 1949**

(6) Nothing in sub clause (g) of the said clause shall affect the operation of any existing law in so far as it imposes, or prevent the State from making any law imposing, in the interests of the general public, reasonable restrictions on the exercise of the right conferred by the said sub clause, and, in particular, nothing in the said sub clause shall affect the operation of any existing law in so far as it relates to, or prevent the State from making any law relating to,

(i) the professional or technical qualifications necessary for practising any profession or carrying on any occupation, trade or business, or

(ii) the carrying on by the State, or by a corporation owned or controlled by the State, of any trade, business, industry or service, whether to the exclusion, complete or partial, of citizens or otherwise

of a public street vested in the State as a beneficiary but this right is subject to such reasonable restrictions as the State may choose to impose. Street-trading is albeit a fundamental right under Article 19(1)(g) of the Constitution but it is subject to reasonable restrictions which the State may choose to impose by virtue of Clause (6) of Article 19 of the Constitution. The right to street-trading under Article 19(1)(g)[6]. of the Constitution does not, however, extend to a citizen occupying or squatting on any specific place of his choice on the pavement regardless of the rights of others, including pedestrians, to make use of the pavements. In other words the law laid down by the Constitution Bench permits a citizen to hawk on the street pavements by moving from one place to another without being stationary on any part of the pavement vested in the State. After laying down the law on the point in the context of Articles 14[7], 19[8] and 21[9] of the Constitution, the Constitution Bench remitted all the petitions to. a proper Division Bench of this Court for final disposal.

Municipal Corporation of Delhi v. Gurnam Kaur [10] held that when the citizens by gathering meager resources try to employ themselves as hawkers and street traders, they cannot be subjected to a deprivation on the pretext

---

[6] **Article 19(1)(g) in The Constitution Of India 1949**

(g) to practise any profession, or to carry on any occupation, trade or business

[7] **Article 14 in The Constitution Of India 1949**

14. Equality before law The State shall not deny to any person equality before the law or the equal protection of the laws within the territory of India Prohibition of discrimination on grounds of religion, race, caste, sex or place of birth

[8] **Article 19 in The Constitution Of India 1949**

19. Protection of certain rights regarding freedom of speech etc

(1) All citizens shall have the right

(a) to freedom of speech and expression;

(b) to assemble peaceably and without arms;

(c) to form associations or unions;

(d) to move freely throughout the territory of India;

(e) to reside and settle in any part of the territory of India; and

(f) omitted

(g) to practise any profession, or to carry on any occupation, trade or business

[9] **Article 21 in The Constitution Of India 1949**

21. Protection of life and personal liberty No person shall be deprived of his life or personal liberty except according to procedure established by law

[10] (19.89) 1 SCC 101

that they have no right. The learned Judge deplored that despite repeated, suggestions by this Court, the Government has not yet framed regulations for regulating citizen's right to carry on hawking business on the, streets.

In the meantime, the writ petition No. 1699/87 *Gainda Ram and Ors. v. MCD*[11] was disposed of by High Court by its judgment and order dated 12th May 1993

Decision by Supreme Court:

Court held that the hawkers' and squatters' or vendors' right to carry on hawking has been recognized as fundamental right under Article 19(1)(g). At the same time the right of the commuters to move freely and use the roads without any impediment is also a fundamental right under Article 19(1)(d). These two apparently conflicting rights must be harmonized and regulated by subjecting them to reasonable restrictions only under a law. The fundamental right of the hawkers, just because they are poor and unorganized, cannot be left in a state of limbo nor can it left to be decided by the varying standards of a scheme which changes from time to time.

---

[11] MANU/SC/0523/1993: (1993) 3 SCC 178.

51

Medical negligence and the liability of Medical Professionals[1]

Facts in Nutshell:

The plaintiffs-respondents, respectively husband and wife, filed a suit against the State of Punjab, the appellant and a lady surgeon who was in the State Government's employment at the relevant time, for recovery of damages to the tune of Rs. 3,00,000/- on account of a female child having been born to them in spite of the wife-respondent No. 2 having undergone a tubectomy operation performed by the lady surgeon. According to the plaintiffs-respondents, they already had a son and two daughters from the wed-lock lasting over 17 years. In response to a publicity campaign carried out by the Family Welfare Department of the appellant-State, respondent No. 2 with the consent of respondent No. 1, underwent a sterilization operation on 1.8.1984. A certificate in this regard bearing mark of identification No. 505, duly signed by the lady surgeon who performed the said surgery, was issued to her. She was given a cash award of Rs. 150/- as an incentive for the operation. On 4.10.1991, respondent No. 2 gave birth to a female child. After serving a notice under Section 80[2] of the Code of Civil Procedure, a

---

[1] Appellants: **State of Punjab Vs.** Respondent: **Shiv Ram and Ors.**
   AIR2005SC3280
   Hon'ble Judges: R. C. Lahoti, C.J., C. K. Thakker and P. K. Balasubramanyan, JJ.

[2] **Section 80 Civil Procedure Code**
   Notice:
   [Save as otherwise provided in sub-section (2), no suits [shall be instituted] against the Government (including the Government of the State of Jammu & Kashmir)] or against a public officer in respect of any act purporting to be done by such officer in his official capacity, until the expiration of two months next after notice in writing has been [delivered to, or left at the office of]-

suit for recovery of damages was filed on 15.5.92 attributing the birth of the child to carelessness and negligence of the lady surgeon. The plaint alleged *inter alia* that the respondents considered abortion to be a sin and that is why after knowing of the conception they did not opt for abortion. The State was impleaded as defendant No. 1 and the lady surgeon who performed the surgery was impleaded as defendant No. 2.

The defendants submitted that there was no negligence or carelessness in the performance of the surgery. It is stated in authoritative text books of medical science that pregnancy occurring after sterilization may be attributable to natural failure. It was also submitted that the plaintiffs having learnt of the unwanted pregnancy, should have sought medical opinion and opted for medical termination of pregnancy within 20 weeks which is permissible and legal[3].

(a) in the case of a suit against the Central Government, [except where it relates to a railway], a Secretary to that Government;

[[(b)] in the case of a suit against the Central Government where it relates to railway, the General Manager of that railway];

[(bb) in the case of a suit against the Government of the State of Jammu and Kashmir the Chief Secretary to that Government or any other officer authorised by that Government in this behalf;]

(c) in the case of a suit against [any other State Government], a Secretary to that Government or the Collector of the district;

[3] **Section 3 in The Medical Termination Of Pregnancy Act, 1971**

When pregnancies may be terminated by registered medical practitioners.

(2) Subject to the provisions of sub- section (4), a pregnancy may be terminated by a registered medical practitioner,-

(a) where the length of the pregnancy does not exceed twelve weeks, if such medical practitioner is, or

(b) where the length of the pregnancy exceeds twelve weeks but does not exceed twenty weeks, if not less than two registerd medical practitioners are of opinion, formed in good faith, that-

(i) the continuance of the pregnancy would involve a risk to the life of the pregnant woman or of grave injury to her physical or mental health; or

(ii) there is a substantial risk that if the child were born, it would suffer from such physical or mental abnormalities as to be seriously handicapped. Explanation I.- Where any pregnancy is alleged by the pregnant woman to have been caused by rape, the angwish caused by such pregnancy shall be presumed to constitute a grave injury to the mental health of the pregnant woman. Explanation II.- Where any pregnancy occurs as a result of failure of any device or method used by any married woman or her husband for the purpose of limiting the number of children, the anguish caused by such unwanted pregnancy may be presumed to constitute a grave injury to the mental health of the pregnant woman.

(3) In determining whether the continuance of a pregnancy would involve such risk of injury to the health as is mentioned in sub- section (2), account may be taken of the pregnant woman' s actual or reasonably foreseeable environment.

(4) (a) No pregnancy of a woman, who has not attained the age of eighteen years, or, who, having attained the age of eighteen years, is a lunatic, shall be terminated except with the consent in writing of her guardian.

(b) Save as otherwise provided in clause (a), no pregnancy shall be terminated except with the consent of the pregnant woman.

Decision by Trial Court:

Court held that on the birth of a child to a woman who was allured into undergoing sterilization operation by the State in pursuance of its Family Planning Schemes, the State was liable to compensate for the consequences of the operation having failed. The suit was decreed for Rs. 50,000/- with interest and costs. The decree for compensation passed by the trial court has been upheld by the first appellate court. The second appeal preferred by the State has been summarily dismissed.

Principles on which the liability of a medical professional is determined:

Reference was made to *Jacob Mathew v. State of Punjab and Anr.*[4]

The relevant principles culled out from the case of **Jacob Mathew** read as under:

(1) Negligence is the breach of a duty caused by omission to do something which a reasonable man guided by those considerations which ordinarily regulate the conduct of human affairs would do, or doing something which a prudent and reasonable man would not do. The definition of negligence as given in Law of Torts, Ratanlal & Dhirajlal (edited by Justice G.P. Singh), referred to hereinabove, holds good. Negligence becomes actionable on account of injury resulting from the act or omission amounting to negligence attributable to the person sued. The essential components of negligence are three: 'duty', 'breach' and 'resulting damage'.

(2) A simple lack of care, an error of judgment or an accident, is not proof of negligence on the part of a medical professional. So long as a doctor follows a practice acceptable to the medical profession of that day, he cannot be held liable for negligence merely because a better alternative course or method of treatment was also available or simply because a more skilled doctor would not have chosen to follow or resort to that practice or procedure which the accused followed. When it comes to the failure of taking precautions what has to be seen is whether those precautions were taken which the ordinary experience of men has found to be sufficient; a failure to use special or extraordinary precautions which might have prevented the

---

[4] 2005CriLJ3710

particular happening cannot be the standard for judging the alleged negligence.

(3) A professional may be held liable for negligence on one of the two findings: either he was not possessed of the requisite skill which he professed to have possessed, or, he did not exercise, with reasonable competence in the given case, the skill which he did possess. The standard to be applied for judging, whether the person charged has been negligent or not, would be that of an ordinary competent person exercising ordinary skill in that profession. It is not possible for every professional to possess the highest level of expertise or skills in that branch which he practices. A highly skilled professional may be possessed of better qualities, but that cannot be made the basis or the yardstick for judging the performance of the professional proceeded against on indictment of negligence.

The Court has further held in *Jacob Mathew's case* :-

"Accident during the course of medical or surgical treatment has a wider meaning. Ordinarily, an accident means an unintended and unforeseen injurious occurrence; something that does not occur in the usual course of events or that could not be reasonably anticipated[5] . Care has to be taken to see that the result of an accident which is exculpatory may not persuade the human mind to confuse it with the consequence of negligence."

Decision by Supreme Court:

The plaintiffs have not alleged that the lady surgeon who performed the sterilization operation was not competent to perform the surgery and yet ventured into doing it. It is neither the case of the plaintiffs, nor has any finding been arrived at by any of the courts below that the lady surgeon was negligent in performing the surgery. The present one was not a case where the surgeon who performed the surgery has committed breach of any duty cast on her as a surgeon. The surgery was performed by a technique known and recognized by medical science. It is a pure and simple case of sterilization operation having failed though duly performed. The appeal was allowed. The judgment and decree passed by the trial court and upheld by the first appellate court and the High Court were set aside. The suit filed by the

---

[5] See, Black's Law Dictionary, 7th Edition

plaintiffs- respondents was dismissed. However, court held that the amount of Rs. 50,000/- if already paid to the plaintiff-respondent shall not be liable to be refunded by way of restitution[6].

---

[6] **Restitution** 1) returning to the proper owner property or the monetary value of loss. Sometimes restitution is made part of a judgment in negligence and/or contracts cases. 2) in criminal cases, one of the penalties imposed is return of stolen goods to the victim or payment to the victim for harm caused. Restitution may be a condition of granting defendant probation or giving him/her a shorter sentence than normal.

301

52

Death due to Pothole and Maintenance of Roads[1]

Facts in Nutshell:

The petitioner-Ms. Madhu Kaur mother of late Mr. Harpreet Singh, who expired in road accident. The petitioner claimed that the road accident in which she lost her son, aged about 22-24 years, was directly attributable to negligence of the respondents Government of NCT of Delhi and Municipal Corporation of Delhi as they had failed to maintain the road in front of base hospital near Balaji temple at Brar Square, Naraina, Delhi. It was stated that the deceased, who was driving a scooter at about 9:30 p.m. at night on 4th May, 2006 got imbalanced and died after hitting a pit (khada), which was more than 4 inches below the regular tarred surface of the main road. The petitioner claims compensation of Rs. 50 lacs from the respondents alleging negligence[2] due to failure to maintain road and to display sign boards of caution in case the road had a pit or a khada, which required repairs.

---

[1] Appellants: **Madhu Kaur** Vs. Respondent: **Govt. of NCT of Delhi an Anr.**
2010ACJ1798

Hon'ble Judges: Sanjiv Khanna, J.

[2] Negligence means failure to exercise due care expected from a reasonable prudent person. It is breach of a duty to take care for safety of others. Negligence implies breach of duty or lack of proper care in doing something. In short, it is want of attention and doing something which a prudent and reasonable man would or would not do. Clerk & Lindsell on Torts (18th Ed.) sets out four requirements of the tort of negligence and the same read:

(1) the existence in law of duty of care situation, i.e. one in which the law attaches liability to carelessness. There has to be recognition by law that the careless infliction of the kind of damages in suit on the class of person to which the claimant belongs by the class of person to which the defendant belongs is actionable;

(2) breach of duty of care by the defendant, i.e. that it failed to measure up to the standard set by law;

(3) casual connection between the defendant's careless conduct and the damage;

(4) that the particular kind of damage to the particular claimant is not so unforeseeable as to be too remote.

Road Maintenance:

The road in question was maintained and under the supervision and control of Government of NCT of Delhi. Roads are meant for being used by vehicles including two wheelers in Delhi. It is/was the responsibility and obligation of the Government of NCT of Delhi to maintain the said road in question. As a reasonable person, Government of NCT of Delhi is/was aware that in case there are/were pits on the road, a person driving a two wheeler can lose balance and suffer injuries including fatal injury. Government of NCT of Delhi was required to act in a prudent manner and ensure that the road in question was properly maintained and not act in a manner which would show a shameful disregard of safety of persons using the road. Failure to properly maintain the road and display caution notice/sign when a road is damaged results in failure to take due care as was expected of a reasonable prudent person and amounts to negligence. The fact that the respondent Government of NCT of Delhi had appointed a contractor does not absolve them from their own responsibility. It was the duty of the Government of NCT of Delhi to see that the contractor was properly performing the work and task entrusted to them.

Judgments Cited:

The Delhi High Court has taken the view that improper maintenance of roads amounts to negligence and in such cases when an accident occurs the road maintaining agency is liable to pay compensation for the loss suffered and damage caused. In *Raj Kumar v. Union of India and Anr.*[3] , a scooterist drove over a manhole which was three inches below surface of the road and lost control and died after hitting the side/divider railing. The road maintenance agencies, viz. MCD as well as Delhi Jal Board who were required to maintain and repair manhole were found guilty and the compensation was awarded. Appeal filed by Delhi Jal Board before the Division Bench was dismissed by a detailed judgment in *Delhi Jal Board v. Raj Kumar and Ors.*[4] The Division Bench noted that when power is given to do some act, it also implies duty to act properly.

---

[3] 124(2005)DLT218

[4] AIR2006Delhi75

Decision by High Court:

The respondent authorities should be conscious and aware of their duty to maintain roads and ensure that the road surface does not have any pits or khada so as to cause accidents, thus resulting in injuries and even loss of life. It is the obligation and responsibility of the road owning agencies to ensure that the roads are maintained properly and repairs undertaken. Even if they have entered into third party contracts for road maintenance, road users should not suffer injuries fatal or otherwise because of lack of maintenance, proper care and repairs. In case road is found to be damaged, necessary caution board/sign boards or barricades should be fixed. In case accidents take place as a result of negligence and failure to maintain roads, damages can always be awarded to persons who have suffered or lost a near and dear one. Loss of life because of negligence of state instrumentalities results in violation of right to life and liberty under Article 21 of the Constitution[5]. In such cases of violation of fundamental right to life, a High Court under Article 226 of the Constitution[6] has power to award

---

[5] **Article 21 in The Constitution Of India**
Protection of life and personal liberty No person shall be deprived of his life or personal liberty except according to procedure established by law

[6] **Article 226 of the Indian Constitution, 1950**: Power of High Courts to issue certain writs.
(1) Notwithstanding anything in Article 32 every High Court shall have powers, throughout the territories in relation to which it exercise jurisdiction, to issue to any person or authority, including in appropriate cases, any Government, within those territories directions, orders or writs, including writs in the nature of habeas corpus, mandamus, prohibitions, quo warranto and certiorari, or any of them, for the enforcement of any of the rights conferred by Part III and for any other purpose.
(2) The power conferred by clause (1) to issue directions, orders or writs to any Government, authority or person may also be exercised by any High Court exercising jurisdiction in relation to the territories within which the cause of action , wholly or in part, arises for the exercise of such power, notwithstanding that the seat of such Government or authority or the residence of such person is not within those territories.
(3) Where any party against whom an interim order, whether by way of injunction or stay or in any other manner, is made on, or in any proceedings relating to, a petition under clause (1), without-
(a) furnishing to such party copies of such petition and all documents in support of the plea for such interim order; and
(b) giving such party an opportunity of being heard, makes an application to the High Court for the vacation of such order and furnishes a copy of such application to the party in whose favor such order has been made or the counsel of such party, the High Court shall dispose of the application within a period of two weeks from the date on which it is received or from the date on which the copy of such application is so furnished, whichever is later, or where the High Court is closed on the last day of that period, before the expiry of the next day afterwards on which the High Court is open; and if the application is not so disposed of, the interim order shall, on the expiry of that period, or , as the case may be, the expiry of the aid next day, stand vacated.
(4) The power conferred on a High Court by this article shall not be in derogation of the power conferred on the Supreme court by clause (2) of Article 32.

compensation and direct the State instrumentality or its servants to ensure enforcement of fundamental rights. This remedy is available in public law.

Compensation in case of loss of life is calculated on the basis of pecuniary loss and non pecuniary loss. Pecuniary loss compensates a person/ claimant of the financial loss suffered. As the financial loss suffered pertains to uncertain future, arithmetical niceties are not required and a rough and a fair estimate is made on the basis of evidence and material placed on record. For calculating pecuniary loss or loss of dependency, the Court has repeatedly held that it is the multiplier method which should be applied. The said method is based upon the principle that the claimant must be paid a capital sum, which would yield sufficient interest to provide material benefits of the same standard and duration as the deceased would have provided for the dependents, if the deceased had lived and earned. The multiplier method is based upon the assessment that yearly loss of dependency should be equal to interest that could be earned in normal course on the capital sum invested. The capital sum would be the compensation for loss of dependency or the pecuniary loss suffered by the dependents. Needless to say, uniform application of the multiplier method ensures consistency and certainty and prevents different amounts being awarded in different cases. For calculating the yearly loss of dependency the starting point is the wages being earned by the deceased, less his personal and living expenses. This provides a basic figure. Thereafter, effect is given to the future prospects of the deceased, inflation and general price rise that erodes value and the purchasing power of money. To the multiplicand so calculated, multiplier is to be applied. The multiplier is decided and determined on the basis of length of dependency, which must be estimated. This has to be necessarily discounted for contingencies and uncertainties.

The multiplier method involves ascertaining of loss of dependency or the multiplicand having regard to the circumstances of the case and capitalizing the multiplicand by appropriate multiplier. The multiplier is determined by the age of the deceased or the claimant. The object is to compute a capital sum which if invested would yield interest in a stable economy equal to the annual dependency. While ascertaining the dependency, regard is to be also given to the fact that ultimately the capital sum should be consumed over a period of time for which the dependency is expected to last.

It is, therefore, safe to presume that the deceased was working as a sales executive and drawing about Rs. 6,500/- per month as salary. In normal course, the deceased would have got married and had his own immediate family. Only a proportion of his income would have been used and was for benefit of the petitioner. Normally in such cases, 50% is deducted towards his personal and immediate family expenses. In some cases future prospects due to possible increase in income of the deceased during the period of dependency have been taken into consideration. In these circumstances, the average monthly wage of the deceased considering the future prospects can be taken as Rs. 8,000/- per month, out of which the petitioner's dependency is presumed to be 50% or Rs. 4,000/-. The annual dependency is Rs. 4000/- x 12= Rs. 48,000. Multiplier of 11 is applied in the present case keeping in view the probable age of the petitioner. The total pecuniary compensation payable is Rs 5,28,000/-. Loss of company, loss of protection and motherhood is to be compensated. Compensation of Rs. 1 lac is awarded on that account. In other words, total compensation of Rs. 6,28,000/- was paid by the respondent No. 1, Government of NCT of Delhi to the petitioner.

53

No one shall be imprisoned merely on the ground of inability to fulfill a contractual obligation[1]

Facts in Nutshell:

Debtors[2] (the appellants) whose personal freedom is in peril because a court warrant for arrest and detention in the civil prison is chasing them for non-payment of an amount due to a bank (the respondent).

The debtors (appellants) suffered a decree[3] against them in a sum of Rs. 2.5 lakhs, the respondent-bank being the decree-holder[4]. There are two other money decrees against the appellants, the total sum payable by them being over Rs. 7 lakhs. In execution of the decree in question a warrant[5] for arrest and detention in the civil prison was issued to the appellants

---

[1] Appellants: **Jolly George Varghese and Anr. Vs.** Respondent: **The Bank of Cochin**
AIR1980SC470

   Hon'ble Judges: R. S. Pathak and V. R. Krishna Iyer, JJ.

[2] A person who owes a creditor; someone who has the obligation of paying a debt

[3] **Civil Procedure Code 1908**

   Section 2. Definitions

   "decree" means the formal expression of an adjudication which, so far as regards the Court expressing it, conclusively determines the rights of the parties with regard to all or any of the matters in controversy in the suit and may be either preliminary or final.

[4] **Civil Procedure Code 1908**

   Section 2. Definitions

   Section 3 "decree-holder" means any person in whose favour a decree has been passed or an order capable of execution has been made;

[5] A written order issued by a judicial officer or other authorized person commanding a law enforce ment officer to perform some act incident to the administration of justice

under Section 51[6] and Order 21, Rule. 37 of the Civil Procedure Code[7]. Besides this process, the decree-holders had proceeded against the properties of the judgment-debtors and in consequence, all these immovable properties had been attached for the purpose of sale in discharge of the decree debts.

Question before the Court:

The question before the court was whether personal freedom of the judgment-debtors can be held in ransom until repayment of the debt and whether such deprivation of liberty illegal? From the perspective of international law the question posed is whether it is right to enforce a contractual liability by imprisoning a debtor in the teeth of Article 11 of the International Covenant on Civil and Political Rights. The Article reads:

No one shall be imprisoned merely *on the ground of inability to fulfil a contractual obligation.*

The Covenant bans imprisonment merely for not discharging a decree debt. Unless there be some other vice or mens ret apart from failure to foot the decree, international law frowns on holding the debtor's person in civil prison, as hostage by the court. India is now a signatory to this Covenant and

---

[6] **Section 51 runs thus:**

51. Subject to such conditions and limitations as may be prescribed, the Court may, on the application of the decree-holder, order execution of the decree-

(a) by delivery of any property specifically decreed;

(b) by attachment and sale or by sale without attachment of any property;

(c) by arrest and detention in prison;

(d) by appointing a receiver; or

(e) in such other manner as the nature of the relief granted may require.

[7] **Order 21 Rule 37:**

37. (1) Notwithstanding anything in these rules, where an application is for the execution of a decree for the payment of money by the arrest and detention is the civil prison of a judgment-debtor who is liable to be arrested in pursuance of the application, the Court shall, instead of issuing a warrant for his arrest, issue a notice calling upon him to appear before the Court op. a day to be specified in the notice and show cause why he should not be committed to the civil prison:

Provided that such notice shall not be necessary if the Court is satisfied, by affidavit, or otherwise, that, with the object or effect of delaying the execution of the decree, the judgment-debtor is likely to abscond or leave the local limits of the jurisdiction of the Court.

(2) Where appearance is not made in obedience to the notice, the Court shall, if the decree-holder so requires, issue a warrant for the arrest of the judgment-debtor.

Article 51(c) of the Constitution[8] obligates the State to "foster respect for international law and treaty obligations in the dealings of organised peoples with one another".

Poverty and Prison (Para 16 of the Judgment)

To cast a person in prison because of his poverty and consequent inability to meet his contractual liability is appalling. To be poor, in this land of daridra Narayana, is no crime and to 'recover' debts by the procedure of putting one in prison is too flagrantly violative of Article 21[9] unless there is proof of the minimal fairness of his wilful failure to pay in spite of his sufficient means and absence of more terribly pressing claims on his means such as medical bills to treat cancer or other grave illness.

Decision of the Court:

In the present case the debtors were in distress because of the blanket distraint of their properties.

Court set aside the arrest of Debtors.

---

[8] **Article 51(c) in The Constitution Of India 1949**

(c) foster respect for international law and treaty obligations in the dealings of organised peoples with one another; and encourage settlement of international disputes by arbitration PART IVA FUNDAMENTAL DUTIES

[9] **Article 21 in The Constitution Of India**

Protection of life and personal liberty No person shall be deprived of his life or personal liberty except according to procedure established by law

Right to Information

Right to Information

The **Right to Information Act 2005 (RTI)** is an Act of the Parliament of India "to provide for setting out the practical regime of right to information for citizens." The Act applies to all States and Union Territories of India except the State of Jammu and Kashmir. Jammu and Kashmir has its own act called Jammu & Kashmir Right to Information Act, 2009. Under the provisions of the Act, any citizen may request information from a "public authority" (a body of Government or "instrumentality of State") which is required to reply expeditiously or within thirty days. The Act also requires every public authority to computerize their records for wide dissemination and to pro-actively publish certain categories of information so that the citizens need minimum recourse to request for information formally.

Seeds for the Legislation on Right to Information

In 1966, the right to information was established for the federal government agencies when the United States adopted the Freedom of Information Act (FOIA). After the resignation of President Richard Nixon in 1974, FOIA strengthened and became the model for other states of the US who adopted similar statutes. FOIA also became the model for other countries, such as Canada, Australia, and New Zealand – all of which adopted similar laws in 1982. By 1990, fifteen other nations, mainly the developed countries in Europe had similar statutes. In the next two decades, similar statutes were adopted by some of the other developed countries like Germany, United Kingdom and Japan. While acting as per the advice of international institutions like World Bank, the FOIA style laws were also adopted by some of the governments later on. By 2010, over seventy nations had adopted the FOIA style of laws. Even in China, a right to information was provided by way of adopting certain regulations. The laws adopted by most of the countries over the last two decades, however, differ in many respects from the United States and the other countries who had adopted it earlier.

The RTI Act under section 27(1) and 28(1) specifies to the appropriate Governments and the Competent Authorities to make rules pertaining to implementation of the Act. Under Section 6 of the RTI Act, PIOs are required to provide reasonable assistance to the applicant in drafting and submission of the application. But unfortunately the implementation of these clauses seems to far short of satisfaction. Unless the various problems attached to implementation of RTI ACT are addressed comprehensively by the appropriate Government and Public Authority in tandem, it would continue to be an issue

Right to Information as a tool to Combat Corruption

In India today, being a welfare-state, the state has spread its tentacles to virtually every aspect of public life. The person on the street is condemned to grapple hopelessly with corruption in almost every aspect of daily work and living. Information is power, and the executive at all levels attempts to withhold information to increase its scope for control, patronage, and the arbitrary, corrupt and unaccountable exercise of power. Ultimately the most effective systemic check on corruption would be where the citizen herself or himself has the right to take the initiative to seek information from the state, and thereby to enforce transparency and accountability. It is in this context that the movement for right to information is so important. The statutory right to information gives a legal right to have access to government-held information strengthens democracy by ensuring transparency and accountability in the actions of public bodies. It enhances the quality of citizen-participation in governance from mere vote-casting, to involvement in the decision-making that affects her or his life.[1]

The most effective check on corruption would be where the citizen has the right to take the initiative to seek information from the state, and thereby to enforce transparency and accountability. This would enhance the quality of participatory political democracy.

---

[1] SHALU NIGAM, *Right to Information Law & Practice*, at p. 4.

Although the right to information is implicit in the Constitution of India the dominant culture of the executive has been one of secrecy and resolute denial of access to information. Demystification of rules and procedures and pro-active dissemination of relevant information amongst the public serves as a very strong safeguard against corruption.

To this end the RTI Act empowers ordinary citizens to exercise far greater control over corrupt and arbitrary exercise of state power. It increases transparency and takes away excuses provided under the Official Secrets Act, 1923 and the Freedom to Information Act, 2000 to evade accountability. It grants citizens access to government information and a mechanism to control public spending.

RTI act requires government officials to furnish information requested by citizens or face punitive action and provides for computerisation of services. This along with the various central and state government established vigilance commissions has considerably reduced corruption and has opened up avenues to redress grievances.

In a recent case the finance ministry under-secretary Jagbir Sigh Phaugat said while deeming a settlement between the Central Bank of India and whistleblower Abhijit Ghosh illegal that "The agreement debars Ghosh from his constitutional rights of freedom of press and no one can debar a person form invoking the provisions of the RTI act."[2]

---

[2] Marpakwar, Prafulla, "Bank-whistleblower deal illegal", TOI Dec 24, 2010.

54

Under RTI Candidate is Entitled to Have A Copy of Answer Sheet[1]

Facts in Nutshell: The first Respondent appeared for the Secondary School Examination, 2008 conducted by the Central Board of Secondary Education (for short 'CBSE' or the 'Appellant'). When he got the mark sheet he was disappointed with his marks. He thought that he had done well in the examination but his answer-books were not properly valued and that improper valuation had resulted in low marks. Therefore he made an application for inspection and re-evaluation of his answer-books. CBSE rejected the said request by letter dated 12.7.2008. The reasons for rejection were:

i) The information sought was exempted under Section 8(1)(e)[2] of RTI Act, 2005

(ii) The Examination Bye-laws of the Board provided that no candidate shall claim or is entitled to re-evaluation of his answers or disclosure or inspection of answer book(s) or other documents.

(iii) The larger public interest does not warrant the disclosure of such information sought.

---

[1] Appellants: **Central Board of Secondary Education and Anr**. Vs.Respondent: **Aditya Bandopadhyay and Ors.**

2011 6 AWC(Supp)5567SC, 2011(4)JCR14(SC)

Hon'ble Judges: R.V. Raveendran and A.K. Patnaik, JJ.

[2] **Section 8(1)(e) of RTI, Act, 2005**: 8(1) (e) information available to a person in his fiduciary relationship, unless the competent authority is satisfied that the larger public interest warrants the disclosure of such information;

Writ Petition in High Court by First Respondent: Feeling aggrieved the first Respondent filed W.P. No. 18189(W)/2008 before the Calcutta High Court and sought the following reliefs:

(a) For a declaration that the action of CBSE in excluding the provision of re-evaluation of answer-sheets, in regard to the examinations held by it was illegal, unreasonable and violative of the provisions of the Constitution of India;

(b) For a direction to CBSE to appoint an independent examiner for re-evaluating his answer-books and issue a fresh marks card on the basis of re-evaluation;

(c) For a direction to CBSE to produce candidate answer-books in regard to the 2008 Secondary School Examination so that they could be properly reviewed and fresh marks card can be issued with re-evaluation marks;

(d) For quashing the communication of CBSE dated 12.7.2008 and for a direction to produce the **answer**-books into court for inspection by the first Respondent.

The Respondent contended that Section 8(1)(e)[3] of **Right to Information Act**, 2005 ('**RTI** Act' for short) relied upon by CBSE was not applicable and relied upon the provisions of the RTI Act to claim inspection.

Decision by High Court: The High Court held that the evaluated answer-books of an examinee writing a public examination conducted by statutory bodies like CBSE or any University or Board of Secondary Education, being a 'document, manuscript record, and opinion' fell within the definition of "information" as defined in Section 2(f)[4] of the RTI Act. Court directed CBSE to grant inspection of the answer books to the examinees who sought information. The High Court however rejected the prayer made by the examinees for re-evaluation of the answer-books, as that was not a relief that was available under RTI Act.

---

[3] **Section 8(1)(e) of RTI, Act, 2005**: 8(1) (e) information available to a person in his fiduciary relationship, unless the competent authority is satisfied that the larger public interest warrants the disclosure of such information;

[4] **Section 2(f) of the RTI Act, 2005:** (f) " information" means any material in any form, including records, documents, memos, e- mails, opinions, advices, press releases, circulars, orders, logbooks, contracts, reports, papers, samples, models, data material held in any electronic form and information relating to any private body which can be accessed by a public authority under any other law for the time being in force;

Action by C.B.S.E:

Feeling aggrieved by the direction of the High Court **to** grant inspection, CBSE filed appeal by special leave in Hon'ble Supreme Court.

Questions before the Supreme Court:

(1) Whether the candidate is entitled for revaluation of answer sheet.

(2) Whether the examinee is entitled to inspect his evaluated answer-books or take certified copies thereof.

Decision by Supreme Court:

RTI Act which enables citizens and entitles them to have access to the answer books as 'information' and inspect them and take certified copies thereof. Section 22 of RTI Act, 2005[5] provides that the provisions of the said Act will have effect notwithstanding anything inconsistent therewith contained in any other law for the time being in force. The examining body will be bound to provide access to an examinee to inspect and take copies of his evaluated answer-books, even if such inspection or taking copies is barred under the rules/bye-laws of the examining body governing the examinations. Appeal of C.B.S.E was rejected.

---

[5] **Section 22 of the RTI Act, 2005:** The provisions of this Act shall have effect notwithstanding anything inconsistent therewith contained in the Official Secrets Act, 1923, and any other law for the time being in force or in any instrument having effect by virtue of any law other than this Act.

55

RTI do not apply to Judgments[1]

Facts in Nutshell:

The facts and circumstances giving rise to this case are, that the petitioner claimed to be in exclusive possession of the land in respect of which civil suit was filed before Additional Civil Judge, Ranga Reddy District praying for perpetual injunction[2] by Dr. Mallikarjina Rao against the petitioner and another, from entering into the suit land. Application filed for interim relief[3] in the said suit stood dismissed. Being aggrieved, the plaintiff therein preferred CMA No. 185 of 2002 and the same was also dismissed. Two other suits were filed in respect of the same property impleading the Petitioner also as the defendant. In one of the suits the Trial Court granted temporary injunction against the Petitioner. Being aggrieved, Petitioner preferred the CMA No. 67 of 2005, which was dismissed by the Appellate Court.

Petitioner filed an application dated 15.11.2006 under Section 6 of the RTI Act[4] before the Administrative Officer-cum-Assistant State Public Information Officer (respondent No. 1) seeking information to the queries mentioned therein. The said application was rejected vide order dated

---

[1] Appellants: **Khanapuram Gandaiah Vs.** Respondent: **Administrative Officer and Ors.** AIR2010SC615

Hon'ble Judges: K. G. Balakrishnan, C.J. and B. S. Chauhan, J.

[2] A *perpetual injunction* is an injunction that is directed towards the final settlement and enforcement of the rights of the parties that are in dispute....

[3] *Interim Relief:* Preliminary relief, such as an injunction, granted by the court to preserve the status quo pending trial.

[4] **Section 6 in The Right To Information Act, 2005**

6. Request for obtaining information.-

(1) A person, who desires to obtain any information under this Act, shall make a request in writing or through electronic means in English or Hindi or in the official language of the area in which the application is being made, accompanying such fee as may be prescribed, to-

23.11.2006 and an appeal against the said order was also dismissed vide order dated 20.1.2007. Second Appeal against the said order was also dismissed by the Andhra Pradesh State Information[5] Commission vide order dated 20.11.2007. The petitioner challenged the said order before the High Court, seeking a direction to the Respondent No. 1 to furnish the information as under what circumstances the Respondent No. 4 had passed the Judicial Order dismissing the appeal against the interim relief granted by the Trial Court. The Respondent No. 4 had been impleaded as respondent by name. The Writ Petition had been dismissed by the High Court on the grounds that the information sought by the petitioner cannot be asked for under the RTI Act.

Thus, the application was not maintainable. More so, the judicial officers are protected by the Judicial Officers' Protection Act, 1850 (hereinafter called the "Act 1850"). Hence, special leave petition[6] was filed by petitioner.

(a) the Central Public Information Officer or State Public Information Officer, as the case may be, of the concerned public authority;

(b) the Central Assistant Public Information Officer or State Assistant Public Information Officer, as the case may be, specifying the particulars of the information sought by him or her: Provided that where such request cannot be made in writing, the Central Public Information Officer or State Public Information Officer, as the case may be, shall render all reasonable assistance to the person making the request orally to reduce the same in writing.

(2) An applicant making request for information shall not be required to give any reason for requesting the information or any other personal details except those that may be necessary for contacting him.

(3) Where an application is made to a public authority requesting for an information,-

(i) which is held by another public authority; or

(ii) the subject matter of which is more closely connected with the functions of another public authority, the public authority, to which such application is made, shall transfer the application or such part of it as may be appropriate to that other public authority and inform the applicant immediately about such transfer: Provided that the transfer of an application pursuant to this sub- section shall be made as soon as practicable but in no case later than five days from the date of receipt of the application.

5   Under the RTI Act "information" is defined under Section 2(f) which provides:

information" means any material in any form, including records, documents, memos, e-mails, opinions, advices, press releases, circulars, orders, logbooks, contracts, report, papers, samples, models, data material held in any electronic form and information relating to any private body which can be accessed by a public authority under any other law for the time being in force.

6   Article 136 of Constitution, states that the Supreme Court may in its discretion, grant special leave to appeal from any judgment, decree, determination, sentence or order in any cause or matter passed or made by any court or tribunal in the territory of India.

Arguments by Petitioner's Counsel:

Learned Senior Counsel appearing for the petitioner had submitted that right to information is a fundamental right of every citizen. The RTI Act does not provide for any special protection to the Judges, thus petitioner has a right to know the reasons as to how the Respondent No. 4 has decided his appeal in a particular manner. Therefore, the application filed by the petitioner was maintainable.

Decision by Supreme Court:

Under the RTI Act "information" is defined under Section 2(f) which provides:

information" means any material in any form, including records, documents, memos, e-mails, opinions, advices, press releases, circulars, orders, logbooks, contracts, report, papers, samples, models, data material held in any electronic form and information relating to any private body which can be accessed by a public authority under any other law for the time being in force.

This definition shows that an applicant under Section 6 of the RTI Act can get any information which is already in existence and accessible to the public authority under law. Of course, under the RTI Act an applicant is entitled to get copy of the opinions, advices, circulars, orders, etc., but he cannot ask for any information as to why such opinions, advices, circulars, orders, etc. have been passed, especially in matters pertaining to judicial decisions. A judge speaks through his judgments or orders passed by him. If any party feels aggrieved by the order/judgment passed by a judge, the remedy available to such a party is either to challenge the same by way of appeal or by revision or any other legally permissible mode. No litigant can be allowed to seek information as to why and for what reasons the judge had come to a particular decision or conclusion. A judge is not bound to explain later on for what reasons he had come to such a conclusion. A judge cannot be expected to give reasons other than those that have been enumerated in the judgment or order. The application filed by the petitioner before the public authority is *per se* illegal and unwarranted. A judicial officer is entitled to get protection and the object of the same is not to protect malicious or corrupt judges, but to protect the public from the dangers to which the administration of justice would be exposed if the concerned judicial officers were subject to inquiry as to malice, or to litigation with those whom their decisions might offend. If anything is done contrary to this, it would certainly affect the independence of the judiciary. A judge should be free to make independent decisions. Therefore the court dismissed the special leave petition by petitioner.

Miscellaneous
(Right to Education, Consumer law)

Miscellaneous

(Right to Education, Consumer law)

Right to Education

The **right to education** is a universal entitlement to education, a right that is recognized as a human right. According to the International Covenant on Economic, Social and Cultural Rights the right to education includes the right to free, compulsory primary education for all, an obligation to develop secondary education accessible to all, in particular by the progressive introduction of free secondary education, as well as an obligation to develop equitable access to higher education, ideally by the progressive introduction of free higher education. The right to education also includes a responsibility to provide basic education for individuals who have not completed primary education. In addition to these access to education provisions, the right to education encompasses the obligation to rule out discrimination at all levels of the educational system, to set minimum standards and to improve quality of education.

The Right of Children to Free and Compulsory Education Act or **Right to Education Act (RTE)**, which was passed by the Indian parliament on 4 August 2009, describes the modalities of the importance of free and compulsory education for children between 6 and 14 in India under Article 21a of the Indian Constitution. The Act makes education a fundamental right of every child between the ages of 6 and 14 and specifies minimum norms in elementary schools. It requires all private schools to reserve 25% of seats to children from poor families (to be reimbursed by the state as part of the public-private partnership plan). It also prohibits all unrecognized schools from practice, and makes provisions for no donation or capitation fees and no interview of the child or parent for admission. The Act also provides that no child shall be held back, expelled, or required to pass a board examination until the completion of elementary education. There is also a provision for special training of school drop-outs to bring them up to par with students of the same age.

The RTE act requires surveys that will monitor all neighbourhoods, identify children requiring education, and set up facilities for providing it. The World Bank education specialist for India, Sam Carlson, has observed: The RTE Act is the first legislation in the world that puts the responsibility of ensuring enrollment, attendance and completion on the Government. It is the parents' responsibility to send the children to schools in the U.S. and other countries. The Right to Education of persons with disabilities until 18 years of age is laid down under a separate legislation- the Persons with Disabilities Act. A number of other provisions regarding improvement of school infrastructure, teacher-student ratio and faculty are made in the Act.

The Act provides for a special organization, the National Commission for the Protection of Child Rights, an autonomous body set up in 2007, to monitor the implementation of the act, together with Commissions to be set up by the states.

The act has been criticized for being hastily-drafted, not consulting many groups active in education, not considering the quality of education, infringing on the rights of private and religious minority schools to administer their system, and for excluding children under six years of age. Many of the ideas are seen as continuing the policies of **Sarva Shiksha Abhiyan** of the last decade, and the World Bank funded District Primary Education Programme DPEP of the '90s, both of which, while having set up a number of schools in rural areas, have been criticized for being ineffective and corruption-ridden.

Consumer Law

Consumer protection consists of laws and organizations designed to ensure the rights of consumers as well as fair trade competition and the free flow of truthful information in the marketplace. The laws are designed to prevent businesses that engage in fraud or specified unfair practices from gaining an advantage over competitors and may provide additional protection for the weak and those unable to take care of themselves. Consumer protection laws are a form of government regulation, which aim to protect the rights of consumers. For example, a government may require businesses to disclose detailed information about products—particularly in areas where safety or public health is an issue, such as food. Consumer protection is linked to the idea of "consumer rights" (that consumers have various rights as consumers), and to the formation of consumer organizations, which help consumers make better choices in the marketplace and get help with consumer complaints.

Other organizations that promote consumer protection include government organizations and self-regulating business organizations such as consumer protection agencies and organizations, the Federal Trade Commission, ombudsmen, Better Business Bureaus, etc. A consumer is defined as someone who acquires goods or services for direct use or ownership rather than for resale or use in production and manufacturing. Consumer interests can also be protected by promoting competition in the markets which directly and indirectly serve consumers, consistent with economic efficiency, but this topic is treated in competition law. Consumer protection can also be asserted via non-government organizations and individuals as consumer activism.

The definition of Consumer right is 'the right to have information about the quality, potency, quantity, purity, price and standard of goods or services', as it may be the case, but the consumer is to be protected against any unfair practices of trade. It is very essential for the consumers to know these rights. However there are strong and clear laws in India to defend consumer rights, the actual plight of consumers of India can be declared as completely dismal. Out of the various laws that have been enforced to protect the consumer rights in India, the most important is the Consumer Protection Act, 1986. According to this law, everybody, including individuals, a firm, a Hindu undivided family and a company, have the right to exercise their consumer rights for the purchase of goods and services made by them. It is significant that, as consumer, one knows the basic rights as well as about the courts and procedures that follow with the infringement of one's rights.

In general, the consumer rights in India are listed below:

- The right to be protected from all kind of hazardous goods and services

- The right to be fully informed about the performance and quality of all goods and services

- The right to free choice of goods and services

- The right to be heard in all decision-making processes related to consumer interests

- The right to seek redressal, whenever consumer rights have been infringed

- The right to complete consumer education

The Consumer Protection Act, 1986 and several other laws like the Weights, Standards & Measures Act can be formulated to make sure that there is fair competition in the market and free flow of correct information from goods and services providers to the ones who consume them. In fact, the degree of consumer protection in any country is regarded as the right indicator of the progress of the country. There is high level of sophistication gained by the goods and services providers in their marketing and selling practices and different types of promotional tasks viz. advertising resulted in an increasing requirement for more consumer awareness and protection. The government of India has realized the condition of Indian consumers therefore the Ministry of Consumer Affairs, Food and Public Distribution has incorporated the Department of Consumer Affairs as the nodal organization to protect the consumer rights, redress the consumer grievances and promote the standards governing goods and services provided in India.

If there is infringement of rights of consumer then a complaint can be made under the following circumstances and reported to the close by designated consumer court:

- The goods or services purchased by a person or agreed to be purchased by a person has one or more defects or deficiencies in any respect

- A trader or a service provider resort to unfair or restrictive practices of trade

- A trader or a service provider if charges a price more than the price displayed on the goods or the price that was agreed upon between the parties or the price that was stipulated under any law that exist Goods or services that bring a hazard to the safety or life of a person offered for sale, unknowingly or knowingly, that cause injury to health, safety or life.

Even though strong and clear laws exist in India to protect consumer rights, the actual plight of Indian consumers could be declared as completely dismal. Very few consumers are aware of their rights or understand their basic consumer rights.

56

Court Cannot Award Marks[1]

Facts in Nutshell: The facts very briefly are that the Respondent[2] No. 1(Khushboo Shrivastava) appeared in the All India Pre-Medical/Pre-Dental Entrance Examination, 2007 conducted by the Central Board of Secondary Education (for short 'the CBSE'). She submitted a representation dated 07.06.2007 through her advocate to the CBSE for re-examination and re-totaling of her marks in Physics, Chemistry and Biology. The CBSE informed the advocate of Respondent No. 1 by letter that there was no provision for re-checking/re-evaluation of answer sheets of the candidates. Aggrieved by the response Respondent No. 1 and others filed writ petition[3], in the Patna High Court under Article 226[4] of the Constitution for directing the CBSE to conduct a **re-evaluation** of her answer sheets and to **re-total** the marks and publish the result.

---

[1] Appellants: **The Secretary, All India Pre-Medical/Pre-Dental Examination, C.B.S.E. and Ors.** Vs. Respondent: **Khushboo Shrivastava and Ors.**
2012(1)ALLMR436, 2012(1)JCR16(SC)
Hon'ble Judges: R.V. Raveendran and A.K. Patnaik, JJ.

[2] A respondent is a person who is called upon to issue a response to a communication made by another. In legal usage, this specifically refers to the defendant in a legal proceeding commenced by a petition, or to an appellee, or the opposing party, in an appeal of a decision by an initial fact-finder.

[3] A writ petition is a right endowed by the law for a person to seek speedy trial before an appellate court after a trial court's judgment on his case. The petitioner seeks to rush his case to prevent irreparable harm.

[4] **Article 226 of the Indian Constitution, 1950**: Power of High Courts to issue certain writs.

(1) Notwithstanding anything in Article 32 every High Court shall have powers, throughout the territories in relation to which it exercise jurisdiction, to issue to any person or authority, including in appropriate cases, any Government, within those territories directions, orders or writs, including writs in the nature of habeas corpus, mandamus, prohibitions, quo warranto and certiorari, or any of them, for the enforcement of any of the rights conferred by Part III and for any other purpose.

(2) The power conferred by clause (1) to issue directions, orders or writs to any Government, authority or person may also be exercised by any High Court exercising jurisdiction in relation to the territories within which the cause of action , wholly or in part, arises for the exercise of such power, notwithstanding that the seat of such Government or authority or the residence of such person is not within those territories.

Reply By C.B.S.E:

The CBSE filed a reply contending inter alias that under the examination bye-laws pertaining to the All India Pre-Medical/Pre-Dental Entrance Examination, there was no provision for re-evaluation.

Decision by High Court:

The learned Single Judge of the Patna High Court passed orders directing the CBSE to produce the answer sheets of Respondent No. 1 on the condition that Respondent No. 1 would deposit Rs. 25,000/- to prove her bonafide that her answer sheets were wrongly evaluated. The learned Single Judge was of the view that if the answer sheets of Respondent No. 1 were correctly evaluated she would have got two more marks.

The Division Bench of the High Court directed that Respondent No. 1 be admitted in the MBBS Course in the next academic session 2009-2010.

Decision by Supreme Court:

The Hon'ble Judges were of the opinion that, neither the learned Single Judge nor the Division Bench of the High Court could have substituted his/ its own views for that of the examiners and awarded two additional marks to the Respondent No. 1 for the two answers in exercise of powers of judicial review under Article226 of the Constitution as these are purely academic matters. Therefore the appeal was allowed and setting aside the Judgment of learned single judge and the Division bench of High Court and writ was dismissed. Also the first respondent who was admitted to MBBS course, her admission will not be affected.

---

(3) Where any party against whom an interim order, whether by way of injunction or stay or in any other manner, is made on, or in any proceedings relating to, a petition under clause (1), without-

(a) furnishing to such party copies of such petition and all documents in support of the plea for such interim order; and

(b) giving such party an opportunity of being heard, makes an application to the High Court for the vacation of such order and furnishes a copy of such application to the party in whose favor such order has been made or the counsel of such party, the High Court shall dispose of the application within a period of two weeks from the date on which it is received or from the date on which the copy of such application is so furnished, whichever is later, or where the High Court is closed on the last day of that period, before the expiry of the next day afterwards on which the High Court is open; and if the application is not so disposed of, the interim order shall, on the expiry of that period, or , as the case may be, the expiry of the aid next day, stand vacated.

(4) The power conferred on a High Court by this article shall not be in derogation of the power conferred on the Supreme court by clause (2) of Article 32.

57

Non Lawyers Can appear for others under Consumer Protection Act (CPA)[1]

Facts in Nutshell:

A complaint bearing No. 428 of 2000 of alleged deficiency in service was filed before the South Mumbai District Consumer Disputes Redressal Forum, Mumbai(for short, Consumer Forum) against the two tour operators. During the pendency of the complaint, applications were filed by the opposite parties contending that the authorized agent should not be granted permission to appear on behalf of the complainants as he was not enrolled as an Advocate. The Consumer Forum considered the applications and held that the authorized agent had no right to act and plead before the Consumer Forum as he was not enrolled as an advocate.

In complaint filed before the Consumer Forum, the majority expressed the view that the authorized agents have a right to file, act, appear, argue the complaint to its logical conclusion before the Consumer Agencies. The issue was taken to the State Consumer Disputes Redressal Commission (for short, State Commission) which stayed the hearing of the matters in which authorized agents were appearing and refused to grant stay where authorized agents were injuncted from appearing before the Consumer Forum. As a result, the proceedings in a large number of cases where the authorized agents were appearing had come to standstill.

The interim order passed by the State Commission was challenged in two writ petitions before the Bombay High Court.

---

[1] Appellants: **C.Venkatachalam** Vs. Respondent: **Ajitkumar C. Shah and Ors**. AND Appellants: **Bar Council of India** Vs. Respondent: **Sanjay R. Kothari and Ors.**
2012(4)BomCR776

Hon'bleJudges: Dalveer Bhandari, Mukundakam Sharma and Anil R. Dave, JJ.

Decision by High Court:

The High Court held that the Consumer Fora constituted under the Consumer Protection Act, 1986 have "trappings of a civil court" but "are not civil courts within the meaning of the provisions of the Code of Civil Procedure." The High Court in the impugned judgment held that a party before the District Consumer Forum/State Commission cannot be compelled to engage services of an advocate.

The High Court further held that the Act of 1986 is a special piece of legislation for the better protection of the interests of consumers. The Act has been enacted to give succour and relief to the affected or aggrieved consumers quickly with nil or small expense. The Division Bench also observed that the right of an advocate to practice is not an absolute right but is subject to other provisions of the Act. According to the Division Bench, permitting the authorized agents to represent parties to the proceedings before the District Forum/State Commission cannot be said to practice law.

The Division Bench also held that there are various statutes like Income Tax Act, Sales Tax Act and the Monopolies and Restrictive Trade Practices Act which permit non-advocates to represent the parties before the authorities under those Acts and those non-advocates appearing before those Forums for the parties cannot be said to practice law. The Rules of 2000 framed under Act of 1986 permit authorized agents to appear for the parties and such appearance of authorized agents cannot be said to be inconsistent with Section 33 of Advocates Act[2].

The Division Bench also dealt with the disciplinary aspect of the matter and held that if authorized agent appearing for the party to the proceedings misbehaves or exhibits violent behaviour or does not maintain the decency and decorum of the District Forum or State Commission or interferes with the smooth progress of the case then it is always open to such District

---

[2] **Section 33 of the Advocates Act, 1961** says that no person shall, on or after the appointed day, be entitled to practise in any court or before any authority unless he is enrolled as an advocate.

Section 33 reads as under: Advocates alone entitled to practise - Except as otherwise provided in this Act or in any other law for the time being in force, no person shall, on or after the appointed day, be entitled to practise in any court or before any authority or person unless he is enrolled as an advocate under this Act.

Forum or State Commission to pass an appropriate order refusing such authorized agent the audience in a given case. Appeal was filed in Supreme Court against the judgment of High Court.

Question before Supreme Court:

The basic issue involved in appeals is whether a person under the purported cover of being an "agent"[3] can represent large number of persons before the forums created under the Consumer Protection Act, 1986 (In short the 'Act') and the Rules made there under.

Decision by Supreme Court:

Ordinarily right to practice has been given only to advocates who are enrolled with the Bar Council of a State. Section 29 of the Advocates Act, 1961 recognised advocates as class of persons entitled to practise the profession of law. Court held that non-lawyers can appear for other under Consumer Protection Act and view taken by High Court in there judgment cannot be said to be erroneous and unsustainable in law. Appeal was dismissed.

---

[3] **Rule 2(b) of the Consumer Protection Rules**, 1987 (in short the 'The Rules') defines an 'agent' as under:

agent means a person duly authorized by a party to present any complaint, appeal or reply on its behalf before the National Commission.

IF YOU THINK[*]

If you think you are beaten, you are

If you think you dare not, you don't!

If you like to win, but think you can't,

It's almost a cinch you won't

If you think you'll lose, you're lost;

For out in the world we find

Success begins with a fellow's will;

It's all in the state of mind.

If you think you are outclassed, you are,

You've got to think high to rise;

You've got to be sure of yourself before

You can ever win a prize

Life's battles don't always go

To the stronger and faster man,

But sooner or later the man who wins

Is the man who thinks he can.

---

[*] You Can Win, Page 55-56